ALS
Advances in Life Sciences

Social Systems and Population Cycles in Voles

Edited by
R.H. Tamarin
R.S. Ostfeld
S.R. Pugh
G. Bujalska

1990

Birkhäuser Verlag
Basel · Boston · Berlin

Editors' addresses:

Dr. Robert H. Tamarin
Dr. Stephen R. Pugh
Biology Department
Boston University
Boston, MA 02215
USA

Dr. Richard S. Ostfeld
Institute of Ecosystem Studies
The New York Botanical Garden
Millbrook, N.Y. 12545 – 0129
USA

Dr. Gabriela Bujalska
Institute of Ecology
PAS
05–092 Dziekanow Lesny
Poland

The use of registered names, trademarks, etc. in this publication does not imply, even in the absence of a specific statement, that such names are exempt from the relevant protective laws and regulations and therefore free for general use.

The publisher cannot assume any legal responsibility for given data, especially as far as directions for the use and the handling of chemicals and drugs are concerned. This information can be obtained from the manufacturers.

Library of Congress Cataloging-in-Publication Data
Social systems and population cycles in voles / edited by R.H. Tamarin ... [et al.].
    p. cm. – (Advances in life sciences)
    Includes bibliographical references and index.
    ISBN 3-7643-2437-6. – ISBN 0-8176-2437-6 (U.S.)
    1. Voles – Behavior. 2. Mammal populations. 3. Social behavior in animals.
I. Tamarin, Robert H. II Series.
QL737.R638S58   1990
599.32'33 – dc20

Deutsche Bibliothek Cataloging-in-Publication Data
Social systems and population cycles in voles / ed. by R.H. Tamarin ... – Basel; Boston;
Berlin: Birkhäuser, 1990
(Advances in life sciences)
ISBN 3-7643-2437-6
NE: Tamarin, Robert H. [Hrsg.]

© 1990 Birkhäuser Verlag
        P.O. Box 133
        4010 Basel
        Switzerland

Printed from the author's manuscript
on acid-free paper in Germany
ISBN 3-7643-2437-6
ISBN 0-8176-2437-6

CONTENTS

PAGE

VI

SPECIES STUDIES: *Arvicola*

PREFACE

This volume is the outgrowth a symposium held 26 August 1989 in Rome, Italy at the Fifth International Theriological Congress. The symposium, convened by Robert Tamarin and Gabriela Bujalska, was held as a follow-up of a symposium held at the Fourth International Theriological Congress in Edmonton, Alberta, convened by Arvo Myllmäki and Tamarin at the urging of William Fuller, Chairman of the Secretariat. The Edmonton symposium, entitled: "Social Systems in *Microtus*" was so well received that it was deemed appropriate to follow it up in Rome. The title of the Rome symposium was: "The Relationship Between Social Systems and Population Dynamics in Microtine Rodents." Andreas Bally, Biology Editor of Birkhäuser Verlag, encouraged us to publish the symposium. Richard Ostfeld and Stephen Pugh, two participants in the symposium, became the editors who interacted directly with the authors.

All of the papers in this volume, as well as the talks and posters, had the common theme of investigations of some aspect of social behavior and population dynamics in voles, in the genera *Microtus, Clethrionomys,* and *Arvicola.* Although there are several ways to arrange these papers, we have chosen to group them in two general areas: overview and species studies. Within each area the papers are arranged alphabetically by the last name of the senior author.

Overview Studies

The conceptual group contains four papers. The paper by Donald Dewsbury (U.S.A.) provides an update on his studies of the comparative ethology of *Microtus* species. Dewsbury has selected two vole species known from field studies to exhibit monogamous tendencies *(M. ochrogaster* and *M. pinetorum)* and two known to be nonmonogamous under most conditions *(M. pennsylvanicus* and *M. montanus).* He then compares species by summarizing laboratory studies of morphology, development, copulatory behavior, ejaculate capacity, parental behavior, and general contact-proneness. Dewsbury's main finding is that the monogamous species are generally similar to each other and dissimilar to the nonmonogamous species with respect to the suite of behaviors studied. Dewsbury demonstrates that mating systems are the result of the often subtle and complex behaviors of individual voles that respond evolutionarily and ecologically to the social environment provided by their conspecifics.

Michael Ferkin (U.S.A.) reviews the mechanism and function of kin recognition in voles emphasizing how kin recognition may influence the social structure and population regulation of vole species. Familiarity based on association before weaning is the principle mechanism voles use to recognize relatives. Therefore, the ability of voles to recognize kin may be limited, especially in species that form extensive communal groups of unrelated individuals or in species with sexually dimorphic natal dispersal patterns. Models of population regulation based on kin recognition, such as Charnov and Finerty's sociobiological hypothesis, may have limited utility.

The paper by Dale Madison (U.S.A.) is a response to the lack of clear terminology in describing the social systems of microtine rodents. Madison emphasizes that species do not have a single type of social organization; rather, each species has a social system consisting of a series of social organizational modes that vary seasonally, spatially, and with population density. Although species of voles may be quite distinct with respect to their social systems, they may share social organizational modes in common under certain conditions. Madison then relates modal variation to population dynamics, arguing that the increased social tolerance of many species in autumn and winter (usually the season of steep declines in density) may affect population cycles more than the mode consisting of individual aggressiveness and solitary living. He also asserts that interspecific differences in social plasticity may influence the tendency to undergo cycles. Species (or populations) that are able to assume different social modes may be better able to adapt to changing environmental conditions, and therefore be more stable, than those that have a single or few modes.

Richard Ostfeld and Lorrie Klosterman (U.S.A.) reflect a similar theme that individuals are behaviorally plastic and therefore a species cannot be assigned to a single social system. After reviewing several cases of intraspecific variability in vole social organization, they explore the implications of behavioral plasticity for the study of the adaptive significance of social systems. They find that some key assumptions of the evolutionary comparative method are violated when phenotypic plasticity is common. They suggest that a comparative method be used to study the adaptive nature of this plasticity.

Species Studies

Microtus *studies.*—The second group of papers includes studies of social systems of various species. Ten studies are devoted to *Microtus* species. Sam Erlinge and his colleagues (Sweden) describe studies of *M. agrestis.* They arrive at the conclusion that social behavior is not a cause of the pattern of population dynamics of this species. Erlinge and his colleagues examine use of space and aggressive behavior of voles over a period of fluctuating population size that included a predator exclusion experiment. Their main findings are that aggressive behavior remained roughly the same from year to year, that population growth was related to productivity of food plants, and that the timing and extent of declines were strongly influenced by predation. Social behavior affected the population response to food and predation, but did not by itself have much influence on population dynamics.

Michael Gaines and his colleagues (U.S.A.) tested the hypothesis that aggression is the proximate stimulus for dispersal in the prairie vole, *M. ochrogaster*. They treated subadult males on an enclosed trapping grid with implanted testosterone capsules while animals on a control grid received sham treatment. They found increased wounding rates of males and higher dispersal rates in the treated population providing support for their hypothesis.

The social system of the prairie vole, *M. ochrogaster*, has been described previously as being based on monogamous pairs. Lowell Getz and his colleagues (U.S.A.) present evidence in their chapter that the basic social unit of the prairie vole is the communal nesting group derived from an original monogamous-pair breeding unit. Communal groups form primarily by the addition of young of the original monogamous pair although some groups include unrelated adults. Communal groups are more prevalent in the winter. During late autumn and winter juvenile survivorship increases when snakes, the principle predators, enter hibernation. The authors suggest that snake predation prevents the formation of communal groups in spring and summer.

Frederick Jannett (U.S.A.) presents data on a relatively unstudied microtine, the rock vole, *M. chrotorrhinus*. Six to seven years of annual censuses revealed that Jannett's population is one of the most stable rodent populations studied to date. Since the social system of this species is not well understood, its potential role in the stable population dynamics remains to be elucidated. Compared to most other *Microtus* species, the rock vole is a habitat specialist, commonly associated with rock or talus in forest, and this may contribute to its density stability.

Traditionally, female voles have been thought to exert a greater influence on population dynamics than males, especially in species with female territoriality. Betty McGuire and her colleagues (U.S.A.) suggest that in *M. ochrogaster*, a species with a mating system based on monogamous pairs or communal groups, males may play a role in regulating density. This assertion is based on extensive trapping data both at prairie vole nests and at the periphery of their home ranges. The presence of a resident male deterred visits by nonresident males, which in turn influenced the reproductive condition of their daughters. Females became reproductive at an earlier age if no resident males were present.

William McShea (U.S.A.) examines the rates and patterns of predation on meadow voles, *M. pennsylvanicus*, based on the fates of individuals followed by radiotelemetry. Predation rates were highest in the winter and lowest in the Autumn. Lactating females were the most susceptible in the first week postpartum. Predation by specialist predators (e.g., weasels) was highest in the spring. McShea suggests that specialist predators may have more of an impact on vole population dynamics because of their impact on dispersal tendencies.

Stephen Pugh and Robert Tamarin (U.S.A.) evaluated Charnov and Finerty's model of population cycles, which is based on kin selection. An assumption in the model is that voles in low density populations occur in close proximity to their kin and kin selection favors cooperative behavior. Population growth ensues; dispersal follows, which erodes the degree of relatedness among neighbors and eliminates the evolutionary impetus for behaving amicably. Increasingly agonistic behavior among increasingly less-related neighbors results in a population crash. Pugh and Tamarin were able to test this scenario by following the spatial relationships among meadow voles of known genetic relatedness during periods of low-to-moderate density. Since they found neither a high degree of relatedness among neighbors at low density nor a consistent reduction in degree of relatedness among neighbors as density increased, they did not support Charnov and Finerty's hypothesis. They point out that Charnov and Finerty's prediction that voles behave more amicably toward relatives than toward nonrelatives has not been adequately tested. Nevertheless, the applicability of this model to vole cycles has not been supported.

Margaret Schadler (U.S.A) reviews 14 years of laboratory research on the factors limiting reproduction in colonies of pine voles, *M. pinetorum*. Colonies were self limiting at a mean density of 16 animals per colony. Reproduction in colonies ceased when populations grew because litter survival dropped to zero or because one or both of the founding pair died. Neither stimulation of estrus in nonreproducing females by injection of sex hormones, nor the introduction of strange males, stimulated their reproduction when a mature reproductive female was present; mature females inhibited reproduction in young females.

Jussi Viitala and Jyrki Pusenius (Finland) describe the social organization of *M. oeconomus* and *M. agrestis* in northern Finland. They conclude that mating systems were much more variable, both between and within species of *Microtus,* than in *Clethrionomys*. The differences in spacing behavior between the two genera had different effects on population regulation, with a temporary decline in density occurring in mid summer in *Microtus* and in the beginning of the breeding season in *Clethrionomys*. Despite these differences, both *Microtus* and *Clethrionomys* cycle synchronously in northern Fennoscandia.

Ken Zwicker (U.S.A.) presents a summary of the natural history and social biology of the beach vole, *M. breweri,* an island endemic descended from the meadow vole, *M. pennsylvanicus*. From his radiotelemetry studies he notes a general similarity between beach and meadow voles. The main differences are that male and female beach voles are most active at different times of day, and that home ranges of male and female beach voles are of equal size and larger than those of female meadow voles. Zwicker discusses the fact that the beach vole population is quite constant at levels roughly equivalent to peak densities of meadow voles. In reviewing several models of population regulation in microtines, he finds that no single model seems adequate to explain cycles in other species and stability in beach voles. Such factors as lack of a dispersal sink, near absence of predation, constant food supply, and low heritability of behavior may contribute to the stability of the beach vole population.

Clethrionomys *studies.*—Five papers are concerned with *Clethrionomys* species. Gabriela Bujalska (Poland) provides a detailed update on the social system of the bank vole *(C. glareolus)*. She describes a unit of social structure, the breeding colony, as being composed of <7 territorial adult females and <6 nonterritorial males, the latter constituting a "clan." Mature females limit maturation and recruitment of immature females into the breeding population. However, Bujalska points out that the bank vole's social system does not conform to models of density-dependent population growth since population density has little effect on reproduction in mature females. Instead, Bujalska finds it useful to focus on the breeding colony (rather than the population) as the unit of social regulation, arguing that the effects of density do not extend beyond the local neighborhood. The stable social structure described for bank voles by Bujalska contrasts somewhat with that described by Ylönen and Viitala and Pusenius; this may result from geographic differences in vole behavior, or from different research methods.

Joanna Gliwicz (Poland) investigated the reproductive performance of *C. glareolus.* Female reproductive success was estimated based on the number of pregnancies and reproductive opportunity of males was based on the degree of inter- and intrasexual overlap of males at the time of conception. Overwintered voles of both sexes had higher reproductive success than young of the year in optimal habitat. However, overwinter survival rates were low. Young voles seem to have two viable reproductive alternatives: either remain in optimal habitat and attempt to survive the winter and breed in the following season or disperse and settle in suboptimal habitat and breed immediately.

A. D. Mironov (U.S.S.R.) describes the aboveground activity patterns of the bank vole based on direct observations of marked individuals. He finds differences in activity patterns based on sex, age, and physiological condition of the voles. Activity patterns did not vary seasonally. In an age when research in behavioral ecology is so dependent on "high tech" methods, such as radiotelemetry and DNA fingerprinting, it is refreshing to see a study based on direct visual observation.

Michał Sikorski and Anna Wójcik (Poland) examine the mating system of the bank vole using mark-recapture and electrophoretic techniques. After gathering data on free-ranging population of overwintered voles, all voles were removed to the lab, and after parturition, putative fathers were assigned to litters using paternity analysis. Although no evidence of multiple paternity was found, Sikorski and Wójcik confirm that bank voles have a promiscuous mating system. Mating success of males was unequal, but those who successfully sired offspring were not readily distinguishable from the others except for their tendency to be older. The data also indicate that the relationship between breeding synchrony of females and space-use strategies of males may be more complex than previously thought.

Hannu Ylönen (Finland) combines a review of the social organization of the genus *Clethrionomys* with a summary of his experiments on *C. glareolus* in central Finland. Similar to Madison, Ostfeld and Klosterman, and Viitala and Pusenius, Ylönen questions the assumption that social organization is rigid within species. His experiments show that female bank voles relax their strict territoriality when food is abundant, when surrounded by relatives, and when population density is high. However, he concludes that *Clethrionomys* is less variable than *Microtus*. Despite differences in social systems of *Microtus* and *Clethrionomys,* in northern Fennoscandia they cycle in synchrony, leading Ylönen to conclude that factors extrinsic to the voles themselves, such as habitat patchiness, food availability, and predation, which all species should experience together, combine to produce cyclic fluctuations. He views changing social behavior as a consequence, rather than a cause, of cycles.

Arvicola *study.*—Boel Jeppsson (Sweden) describes water vole *(Arvicola terrestris)* social systems in a marsh and grassland in Sweden. The degree of intraspecific variability seen in the water vole is comparable to that between species or even genera of other voles. Individuals in the marsh population migrated in winter to grassland, whereas the grassland population was resident throughout the year. Voles in the marsh were protected from predation by water and high vegetation, whereas those in the grassland relied entirely on burrows they constructed. Burrows, rather than food, seem to be the limiting resource for both male and female grassland voles, and in this habitat both sexes defended individual territories. In other habitats, the dispersion of females (clumped or uniform) influenced whether males are territorial. Jeppsson's comparison of populations that rely on different resources indicates that previous models of the evolution of social systems in microtine rodents may need to be modified.

Summation

These papers show that there is much research being done on the nature of the social systems of voles and there is as yet no consensus as to the relationships that might exist between social systems and population dynamics. Although a consensus seems to exist regarding the existence of plasticity of vole social systems, much more comparative work is needed. We hope that this volume serves to bring new facts and new ideas to the reader and possibly to encourage investigators to examine further the relationships explored here until such time that a true synthesis might exist.

We thank William Fuller for his help and encouragement over the years. One of us (Tamarin) would like to thank Fuller and others who stood in for him in his absence in Rome. Andreas Bally provided encouragement during the development of this volume. All chapters were peer reviewed anonymously. We thank the many reviewers who have helped to elevate the quality of these articles. Thanking them by name would deny them their anonymity. We hope that a general acknowledgment will convey our gratitude.

15 August 1990

R. Tamarin, Boston

R. Ostfeld, Millbrook

S. Pugh, Boston

G. Bujalska, Dziekanów Leśny

Social Systems and
Population Cycles in Voles
Advances in Life Sciences
© Birkhäuser Verlag Basel

INDIVIDUAL ATTRIBUTES GENERATE CONTRASTING
DEGREES OF SOCIALITY IN VOLES

Donald A. Dewsbury

Department of Psychology, University of Florida, Gainesville, FL 32611 U.S.A.

Summary.—Different species of voles *(Microtus)* live in different mating systems, with prairie and pine voles generally more social and more monogamous than montane and meadow voles. Mating systems are treated as epiphenomena, driven by the actions and adaptations of individual animals. The species differ with respect to morphology, development, male ejaculate capacity, copulatory behavior, parental behavior, and social contact-proneness. Natural selection appears to have acted on suites of traits of individuals and thereby produced contrasting mating systems in the field.

INTRODUCTION

Animal mating systems generally are classified into several categories (monogamy, polygamy, promiscuity). Although these categories are useful at the sociological level of analysis, mating systems are the end product of the behavioral tendencies of individuals, each selected to maximize its lifetime reproductive success. An in-depth understanding of mating systems thus requires a more fine-grained analysis of the behavioral proclivities of the individuals in the mating system. Although the behavior of individuals is affected by their social and ecological milieu, there remain stable species differences in individual behavior and other characteristics among different species.

Different species of *Microtus* generally are characterized by different mating systems. In prairie voles, *Microtus ochrogaster,* and pine voles, *M. pinetorum,* males and females often share nests during the breeding season; there is evidence of monogamy under some conditions (FitzGerald and Madison, 1983; Getz and Hofmann, 1986). By contrast, in montane voles, *M. montanus,* and meadow voles, *M. pennsylvanicus,* male-female cohabitation and monogamy appear rare during summer breeding (Jannett, 1982; Madison, 1980). In prairie and pine voles, males and females have roughly equal home range sizes, whereas in montane and meadow voles, home ranges of males are larger (Gaulin and FitzGerald, 1988). It must be emphasized, however, that these systems are fluid, changing with such factors as season and population density (Getz and Hofmann, 1986; Madison and McShea, 1987). In spite of such variation, there appear to be species-characteristic tendencies toward different individual characteristics and group mating systems.

In this paper I present a progress report for a project in which my associates and I are analyzing the suites of traits that differentiate these four species of voles with different mating systems and that appear to be the primary locus of selection resulting in these systems at the sociological level (Dewsbury, 1988). My purpose is to determine which characteristics will or will not differentiate the two pairs of species with generally similar, though not identical, mating systems.

MORPHOLOGY

There are no differences in overall body mass correlated with mating system (Table 1). Although meadow voles are the largest species and pine voles the smallest, prairie and montane voles are of intermediate mass (Pierce et al., 1990).

It is generally agreed that sexual dimorphism for body mass should be reduced in monogamous species relative to nonmonogamous species (Kleiman, 1977). According to this view, sexual selection is responsible for the development of size and other characteristics in males that lead to mating success in nonmonogamous systems. The data on these four species of voles are rank ordered in a manner consistent with this view (Table 1). As shown by Dewsbury et al. (1980), montane and meadow voles are the most dimorphic species, with 90-day-old males weighing 11.0 and 9.6 grams, respectively, more than their 90-day-old sisters. Although male prairie voles are significantly heavier than females, the difference is not as great (Table 1). Recently, we have found a complete lack of sexual dimorphism for body mass in pine voles (Table 1).

DEVELOPMENT

Species with monogamous mating systems often live in stable environments (Getz, 1978), and are expected to have lower reproductive potentials. Under such conditions a slower rate of physical and behavioral maturation also would be expected (Kleiman, 1977). We have found that montane and meadow voles generally have larger litters than prairie or pine voles (Table 1). This is at least one aspect of reproductive potential; data are needed concerning the number of litters per year.

In general, individual *Microtus* mature rapidly compared to other muroid rodents. However, it is difficult to select appropriate indices of maturation for intrageneric comparisons. Those related to sexual maturation are greatly affected by the physical and social environment and thus are inappropriate. Age at which eyes open often is used as an index of maturation (Dewsbury, 1981a), but the four species are not clearly differentiated with respect to this index (Table 1; Dewsbury, 1981a). In studies with family groups in 1.3 by 1.3 m pens, McGuire and Novak (1984, 1986) found that montane and meadow voles had an earlier age of last nipple attachment and at which the first solid food was eaten, indicating more rapid maturation, than prairie or pine voles (Table 1).

Table 1.—Some characteristics of four species of *Microtus*.

Characteristic	Prairie vole	Pine vole	Montane vole	Meadow vole
Mating system				
Male-female sociality[1-4]	Often strong	Often strong	Generally weak	Generally weak
Home range dimorphism[14]	Equal	Equal	Male larger	Male larger
Morphology				
Male body mass (g)[5]	45.4	20.1	43.0	54.6
Male-female body mass dimorphism[6,7]	6.2	-0.4	11.0	9.6
Development				
Mean litter size[8]	3.6	2.3	6.6	5.1
Percent nursing in day 2 test[7]	95.4	89.6	80.2	57.2
Distance nipple clinging day 2 (cm)[15]	29.4	30.0	8.9	3.7
Mean age eye opening[8,7]	9.1	11.7	10.6	9.4
Age last nipple attachment[9]	20	21	14	13
Age first solid food[9]	15	17	14	13
Male ejaculate capacity				
Testes:body mass ratio[5]	1.2	0.3	0.9	2.2
Mean ejaculation frequency[10-13,5]	2.0, 2.7	2.2, 2.4	5.0, 3.4	5.9, 2.5
Total sperm ejaculated (X10[6])[5]	30.5	3.3	19.0	25.5
Copulatory behavior				
Intromission latency (s)[10-13]	172	550	102	132
Intromission frequency first series[10-13]	9.5	0.4	17.7	14.0
Parental behavior				
Paternal time in nest in enclosure (s)[9]	569	292	9	3
Maternal time in nest in enclosure (s)[9]	486	351	207	144
Maternal time nursing in small cage (s)[7]	786	548	56	145
Social contact proneness				
Male-female time huddling (s)[15,7]	31.2	12.8	1.3	7.0

References: [1]Getz and Hofmann (1986); [2]FitzGerald and Madison (1983); [3]Jannett (1982); [4]Madison (1980); [5]Pierce et al. (1990); [6]Dewsbury et al. (1980); [7]New data, this laboratory; [8]Dewsbury (1981a); [9]McGuire and Novak (1986); [10]Gray and Dewsbury (1973); [11]Dewsbury (1976); [12]Dewsbury (1973); [13]Gray and Dewsbury (1975); [14]Gaulin and FitzGerald (1988); [15]Shapiro et al. (1989)

In a recent study in our laboratory, Salo, Shapiro, and Dewsbury tested the persistence of nipple clinging by pups of these four species at 2, 6, and 10 days of age. Dams were removed from the home cage and small collars were placed around their necks. They were then placed in a new cage and allowed to adapt. The female was then gently led, via a nylon lead, from one end of the cage to the other. The distance each pup remained clinging to the mother's nipple was recorded. More prairie and pine voles than meadow or montane voles were recorded as nursing at the beginning of the test. Prairie and pine vole pups remained on the nipple for nearly all 30-cm tests, whereas montane and meadow vole pups generally lost contact after less than 10 cm (Table 1). Thus, the pups in the more monogamous species remain physically more attached to the mother than those of the nonmonogamous species.

MALE EJACULATE CAPACITY

In species in which more than one male mates with individual females during an estrous period, the conditions for sperm competition exist. One would expect that in such species, generally those that are nonmonogamous, males would produce more sperm, deliver larger ejaculates, and have larger testes, relative to body mass, than in species in which females mate with a single male (Harcourt et al., 1981; Kenagy and Trombulak, 1986). Parameters of male ejaculate capacity were examined for these four species of voles (Table 1; Pierce et al., 1990). Although meadow voles have very large testes and those of pine voles are quite small, the testes of montane and prairie voles are both intermediate. Thus, there exists no simple relationship between testes sizes and mating systems among these four species.

In our initial studies of copulatory behavior in these species, individual male-female pairs were allowed to copulate until they attained an arbitrary, but standard, satiety criterion of 30 min with no intromissions or 1 h with no ejaculations (Dewsbury, 1973, 1976; Gray and Dewsbury, 1973, 1975). Males in the nonmonogamous species attained more ejaculations under these conditions than did males of the monogamous species (Table 1, Fig. 1). In recent work (Pierce et al., 1990), a different female was used for each ejaculation delivered by each male, in order that the number of sperm per ejaculate could be determined. Under these conditions, the ejaculation frequencies of the four species were quite similar. This may be due, in part, to a greater initial resistance offered by unmated female meadow voles; this effect needs quantification.

Pine voles ejaculate fewer sperm per mating episode than the other species. However, as the other monogamous species is not well differentiated from the nonmonogamous ones, this characteristic appears not tightly tied to mating system. In addition, it might be expected that in monogamous species males would deliver a single large ejaculate, whereas in nonmonogamous species males would deliver more ejaculates with fewer sperm per ejaculate (Parker, 1984). However, all species attain multiple ejaculations. Based on pattern of sperm counts per ejaculation over successive ejaculates, when corrected for baseline effects, the species appear rank ordered in a manner consistent with expectation (Fig. 1). In the third ejaculation, montane and meadow voles deposited 43% and 72% of the number of sperm in the first ejaculate, respectively; the comparative values for prairie and pine voles are 19% and 30%.

The reasons for these patterns are not entirely clear. However, what may be critical for the evolution of testes size and sperm numbers may be the frequency with which individual females mate with more than one male per estrous period. Because prairie vole females sometimes may mate with more than one male (Getz and Hofmann, 1986) and montane vole females may not (Wolff, 1985), the results may be consistent with tendencies toward multiple mating though not with the tendency to form stable pair bonds.

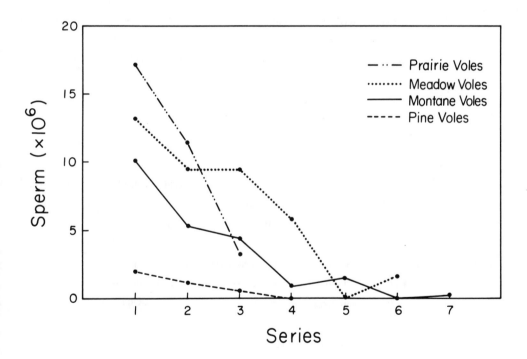

Figure 1. Mean number of sperm per ejaculation for successive ejaculates in four species of *Microtus*.

COPULATORY BEHAVIOR

It might be expected that the initiation of copulatory behavior in unfamiliar male-female pairs would be slower in monogamous species, in which there is a pair bond formed, than in nonmonogamous species (Dewsbury, 1981a). Compared to other species of muroid rodents, voles are quick to initiate copulation. The rank ordering of the four species with respect to intromission latency is generally consistent with this expectation (Table 1).

Before each ejaculation the males of all species of *Microtus* studied thus far display a series of intromissions (mounts with intromission), during which they mount the female, gain vaginal insertion, and display deep pelvic thrusting, but do not ejaculate. The number of these intromissions varies with species (Table 1), with males of the more nonmonogamous species displaying more intromissions than those of more monogamous ones. As these intromissions may function in removing the copulatory plugs of other males (Dewsbury, 1981b), they may be an adaptive characteristic for species with multiple-male mating.

Males of many nonmonogamous species show a "Coolidge effect," a resumption of copulation at satiety when a novel female is presented. This has been found in meadow voles and montane voles, but not in prairie voles (Dewsbury, 1973; Gray and Dewsbury, 1973, 1975). It has not yet been studied in pine voles.

PARENTAL BEHAVIOR

Because a more monogamous system is generally associated with greater parental effort than a nonmonogamous system, one would expect differences in the parental behavior of these species. Recently, we studied maternal behavior in laboratory cages. For each test, pups were distributed across the cage and the latency to and duration of various aspects of maternal behavior were recorded. In general, prairie and pine voles spent more time nursing pups—dams had shorter latencies and longer durations for maternal behavior than did montane and meadow voles (Table 1).

McGuire and Novak (1984, 1986) studied these species in 1.3 by 1.3 m pens. They found that female prairie and pine voles spent more time in nests with their pups than did montane or meadow voles (Table 1).

Because the display of paternal care often is treated as one characteristic of a monogamous system (Dewsbury, 1988), one would expect more paternal care in prairie and pine voles than in montane and meadow voles. The data of McGuire and Novak (1984, 1986) generally confirm this expectation (Table 1). However, these trends appear to vary with prevailing conditions; Storey and Snow (1987) found appreciable paternal care in meadow voles.

SOCIAL CONTACT PRONENESS

Perhaps the most basic trait that might be expected to differentiate these species is the overall tendency toward social contact. We have measured this by placing an unfamiliar male and female together in a neutral cage and determining the amount of time the animals spend in physical contact with each other. Two hours are allowed for habituation, and the behavior during the third hour is analyzed from videotape (Shapiro et al., 1989). The pairs do not copulate under these conditions. Pairs of prairie voles spent more than half of the time huddling, pairs of montane voles were together for just over one minute, and pine and meadow voles spent intermediate times huddling (Table 1). This tendency toward social contact appears related to the contrasting levels of sociality in these species.

CONCLUSIONS

The mating system of a population in the field is the product of the behavior of individuals. However, this behavior is affected by the behavior of other animals in the system and by ecological factors. My focus is upon stable characteristics that differentiate species often found in contrasting mating systems. It is my view that mating systems are the product of these contrasting behavioral tendencies. Natural selection appears generally to work at the level of the individual organism and thus it is on the behavior of the individual organisms that we should concentrate if we wish to relate behavior to evolution. Organisms can be viewed as possessing suites of characteristics that lead them to behave in different ways in different situations. The mating system thus is driven by these behavioral patterns of individuals.

It is not surprising that the relationships between mating system and those characteristics we have measured in the laboratory are not always consistent with expectations. Both the mating system and the behavior displayed in the laboratory change with prevailing conditions. Current theories are not yet sufficiently advanced to permit unambiguous predictions. Nevertheless, there appears to be some remarkable stability of species characteristics across different situations. When characteristics of morphology, development, male ejaculate capacity, copulatory behavior, parental behavior, and proneness to social contact are examined, a consistent pattern emerges. Many differences can be found between prairie and pine voles, on the one hand, and montane and meadow voles, on the other. In general, these tend to be the kind of differences that would generate the kinds of differences in mating systems that have been observed in the field. The interlocking pattern of relationships among different adaptations requires elaboration.

I am especially interested in some of the more subtle aspects of mate choice and individual

8

discrimination in these species. Prairie voles and montane voles differ with respect to choice by females of familiar versus unfamiliar males and of dominant versus subordinate males, choice by males of unmated versus mated females, and the tendency of males to mate with more than one female when four receptive females are present (Dewsbury, 1988). I hope to extend these analyses and others to meadow and pine voles and thus expand the catalog of traits that appear to differentiate species with contrasting mating systems. In so doing, I hope to reveal further the nature of the suites of traits that underlie and drive contrasting mating systems.

ACKNOWLEDGMENTS

This research was supported by Grant BNS-8904974 from the National Science Foundation.

LITERATURE CITED

Dewsbury, D. A. 1973. Copulatory behavior of montane voles *(Microtus montanus)*. Behaviour, 44:186-202.

———. 1976. Copulatory behavior of pine voles *(Microtus pinetorum)*. Perceptual and Motor Skills, 43:91-94.

———. 1981a. An exercise in the prediction of monogamy in the field from laboratory data on 42 species of muroid rodents. Biologist, 63:138-162.

———. 1981b. On the function of the multiple-intromission, multiple-ejaculation copulatory patterns of rodents. Bulletin of the Psychonomic Society, 18:221-223.

———. 1988. The comparative psychology of monogamy. Nebraska Symposium on Motivation, 35:1-50.

Dewsbury, D. J. Baumgardner, R. L. Evans, and D. G. Webster. 1980. Sexual dimorphism for body mass in 13 taxa of muroid rodents under laboratory conditions. Journal of Mammalogy, 61:146-149.

FitzGerald, R. W., and D. M. Madison. 1983. Social organization of a free-ranging population of pine voles, *Microtus pinetorum*. Behavioral Ecology and Sociobiology, 13:183-187.

Gaulin, S. J. C., and R. W. FitzGerald. 1988. Home-range size as a predictor of mating systems in *Microtus*. Journal of Mammalogy, 69:311-319.

Getz, L. L. 1978. Speculation on social structure and population cycles of microtine rodents. Biologist, 60:134-147.

Getz, L. L., and J. E. Hofmann. 1986. Social organization in free-living prairie voles, *Microtus ochrogaster*. Behavioral Ecology and Sociobiology, 18:275-282.

Gray, G. D., and D. A. Dewsbury. 1973. A quantitative description of copulatory behavior in prairie voles *(Microtus ochrogaster).* Brain, Behavior and Evolution, 8:437-452.

———. 1975. A quantitative description of the copulatory behaviour of meadow voles *(Microtus pennsylvanicus).* Animal Behaviour, 23:261-267.

Harcourt, A. H., P. H. Harvey, S. G. Larson, and R. V. Short. 1981. Testis weight, body weight and breeding system in primates. Nature, 293:55-57.

Jannett, F. J., Jr. 1982. Nesting patterns of adult voles, *Microtus montanus,* in field populations. Journal of Mammalogy, 63:495-498.

Kenagy, G. J., and S. C. Trombulak. 1986. Size and function of mammalian testes in relation to body size. Journal of Mammalogy, 67:1-22.

Kleiman, D. G. 1977. Monogamy in mammals. Quarterly Review of Biology, 52:39-69.

Madison, D. M. 1980. An integrated view of the social biology of *Microtus pennsylvanicus.* Biologist, 62:20-33.

Madison, D. M., and W. J. McShea. 1987. Seasonal changes in reproductive tolerance, spacing, and social organization in meadow voles: A microtine model. American Zoologist, 27:899-908.

McGuire, B., and M. Novak. 1984. A comparison of maternal behaviour in the meadow vole *(Microtus pennsylvanicus),* prairie vole *(M. ochrogaster)* and pine vole *(M. pinetorum).* Animal Behaviour, 32:1132-1141.

McGuire, B., and Novak, M. 1986. Parental care and its relationship to social organization in the montane vole *(Microtus montanus).* Journal of Mammalogy, 67:305-311.

Parker, G. A. 1984. Sperm competition and the evolution of animal mating strategies. Pp. 1-60, *in* Sperm competition and the evolution of animal mating systems (R. L. Smith, ed.). Academic Press, Orlando, Florida, 687 pp.

Pierce, J. D., Jr., et al. 1990. Patterns of sperm allocation across successive ejaculates in four species of voles *(Microtus).* Journal of Reproduction and Fertility, 88:141-149.

Shapiro, L. E., M. E. Meyer, and D. A. Dewsbury. 1989. Affiliative behavior in voles: Effects of morphine, nalaxone, and cross-fostering. Physiology and Behavior, 46:719-723.

Storey, A. E., and D. T. Snow. 1987. Male identity and enclosure size affect paternal attendance of meadow voles, *Microtus pennsylvanicus.* Animal Behaviour, 35:411-419.

Wolff, J. O. 1985. Behavior. Pp. 340-372, *in* Biology of New World *Microtus* (R. H. Tamarin, ed.). American Society of Mammalogists, Special Publication, 8:1-893.

KIN RECOGNITION AND SOCIAL BEHAVIOR
IN MICROTINE RODENTS

Michael H. Ferkin

Department of Psychology, University of California, Berkeley, CA 94720 U.S.A.

Summary.—The mechanism and function of kin recognition were examined within the framework of the social systems of vole species. Association is a proximate mechanism that underlies kin recognition for vole species that have been examined. Yet association during preweaning may not be adequate for all species at certain times of year. Some vole species form communal groups during the breeding season, whereas other species nest communally during the nonbreeding season. Moreover, individuals of some species of voles nest together at high densities, whereas individuals of other species disperse at high densities. Familiarity based on association is the cue that voles use to discriminate between close relatives and unrelated individuals. Voles do not recognize unfamiliar close relatives. Consequently, the ability to recognize kin may be limited to individuals that are philopatric or have repeated contacts with close relatives. Therefore, the ability to recognize kin may be dependent on the mating system, social organization, and habitat of a particular species.

INTRODUCTION

Kin recognition functions to reduce agonistic interactions between close relatives, allowing preferential treatment among close kin (Hamilton, 1964; Holmes, 1988). In many animals, kin recognition may aid in the development of kin selection. Animals may modify their behavior to increase the benefits to close kin, or direct behavior preferentially towards or away from close relatives (Alexander, 1979; Hamilton, 1964). The ability to recognize and preferentially respond to close relatives may be especially important to microtine rodents since behavioral interactions affect social organization and population dynamics (Krebs, 1985; Tamarin, 1983).

The proximate and ultimate aspects of microtine social interactions may be influenced by the genetical relatedness of conspecifics (Charnov, 1981; Kawata, 1990; Tamarin, 1988). Proximately, the effects of genetical relatedness on social interactions appear to depend on the rearing environment and function to promote preferential treatment and nepotistic behavior toward close versus distant relatives (Bekoff, 1981a, 1981b; Blaustein et al., 1987a). Ultimately, positive interactions between related individuals may favor higher reproductive success and increase the inclusive fitness of close relatives (Charnov, 1981; Charnov and Finerty, 1980). Although it may not always be adaptive to display nepotistic behavior, rarely will it be adaptive to favor nonrelatives (Dewsbury, 1988; Holmes, 1988).

The ability of individuals to recognize and respond differentially toward related versus unrelated conspecifics may be an inherent feature among animals (Blaustein et al., 1987a, 1987b; Dewsbury, 1988; Hepper, 1986; Holmes and Sherman, 1983; Porter, 1988; Waldman, 1987). For rodents, phenotypic matching and association are the most frequently inferred mechanisms of kin recognition (Holmes and Sherman, 1983). In phenotypic matching an individual learns and recalls the phenotypes of its relatives or itself, and then compares phenotypes of unfamiliar conspecifics to this learned template (Alexander, 1979; Holmes and Sherman, 1983). In spiny mice *(Acomys cahirinus)* and Belding's ground squirrels *(Spermophilus beldingi),* individuals can recognize close relatives independently of previous contact by phenotype matching. However, in species examined to date, microtine rodents behave as if they may not be able to calculate genetic relatedness independently of familiarity. Vole species do not discriminate between or respond differentially to unfamiliar close relatives versus unfamiliar, unrelated conspecifics (Blaustein et al., 1987a, 1987b). For voles, kin recognition appears to be based solely on association before weaning. Individuals may become familiar with their litter and nestmates through repeated contacts (Bekoff, 1981a; Dewsbury, 1988; Holmes, 1988).

In this chapter, I discuss the bases of kin recognition in microtine rodents. Whereas the bases for kin recognition appear to be universal, the functions, as well as the ability of individuals to recognize kin vary across taxa. Factors such as sexually dimorphic patterns of parental care, dispersal, space use, aggression, and seasonal differences in behavior may affect an individual's ability to identify kin. Indeed, sexual dimorphism in kin recognition may be as widespread as interspecies differences if behavioral polymorphisms are maintained by changing environmental conditions and shifting selective pressures (Blaustein et al., 1987b). Accordingly, kin recognition may play a greater role in social organization for some species than others.

PROXIMATE LEVEL - CAUSALITY

Familiarity, based on common rearing, is a proximate cue that voles use to identify and discriminate between kin and nonkin (Blaustein et al., 1987a, 1987b; Ferkin, 1989; Ferkin and Rutka, 1990). Unlike some rodents that are able to recognize close relatives with which they had no prior experience (Hepper, 1986; Holmes and Sherman, 1982; Porter, 1987), evidence suggests that voles may not recognize unfamiliar relatives as kin (Boyd and Blaustein, 1985; Ferkin, 1989; Ferkin and Rutka, 1990; Gavish et al., 1984). Among voles, phenotypic matching does not appear to be a mechanism of kin recognition; voles have not demonstrated an ability to learn their own or their relatives phenotype, a prerequisite for learning the identification of unfamiliar, close relatives.

For many vole species, the rearing environments are structured so that individuals interact solely with close kin (Kawata, 1990). Although there are exceptions (Jannett, 1978; McShea and Madison, 1984), most natal nests do not contain individuals of unequal relatedness. This type of rearing situation may permit a type of kin recognition that allows discrimination between familiar conspecifics (nestmates and littermates) and unfamiliar conspecifics (non-nestmates: Holmes, 1988). Further, by learning to behave preferentially toward nestmates and littermates, individuals may learn to behave nepotistically toward their relatives (Holmes, 1988). Studies on *Microtus pennsylvanicus* provide support for this view (Ferkin, 1989; Ferkin and Rutka, 1990). However, if individuals are cross-fostered at birth to litters containing unrelated individuals, the cross-fostered young treat their foster nestmates preferentially. Voles that were cross-fostered to other litters fail to recognize their genetic siblings and biological parents (Ferkin, 1989; Ferkin and Rutka, 1990). In addition, preferences for individuals of another species may develop if individuals are cross-fostered to individuals of a sympatric species (McDonald and Forslund, 1978; McGuire and Novak, 1987). Thus, when individuals do not share a common rearing environment, they will fail to discriminate between conspecifics on genetic relatedness alone (Bekoff, 1981a, 1981b; Holmes, 1988).

Long-term associations between close relatives may be facilitated by repeated contacts. These would occur in both males and females in species that form family aggregations (e.g., *M. montanus* and *M. pinetorum*), or that are monomorphic in dispersal tendencies (e.g., *M. ochrogaster:* Boonstra et al., 1987), and among females in polygynous species in which males are dispersal-prone and females tend to be philopatric (e.g., *M. pennsylvanicus, M. californicus, Clethrionomys rufocanus,* and *C. glareolus:* Boonstra et al., 1987; Ims, 1989; Kawata, 1987b). Repeated interactions between close relatives may enhance the probability of kin-directed behavior, and increase the likelihood of kin recognition (Ims, 1989). In species in which females are philopatric, sisters had home ranges that were in closer proximity than nonsiblings (Ims, 1989; Kawata, 1987a, 1987b; Pugh, 1989; Ylönen and Viitala, 1987). Within a population of *M. pennsylvanicus,* neighboring females were more closely related than neighboring males (Pugh, 1989), and behavioral encounters between neighboring females contained fewer agonistic acts than encounters between neighboring males (Ferkin, 1988b). Similarly, female red-backed voles, *C. rufocanus,* were better able to acquire an exclusive home range and increase reproductive success when neighbors were sisters (Kawata, 1987b). In adulthood, the ability to recognize neighbors, as well as kin, may be limited to individuals that remain in close proximity to close relatives. Space sharing, increased reproductive success, and reduced agonism resulting from philopatry may promote preferential treatment of relatives and foster kin recognition.

In some species of voles, the opportunity to associate with close relatives in adulthood may be negated by sex-biased natal dispersal (Boonstra et al., 1987; Holmes, 1988). In species that tend to be polygynous (e.g., *M. pennsylvanicus, M. californicus, C. rutilus,* and *C. rufocanus:* Ims, 1989; Kawata, 1987b; Madison, 1980; Ostfeld, 1986; Viitala, 1987), dispersed males may have little or no contact with close relatives. Neighboring male and female meadow voles were not related (Pugh, 1989), and encounters between males and females were not affected by familiarity (Ferkin, 1988b). In addition, neighboring males were not closely related (Pugh, 1989), and encounters between neighboring males were more agonistic than those between non-neighboring males (Ferkin, 1988b). For males in this type of mating system, kin recognition may dissipate with time (Dewsbury, 1982, 1988; Holmes, 1988). In species in which sex-biased dispersal patterns are prevalent, kin recognition among adults may be limited to the philopatric sex.

PROXIMATE LEVEL - CUES

Olfactory cues alone may allow microtine rodents to discriminate between and respond differentially to close relatives and unrelated conspecifics (Ferkin, 1989; Smale et al., 1990). The principal phenotypic cues used for social recognition are chemosignals of low volatility in the urine, saliva, and sebaceous and preputial gland secretions (Brown, 1985a; Rowsemitt et al., 1988). Whether each odor-producing substrate transmits cues that relay specific information is presently unknown. However, the size and activity of the odor producing tissues (Rowsemitt et al., 1988), the saliency of the odor cues that are emitted, and the reactions to these odors may vary seasonally. Peak activity occurs during the breeding season when gonadal titers are high (Brown, 1985b). Therefore, manipulations of estrogen and testosterone levels may affect odor preferences and odors generated by voles. Seasonality may also affect the saliency of chemosignals broadcasted by family members.

Familial chemosignals emitted by *M. ochrogaster* and *M. pinetorum* inhibit puberty and delay maturation and growth (Batzli et al., 1977; Lepri and Vandenbergh, 1986), but do not in *M. pennsylvanicus* and *M. montanus* (Batzli et al., 1977; Cockburn, 1988). Familiarity of odor cues and chemosignals between voles enhances scent marking, investigatory, and affiliative behaviors (Carter et al., 1988; Viitala and Hoffmeyer, 1985), and may expedite kin recognition. The delay or onset of puberty, and the interpretation of priming pheromones may be mediated by the vomeronasal organ (Lepri and Wysocki, 1987). Here, the vole must make direct contact with the odorants, which are high molecular weight, nonvolatile substances (Lepri and Wysocki, 1987). In contrast, the primary olfactory system of voles is dependent on volatile cues, and may mediate hormonal changes in an individual in response to conspecific odors (Brown, 1985a). Although the neural bases of kin recognition are as yet relatively unexplored, in *M. ochrogaster,* behavioral and neuroendocrine changes may be a result of differential responsiveness to familiar individuals (Carter et al., 1988; Smale, 1988).

FUNCTIONS OF KIN RECOGNITION

The effects of kinship on social behaviors remain largely unknown for most microtine rodents. Although the effects of kinship on agonistic acts have been examined by few investigators, it is generally agreed that familiar close kin would behave amicably toward one another (Bekoff, 1981a; Ferkin, 1989; Ferkin and Rutka, 1990). Yet, several other responses to familiar kin are seen in other species. For example, in voles that may be facultatively monogamous, such as *M. ochrogaster* and *M. pinetorum,* kin recognition serves to deter mating with a familiar sibling (Gavish et al., 1984; McGuire and Getz, 1981; Schadler, 1983). These voles also show a preference for a familiar mate as opposed to an unfamiliar one (Newman and Halpin, 1988; Shapiro et al., 1986). By contrast, neither *M. pennsylvanicus* nor *M. montanus* shows a preference between familiar and unfamiliar mates (Cockburn, 1988; Shapiro et al., 1986). Moreover, inbreeding occurs in *M. pennsylvanicus* (Batzli et al., 1977; Pugh and Tamarin, 1988), but not *M. montanus* (Boyd and Blaustein, 1985), which may live in extended families at high densities (Jannett, 1978), whereas *M. pennsylvanicus* remains solitary (Madison, 1980). Differences between these species in avoiding mating with close relatives may have to do with differences in their mating systems.

Common to both monogamous and polygynous species is that kin recognition favors reduced agonistic behavior and affiliative interactions between close relatives (Blaustein et al., 1987b). In *M. ochrogaster, M. pinetorum, M. arvalis, M. montanus,* and *C. rufocanus* kin recognition may aid in the formation of communal groups and extended families during the breeding season (Boyce and Boyce, 1988; FitzGerald and Madison, 1983; Getz and Carter, 1980; Jannett, 1978; Viitala and Hoffmeyer, 1985). To offset the benefits gained by communal nesting, inbreeding is inhibited (Boyd and Blaustein, 1985; Gavish et al., 1984; McGuire and Getz, 1981; Schadler, 1983), and maturation is delayed by odors transmitted by close adult relatives (Batzli et al. 1977; Viitala and Hoffmeyer, 1985). With the exception of montane voles, these species tend to inhabit predictable, stable habitats (Getz, 1985) and may be monogamous under certain conditions (Cockburn, 1988; Wolff, 1985). Here, kin recognition may be enhanced by restricted emigration and immigration into family groups, repeated intragroup social contacts (Holmes, 1988), and monomorphic dispersal tendencies (Boonstra et al., 1987). Presumably, kin recognition may act to reduce intrafamily competition.

In contrast, kin recognition does not appear to inhibit inbreeding and delay maturation in *M. pennsylvanicus* and *M. californicus* (Batzli et al., 1977; Cockburn, 1988; Pugh and Tamarin, 1988; Viitala and Hoffmeyer, 1985). Two characteristics common to these species are that they live in unpredictable, ephemeral habitats (Getz, 1985) and are polygynous during the breeding season (Cockburn, 1988; Wolff, 1985). In these species, male-biased dispersal patterns may limit kin recognition to females (Boonstra et al., 1987). However, these species form communal groups composed of close relatives during the nonbreeding season (Kawata, 1990; Madison et al., 1984; Ylönen et al., 1988). Kin recognition may be involved in the formation of these communal groups. Although a relationship between kin recognition and social systems is emerging, more species should be examined before one can adduce its validity.

Errors in kin recognition may result in preferential treatment toward nonrelatives and a consequent lowering of inclusive fitness among close kin. This situation may arise at high densities in voles that form extended families (Boyce and Boyce, 1988; FitzGerald and Madison, 1983; Jannett, 1978). Increased immigration may permit unrelated individuals to enter these family aggregations (Kawata, 1990). In species that do not form family aggregations in response to high densities during the breeding season (Madison, 1980; Ostfeld, 1986), increased immigration and dispersal may permit individuals to have repeated contacts with unrelated conspecifics (Lidicker, 1985). Small isolated demes that are formed in low density populations become larger and more continuous at higher densities (Lidicker, 1985). If the demes are composed of a small number of related individuals, the average degree of relatedness between individuals would decline as density increases and the population becomes more continuous (Lidicker, 1985). In both of these scenarios, repeated contacts of unrelated individuals may allow them to be identified as close kin, and possibly to receive preferential treatment.

SEASONALITY

The ability to recognize kin may be affected by the seasonal plasticity of social behavior typical of vole species (Madison and McShea, 1987; Viitala, 1977; Ylönen and Viitala, 1987). During the nonbreeding season, agonistic behavior is reduced and voles may display a social preference for same-sex conspecifics (Ferkin, 1988a, 1990; Ferkin and Seamon, 1987). In many vole species territorial boundaries established by females during the breeding season are relaxed during the nonbreeding season when voles nest communally (Karlsson, 1986; Madison et al., 1984; Ylönen et al., 1988). Seasonal shifts in social tolerance may facilitate the formation and determine the composition of overwintering groups (Ferkin and Seamon, 1987; Madison and McShea, 1987; McShea, 1990; Viitala, 1977). These groups may be composed of related individuals (Kawata, 1990; Madison et al., 1984). At high densities, unrelated individuals may be able to infiltrate these groups and benefit from the selective advantages of preferential treatment. Consequently, association may not provide a reliable basis for kin recognition.

In addition, errors in kin recognition may occur during the breeding season when lactating females raise their litters communally (McShea and Madison, 1984). In *M. pennsylvanicus,* for example, fitness may be reduced by preferential treatment toward nephews and nieces versus sons and daughters.

If the lactating females are not close relatives, preferential treatment of distant relatives may lower direct and inclusive fitness among genetic relatives. As the breeding season proceeds, dispersal and fusion of these family groups would reduce the degree of relatedness between neighbors, and thereby reducing inclusive fitness among related individuals.

POPULATION REGULATION

Charnov and Finerty (1980) created a model to describe the relationship among kin selection, social behavior, and populations density. The sociobiological hypothesis or kin-selection model has been used to predict that periodic fluctuations of vole populations may be influenced by the degree of relatedness between conspecifics (Charnov and Finerty, 1980). Central to the kin-selection model is that changes in population density are related to shifts in intraspecific aggression between neighbors, which are dependent on their degree of relatedness. A high coefficient of relatedness between neighbors would favor nepotistic behavior, reduced aggression, and greater reproductive success. From the model, we can predict that in low-density populations, neighboring conspecifics are close relatives, whereas neighbors in high-density populations would not be as closely related. A critical assumption of this model is the ability of individuals to recognize kin and behave accordingly.

The utility of the Charnov and Finerty (1980) hypothesis has been the subject of recent scrutiny (Bekoff, 1981b; Heske et al., 1988; Kawata, 1990; Pugh and Tamarin, this volume). Despite theoretical support (Warkowska-Dratnal and Stenseth, 1985), empirical evidence for the kin-selection model has been equivocal (Boyd and Blaustein, 1985; Ferkin, 1988b, 1989; Ferkin and Rutka, 1990; Ylönen et al., 1990), or lacking (Boonstra and Hogg, 1988; Kawata, 1987a; Pugh, 1989). The lack of agreement concerning the predictive value of this hypothesis may be a consequence of varied interpretation of the model, difficulty of testing a nonmathematical model, and limited consideration for the effects of kin recognition on behavioral interactions.

In recent tests, researchers examined differences in a suite of population characters between field populations that were founded by relatives or nonrelatives (Boonstra and Hogg, 1988; Kawata, 1987a; Ylönen et al., 1990). Unfortunately, the effects of familiarity on kin recognition were not controlled in these studies. It is not unreasonable to assume that neighbors in low density and founding populations may be considered close relatives, independently of genetic relatedness. Indeed, Boonstra and Hogg (1988) and Kawata (1987a) found no differences between populations started by relatives and those by unrelated individuals. Further, in other studies (Kawata, 1987a; Pugh, 1989), populations may not have reached sufficiently high densities, and only at high densities would one expect to see the effects of kinship on population processes (Charnov and Finerty, 1980). Increased dispersal at high densities may dilute the degree of relatedness between neighbors. Neighbors may become surrounded increasingly more by less-closely related individuals, nullifying the positive effects of kin-directed behaviors, and thereby reducing the likelihood of the occurrence of kin recognition (Kawata, 1990; Lidicker, 1985).

As previously mentioned, kin recognition may be sexually dimorphic. Since most vole species are polygynous (Cockburn, 1988; Wolff, 1985), the ability to recognize kin may be limited among males. In these species, sires have no contact with their own offspring prior to weaning (Oliveras and Novak, 1985). Previous association resulted in reduced agonistic behavior between sires and their own offspring (Ferkin, 1989). Sires and offspring were not agonistic if both were reared together. However, this situation is uncommon in field populations. Male-biased dispersal patterns typically found among polygynous voles (Boonstra et al., 1987) may also limit subsequent contacts between males and close relatives. Intra-litter social bonds may become diluted after a few weeks of age as a consequence of natal dispersal (Ferkin, 1988a; Wilson, 1982). In *M. pennsylvanicus* (Pugh, 1989), *C. rufocanus* (Ims, 1989; Ylönen and Viitala, 1987), and *C. rutilus* (Viitala, 1987) neighboring males were not close relatives. Indeed, pairings between neighboring adult male *M. pennsylvanicus* were more agonistic than between non-neighboring adult males (Ferkin, 1988a). These findings support the view that kin recognition dissipates with time, suggesting that the kin-selection model may not be an adequate predictor of the behavior for these individuals (Kawata, 1990).

By contrast, females in both polygynous and monogamous mating systems may be able to recognize kin. Maternal care (McGuire and Novak, 1984) coupled with female philopatry (Boonstra et al., 1987) may increase the likelihood of social interactions among sisters and mother and daughters, and favor the formation of long-term associations between female kin. Pugh (1989) reported that 85% of the female meadow voles in one population settled within two home range lengths from their birth site. In this field population, neighboring females were related (Pugh, 1989), and paired encounters between neighboring females contained fewer agonistic acts than encounters between non-neighboring females (Ferkin, 1988b). Similarly, females in the following species are philopatric and nest adjoining the territories of close female relatives: *C. rutilus* (Viitala, 1987), *C. rufocanus* (Kawata, 1987b; Ylönen and Viitala, 1987), and *C. glareolus* (Ylönen et al., 1988). In these populations sisters were often neighbors. This condition would favor repeated contacts between female siblings, encourage long-term associations, allow preferential treatment toward close relatives, and facilitate identification of close kin.

The duration of kin recognition among microtine rodents may be affected by density and environmental constraints (Blaustein et al., 1987b; Heske et al., 1988; Lidicker, 1985). As density increases past a certain point, neighboring individuals would be less familiar with one another with the consequence that aggression may increase (Lidicker, 1985). Voles that form family groups in response to high densities may be able to discriminate between close relatives and unrelated individuals. Voles that do not form family groups may be unable to recognize kin at high density. Preferential treatment of close relatives over nonrelatives also may not occur when environmental conditions are variable, or if resources are not limited (Blaustein et al., 1987b).

CONCLUSIONS

Vole species appear to use phenotypic cues such as familiarity to recognize close relatives and neighbors. Usually these cues are adequate to distinguish close relatives from unrelated conspecifics, at least at certain times of the year. Although the proximate mechanism that underlies kin recognition appears to be universal for all vole species, association during pre-weaning does not appear to be an adequate system for vole species that nest in multi-family aggregations, raise young communally, and are sexually dimorphic in parental care and dispersal tendencies.

Vole species that differ in social organization, habitat, and mating system appear to have derived different functions for kin recognition. Circumstantial evidence suggests that kin recognition reduces intrafamily competition among species that form assemblages of close relatives in the breeding season, have monomorphic dispersal patterns, are monogamous, and inhabit stable, predictable habitats.

Female philopatry may permit repeated contacts with neighbors that may be close relatives. Long-term associations among females may favor preferential treatment and permit kin recognition. In contrast, the lack of paternal care and male-biased dispersal tendencies in most species, lead me to suggest limited interaction between males and close relatives. Since voles do not appear to be able to recognize close kin by phenotypic matching, kin recognition may dissipate with time, or be rendered unnecessary for males once they disperse from their natal areas. Sexually dimorphic life history patterns of many vole species may create limitations to models of population regulation that are dependent upon kin recognition.

ACKNOWLEDGMENTS

I benefitted from the constructive criticism of S. R. Pugh, R. H. Tamarin, I. Zucker, Z. T. Halpin, M. R. Gorman, and S. B. Ferkin. Preparation of this manuscript was supported by a National Institutes of Health, National Research Service Award postdoctoral fellowship, grant 1F32NS08792-01.

LITERATURE CITED

Alexander, R. D. 1979. Darwinism and human affairs. University of Washington Press, Seattle, 317 pp.

Batzli, G. O., L. L. Getz, and S. S. Hurley. 1977. Suppression of growth and reproduction of microtine rodents by social factors. Journal of Mammalogy, 58:583-591.

Bekoff, M. 1981a. Mammalian sibling interactions: genes, facilitative environments, and the coefficient of familiarity. Pp. 307-346, *in* Parental care in mammals (D. J. Gubernick and P. H. Klopfer, eds.). Plenum Press, New York, 459 pp.

―――. 1981b. Vole population cycles: kin selection or familiarity? Oecologia (Berlin), 45:1-2.

Blaustein, A. R., M. Bekoff, and T. J. Daniels. 1987a. Kin recognition in vertebrates (excluding primates): empirical evidence. Pp. 287-332, *in* Kin recognition in animals (D. J. C. Fletcher and C. D. Michener, eds.). John Wiley and Sons, Chichester, England, 465 pp.

―――. 1987b. Kin recognition in vertebrates (excluding primates): mechanisms, functions, and future research. Pp. 333-358, *in* Kin recognition in animals (D. J. C. Fletcher and C. D. Michener, eds.). John Wiley and Sons, Chichester, England, 465 pp.

Boonstra, R., and I. Hogg. 1988. Friends and strangers: a test of the Charnov and Finerty hypothesis. Oecologia (Berlin), 77:95-100.

Boonstra, R., C. J. Krebs, M. S. Gaines, M. L. Johnson, and I. T. M. Craine. 1987. Natal philopatry and breeding systems in voles *(Microtus* spp.). Journal of Animal Ecology, 56:655-673.

Boyce, C. C. K., and J. L. Boyce, III. 1988. Population biology of *Microtus arvalis*. I. Lifetime reproductive success of solitary and grouped breeding females. Journal of Animal Ecology, 57:711-722.

Boyd, S. K., and A. R. Blaustein. 1985. Familiarity and inbreeding avoidance in the grey-tailed vole. Journal of Mammalogy, 66:348-352.

Brown, R. E. 1985a. The rodents I: effects of odours on reproductive physiology (primer effects). Pp. 245-344, *in* Social odours in mammals (R. E. Brown and D. W. MacDonald, eds.). Clarendon Press, Oxford, 1:1-506.

Brown, R. E. 1985b. The rodents II: suborder Myomorpha. Pp. 345-457, *in* Social odours in mammals (R. E. Brown and D. W. MacDonald, eds.). Clarendon Press, Oxford, 1:1-506.

Carter, C. S., D. M. Witt, G. Thompson, and K. Carlstead. 1988. Effects of hormonal, sexual, and social history on mating and pair bonding in prairie voles. Physiology and Behavior, 44:691-697.

Charnov, E. L. 1981. Vole population cycles: ultimate or proximate explanation? Oecologia (Berlin), 48:132.

Charnov, E. L., and J. P. Finerty. 1980. Vole population cycles. A case for kin-selection? Oecologia (Berlin), 45:1-2.

Cockburn, A. 1988. Social behaviour in fluctuating populations. Croom Helm, London, 239 pp.

Dewsbury, D. A. 1982. Avoidance of incestuous breeding between siblings in two species of *Peromyscus* mice. Biology of Behavior, 7:157-169.

―――. 1988. Kin discrimination and reproductive behavior in muroid rodents. Behavior Genetics, 18:525-536.

Ferkin, M. H. 1988a. Seasonal differences in social behavior among adult and juvenile meadow voles, *Microtus pennsylvanicus*. Ethology, 79:116-125.

————. 1988b. The effect of familiarity on social interactions in meadow voles, *Microtus pennsylvanicus:* a laboratory and field study. Animal Behaviour, 36:1816-1822.

————. 1989. Adult-weanling recognition among captive meadow voles *(Microtus pennsylvanicus).* Behaviour, 118:114-124.

————. 1990. Odor selections of island beach voles during the nonbreeding season. Journal of Mammalogy, 71:397-401.

Ferkin, M. H., and T. F. Rutka. 1990. Sibling recognition in meadow voles, *Microtus pennsylvanicus*. Canadian Journal of Zoology, 68:609-613.

Ferkin, M. H., and J. O. Seamon. 1987. Odor preferences and social behavior in meadow voles, *Microtus pennsylvanicus:* seasonal differences. Canadian Journal of Zoology, 65:2931-2937.

FitzGerald, R. W., and D. M. Madison. 1983. Social organization of a free-ranging population of pine voles, *Microtus pinetorum*. Behavioral Ecology and Sociobiology, 13:183-187.

Gavish, L., J. E. Hofmann, and L. L. Getz. 1984. Sibling recognition in the prairie vole, *Microtus ochrogaster*. Animal Behaviour, 32:362-366.

Getz, L. L. 1985. Habitats. Pp. 286-289, *in* Biology of New World *Microtus* (R. H. Tamarin, ed.). Special Publication, American Society of Mammalogists, 8:1-893.

Getz, L. L., and S. C. Carter. 1980. Social organization in *Microtus ochrogaster* populations. The Biologist, 62:56-69.

Hamilton, W. D. 1964. The genetical evolution of social behaviour, I and II. Journal of Theoretical Biology, 7:1-52.

Heske, E. J., R. S. Ostfeld, and W. Z. Lidicker, Jr. 1988. Does social behavior drive vole cycles? An evaluation of competing models as they pertain to California voles. Canadian Journal of Zoology, 66:1153-1159.

Hepper, P. G. 1986. Kin recognition: functions and mechanisms a review. Biological Reviews, 61:63-93.

Holmes, W. G. 1988. Kinship and the development of social preferences. Pp. 389-414, *in* Handbook of developmental psychology and behavioral neurobiology (E. M. Blass, ed.). Plenum Press, New York, 9:1-476.

Holmes, W. G., and P. W. Sherman. 1982. The ontogeny of kin recognition in two species of ground squirrels. American Zoologist, 22:491-517.

————. 1983. Kin recognition in animals. American Scientist, 71:46-55.

Ims, R. A. 1989. Kinship and origins: effects on dispersal and space sharing in *Clethrionomys rufocanus*. Ecology, 70:607-616.

Jannett, F. J., Jr. 1978. The density dependent formation of extended maternal families of the montane vole, *Microtus montanus nanus.* Behavioral Ecology and Sociobiology, 3:245-263.

Karlsson, A. F. 1986. Effect of conspecifics on winter movements and dispersion in an overwintering bank vole *(Clethrionomys glareolus)* population. Canadian Journal of Zoology, 64:593-598.

Kawata, M. 1987a. The effect of kinship on spacing among female red-backed voles, *Clethrionomys rufocanus bedfordiae.* Oecologia (Berlin), 72:115-122.

———. 1987b. Pregnancy failure and suppression by female-female interaction in enclosed populations of the red-backed vole, *Clethrionomys rufocanus bedfordiae.* Behavioral Ecology and Sociobiology, 20:89-97.

———. 1990. Fluctuating populations and kin interaction in mammals. Trends in Evolutionary Ecology, 5:17-20.

Krebs, C. J. 1985. Do changes in spacing behavior drive population cycles in small mammals? Pp. 295-312, *in* Behavioral ecology: ecological consequences of adaptive behaviour (R. M. Sibly and R. H. Smith, eds.). Blackwell Scientific Publications, Oxford, 420 pp.

Lepri, J. J., and J. G. Vandenbergh. 1986. Puberty in pine voles, *Microtus pinetorum,* and the influence of chemosignals on female reproduction. Biology of Reproduction, 34:370-377.

Lepri, J. J., and C. J. Wysocki. 1987. Removal of the vomeronasal organ disrupts the activation of reproduction in female voles. Physiology and Behavior, 40:349-355.

Lidicker, W. Z., Jr. 1985. Population structuring as a factor in understanding microtine cycles. Acta Zoologica Fennica, 173:23-27.

Madison, D. M. 1980. An integrated view of the social behavior of *Microtus pennsylvanicus.* The Biologist, 69:20-33.

Madison, D. M., and W. J. McShea. 1987. Seasonal changes in reproductive tolerance, spacing, and social organization in meadow voles: a microtine model. American Zoologist, 27:899-908.

Madison, D. M., R. W. FitzGerald, and W. J. McShea. 1984. Dynamics of social nesting in overwintering meadow voles *(Microtus pennsylvanicus):* possible consequences for population cycling. Behavioral Ecology and Sociobiology, 15:9-17.

McDonald, D. L., and L. G. Forslund. 1978. The development of social preferences in the voles *Microtus montanus* and *M. canicaudus.* Effects of cross-fostering. Behavioral Biology, 22:497-508.

McGuire, B., and M. A. Novak. 1984. A comparison of maternal behaviour in the meadow vole *(Microtus pennsylvanicus),* prairie vole *(M. ochrogaster),* and pine vole *(M. pinetorum).* Animal Behaviour, 32:1132-1141.

———. 1987. Effects of cross-fostering on the development of social preferences in meadow voles *(Microtus pennsylvanicus).* Behavior and Neural Biology, 47:167-172.

McGuire, M. R., and L. L. Getz. 1981. Incest taboo between sibling *Microtus ochrogaster.* Journal of Mammalogy, 62:213-215.

McShea, W. J. 1990. Social tolerance and proximate mechanisms of dispersal among winter groups of meadow voles, *Microtus pennsylvanicus.* Animal Behaviour, 39:346-351.

McShea, W. J., and D. M. Madison. 1984. Communal nesting by reproductively active females in a spring population of *Microtus pennsylvanicus.* Canadian Journal of Zoology, 62:344-346.

Newman, K. S., and Z. T. Halpin. 1988. Individual odours and mate recognition in the prairie vole, *Microtus ochrogaster.* Animal Behaviour, 36:1779-1787.

Oliveras, D., and M. A. Novak. 1986. A comparison of paternal behaviour in the meadow vole, *Microtus pennsylvanicus,* the pine vole, *M. pinetorum,* and the prairie vole, *M. ochrogaster.* Animal Behaviour, 34:519-526.

Ostfeld, R. S. 1986. Territoriality and mating system of California voles. Journal of Animal Ecology, 55:691-706.

Porter, R. H. 1987. Kin recognition: functions and mediating mechanisms. Pp. 175-203, *in* Sociobiology and psychology: ideas, issues and applications (C. Crawford, M. Smith, and D. Krebs, eds.). Erlbaum Associates, Hillsdale, New Jersey, 429 pp.

———. 1988. The ontogeny of sibling recognition in rodents: superfamily Muroidea. Behavior Genetics, 18:483-494.

Pugh, S. R. 1989. Relatedness, inbreeding and reproductive success in the meadow vole, *Microtus pennsylvanicus.* Ph.D. Dissertation, Boston University, Boston, 108 pp.

Pugh, S. R., and R. H. Tamarin. 1988. Inbreeding in a population of meadow voles, *Microtus pennsylvanicus.* Canadian Journal of Zoology, 66:1831-1834.

Rowsemitt, C. N., C. J. Walsh, M. C. Kuehl, R. E. Moore, and L. L. Jackson. 1988. Hormonal regulation of preputial gland function in male *Microtus montanus,* the montane vole. Comparative Biochemistry and Physiology, 90A:195-200.

Schadler, M. H. 1983. Male siblings inhibit reproductive activity in female pine voles, *Microtus pinetorum.* Biology of Reproduction, 28:1137-1139.

Shapiro, L. E., D. Austin, S. E. Ward, and D. A. Dewsbury. 1986. Familiarity and female choice in two species of voles *(Microtus ochrogaster* and *Microtus montanus).* Animal Behaviour, 34:90-97.

Smale, L. 1988. Influence of male gonadal hormones and familiarity on pregnancy interruption in prairie voles. Biology and Reproduction, 39:28-31.

Smale, L., J. M. Pedersen, M. L. Block, and I. Zucker. 1990. Investigation of conspecific male odours by female prairie voles. Animal Behaviour, 39:768-774.

Tamarin, R. H. 1983. Animal population regulation through behavioral interactions. Pp. 698-720, *in* Advances in the study of animal behavior (J. F. Eisenberg and D. V. Kleiman, eds.). Special

Publication, The American Society of Mammalogists, 7:1-753.

————. 1988. The role of behavior in models of small rodent population dynamics. Oikos, 52:222-223.

Viitala, J. 1977. Social organization in cyclic subartic populations of the voles *Clethrionomys rufocanus* (Sund.) and *Microtus agrestis* (L.). Annales Zoologici Fennici, 14:53-93.

————. 1987. Social organization of *Clethrionomys rutilus* (Pall.) at Kilpisjarvi, Finnish Lapland. Annales Zoologici Fennici, 24:267-273.

Viitala, J., and I. Hoffmeyer. 1985. Social organization in *Clethrionomys* compared with *Microtus* and *Apodemus:* social odours, chemistry, and biological effects. Annales Zoologici Fennici, 22:359-371.

Waldman, B. 1987. Mechanisms of kin recognition. Journal of Theoretical Biology, 128:159-185.

Warkowska-Dratnal, H., and N. C. Stenseth. 1985. Dispersal and the microtine cycle: comparison of two hypotheses. Oecologia (Berlin), 65:468-477.

Wilson, S. C. 1982. The development of social behaviour between siblings and nonsiblings of the voles, *Microtus ochrogaster* and *Microtus pennsylvanicus.* Animal Behaviour, 30:426-437.

Wolff, J. O. 1985. Behavior. Pp. 340-372, *in* Biology of New World *Microtus.* (R. H. Tamarin, ed.). Special Publication, The American Society of Mammalogists, 8:1-893.

Ylönen, H., and J. Viitala. 1987. Social organization and habitat use of introduced populations of the vole *Clethrionomys rufocanus* (Sund) in central Finland. Zeitschrift für Säugetierkunde, 52:354-363.

Ylönen, H., T. Kojola, and J. Viitala. 1988. Changing female spacing behaviour and demography in an enclosed breeding population of *Clethrionomys glareolus.* Holartic Ecology, 11:286-292.

Ylönen, H., T. Mappes, and J. Viitala. 1990. Different demography of friends and strangers: an experiment on the impact of kinship and familiarity in *Clethrionomys glareolus.* Oecologia (Berlin), 83:333-337.

Social Systems and
Population Cycles in Voles
Advances in Life Sciences
© Birkhäuser Verlag Basel

SOCIAL ORGANIZATIONAL MODES
IN MODELS OF MICROTINE CYCLING

Dale M. Madison

Department of Biological Sciences, State University of New York at Binghamton, Binghamton, NY
13903 U.S.A.

Summary.—An understanding of the social behavior and organization of microtine rodents is relevant
to theory regarding regulation of numbers and population cycles. Unclear or typological concepts of
social organization and inadequate data on year-round social structure are barriers to this
understanding. The social organizational mode is defined as a subunit of social organization within a
species, such as the exclusive territories of breeding female meadow voles. All the modes at any
particular time in a population make up the social organization of that population, whereas the social
system consists of all the social organizations that exist for a species throughout its range and annual
cycle. Defining under what circumstances the modes vary is the approach most likely to show
significant linkages between social behavior and population processes. Social tolerance and modal
diversity may be closely linked to whether populations are likely to fluctuate.

INTRODUCTION

It is an understatement to say that many scientists are concerned with the factors that play
fundamental roles in regulating the density of microtine populations and in causing multiannual cycles.
Much time is spent in recording the vital statistics of populations and trying to associate gains or
losses with a host of independent variables. Some biologists have known for years that species differ in
their social behavior, and population ecologists have noted that different species of small mammals
have different population characteristics and propensities for population cycling. Thus, it is only
natural to ask whether the differences in social behavior between species are linked to interspecific
differences in population processes. Superficially, it seems simple to look for these linkages. One
merely establishes for each species what the social system is and what the vital population statistics
are, and then looks for associations. Comparative studies such as these are often more difficult to
achieve than they appear (Ostfeld and Klosterman, this volume). A corollary approach is to look for
linkages between changes in both population statistics and social behavior within the same population.

One assumption in this approach is that there is a typical, identifiable social organization and set
of population statistics for a population. The reliability of this assumption, and the problem of how

one looks for associations between these behavioral and population variables, must be evaluated. In this paper, I will first review definitions of social system, social organization, and social structure. Then, I will develop the concept of a social organizational mode and relate it to studies attempting to find connections between social behavior and population statistics. I will follow with a brief review of present knowledge concerning social complexity and organizational modes within a few microtine species representing a wide range of social variation. Finally, I will use the concept of the social organizational mode to evaluate the behavioral models that are used to explain population cycling in microtine rodents.

CRITIQUE OF CURRENT DEFINITIONS OF SOCIAL PATTERNS

From a review of a wide range of standard texts in animal behavior I determined that clear definitions of social system, social organization, and social structure were few or nonexistent. I turned to studies of primates for insights regarding definitions, not only because the longer history of intensive studies of social behavior seemed likely to produce a clearer terminology, but also because some studies of primate sociobiology reveal geographic and population variations in social organization within a species (Dunbar, 1979), which may help us in interpreting the role of social behavior in vole cycles.

With few exceptions, the terms "social organization," "social structure," and "social system" are used as synonyms by most investigators probably to avoid repetition of word use in scientific writing. These terms are used interchangeably in major review texts by Bernstein and Smith (1979), Crook (1970), Hinde (1983), and Smuts et al. (1986), to identify the spatio-temporal patterns of distribution of animals within a species that result from the identities (e.g., relatedness, familiarity), characteristics (e.g., size, gender, age, reproductive status), and interactions of the animals. One exception is the use of "social structure" to refer to the pattern of individual occurrence through time and space, and to use "social organization" in reference to the pattern of social interactions (relationships) between conspecifics through time (Rowell, 1979). To study social structure, one therefore represents individuals as points and studies the clustering, density, appearance, disappearance, and movement of these points through time. Social organization is described by the social relationships between these points and how these relationships influence spacing and group affiliation. Differences in relatedness and developmental experience are the focus of studies of "social organization."

Currently, most primate studies emphasize relationships, whereas microtine studies have for the most part emphasized the social structure approach. I believe the dichotomy is in part the result of differences in maturity of the behavioral studies involving the two groups. Past studies emphasized spatial patterns, often attributing these to differential social tolerance between individuals based on such factors as sex, size (mass), reproductive status, and aggressiveness. Species were then quickly "typed" as to the nature of their social organization. Subsequent and especially recent studies motivated by sociobiological theory began to address developmental experiences and kinship as significant factors in grouping patterns. In addition, inter- and intrapopulational variations in grouping patterns have become apparent. As even more extensive studies are conducted on a species, multiple social "strategies" have been revealed among individuals within populations, and the typological concept of a species' social organization becomes difficult to apply in many cases.

Most rodents are too quiet, small and difficult to observe in their natural habitat to allow recording of individual differences in the nature of their interactions and their developmental experiences. Also, the larger litters of rodents complicate developmental experiences. Cross-fostering techniques and the manipulation of litter size are ways of addressing some of the experiential questions. However, for most practical purposes, the study of Rowell's (1979:5) "social organization" in microtines seems to be essentially restricted to kinship studies like those of Kawata (1985), Tamarin et al. (1983), and Sheridan and Tamarin (1986).

My preference is to retain Rowell's (1979) definitions, but to change the terminology to *spatio-temporal structure* (for social structure) and *relational structure* (for social organization). I suggest using *social organization* to include both spatio-temporal and relational structure, but restricting the definition to social patterns at the time and location of the study, such that through the annual cycle and across the geographical range of a species, the species may have several different social organizations. I suggest that the term *social system* be used to refer to the total collection of social organizations that exist for a species, understanding clearly that some types of social organization may not be represented in some populations or at some times.

In applying the terminology, it should be understood that different species may at some point have similar social organizations, but each species is most likely to have a unique social system. Within a species, different populations may have different social organizations and corresponding variation in population characteristics. One microtine species in which this may occur is *Clethrionomys glareolus,* which has northern "cyclic" populations that are reproductively different from southern "noncyclic" populations (Hansson, 1985). Different social organizations may also occur in a single population over time (e.g., meadow voles, *Microtus pennsylvanicus:* Madison and McShea, 1987). The population may also have complex social organizations made up of two or more types of social units (modes of social organization) that are clearly different and may affect the processes of a population in different ways. A thorough understanding of what these modes of social organization are, and how they interact, is fundamental to assessing clearly the relationship between social behavior and population processes in microtine populations.

DEVELOPMENT OF THE CONCEPT OF THE
SOCIAL ORGANIZATIONAL MODE

A mode within the social system is a single type (subunit) of social organization in a population. If the unit of dispersion *(sensu* Brown and Orians, 1970) within the population is the individual, and if all individuals obey the same dispersion rules (e.g., all defend a territory), then the population may have just one organizational mode and be considered unimodal. If different classes of solitary individuals obey different dispersion rules, the populations can be considered multimodal. An example of the latter may be seen in meadow voles during the summer. Breeding females defend exclusive territories, whereas reproductive males overlap and move around in search of receptive females. In cases in which the unit of dispersion is the social group, and if all groups have the same composition, the population would be considered unimodal. If the concurrent groups differ in social organization, such as the monogamous and polyandrous groups in pine voles *(Microtus pinetorum:* FitzGerald and Madison, 1983), or if populations consist of both individual and group units, such as in *M. arvalis* (Boyce and Boyce, 1988a), the social organization would be multimodal.

The time dimension must also be included in discussions of social organizational modes. The examples mentioned above were cases in which different modes occurred concurrently. A population may also be multimodal over the annual cycle but be unimodal at any particular time. Some primate species, such as Hamadryas baboons *(Papio hamadryas),* change their organizational mode through several stages before mid-day, and then gradually reverse the sequence during late afternoon up until nightfall (Kummer, 1971). To my knowledge, no such regular change in mode occurs for microtine rodents.

There are several reasons for defining a social organizational mode. One is that the set of social tolerances expressed by individuals is likely to differ among the different modes, and therefore it is likely that each mode will affect the statistical patterns for the population differently. If the effects are statistically different, population-wide averages are not likely to be meaningful. Furthermore, different modes may have different regulatory mechanisms, which could be antagonistic or synergistic in effect. For clear linkages between population statistics and social behavior, separate characterization of each mode is essential in multimodal populations. An example of this "modal partitioning" would be the comparison of vital statistics of monogamous and polyandrous groups in pine voles (FitzGerald and Madison, 1983) or the grouped and solitary breeding females in *M. arvalis* (Boyce and Boyce, 1988a).

Treatment of modal social groups as miniature demes or populations is not novel (D. S. Wilson, 1975; E. O. Wilson, 1975). The modal groups can be characterized statistically much as populations are. Correlations between organizational mode of groups and their population characteristics (birth rate, dispersal, mortality rate, regulation of group size, etc.) can then be established. In interspecific comparisons, population characteristics of similar modes can be compared to look for rules across species or for fundamental differences between species. For example, the monogamous groups of prairie voles *(Microtus ochrogaster:* Getz and Hofmann, 1986) could be compared to the same social modes in pine voles (Fitzgerald and Madison, 1983) to look for similarities or differences in population processes. However, considerable care should be taken in comparing mating systems among species because of their polythetic nature (Dewsbury, 1988:16, "classified with respect to a cluster of characteristics, no one of which is critical") and different phylogenetic histories (Ostfeld and Klosterman, this volume).

In applying the revised classification and the organizational mode concept to the present volume, it would be premature and even ill-advised to think that we can immediately look for relations between social systems and population statistics. Our descriptions of social organizational complexity and modes for microtine species through the annual cycle in the field are very incomplete. However, we can begin to look within and, to some extent, among species for relationships between social behavior and population statistics for the social modes that we know something about.

I will now briefly review the social organizations and modes of several species of microtine rodents. I will emphasize those that seem to be ideal for modal comparisons. It is becoming clear that many species are probably unimodal at certain times or places, that probably every microtine species has a multimodal social system, that there are many modal similarities among species, and that despite these similarities, every species probably has its own social system—a distinctive spatio-temporal set of social organizational modes.

THE MODAL CONCEPT AND MICROTINE SOCIAL COMPLEXITY

Much of what is known about the social organization of microtine rodents in the field comes from species that have been tracked (with radiotransmitters or other methods) during most of the annual cycle. Systematic, long-term mark and recapture studies may give reliable evidence of social relationships in a population, although information on co-nesting (not to be confused with living within the same burrow system) is inferential. Co-nesting is a direct measure of social tolerance and affiliation between individuals. Tracking techniques generally yield excellent information on social spacing and co-nesting and allow investigators to locate nests, identify which females reproduce, determine whether males occupy the nest chamber (possibly a measure of paternal care), and record which young are weaned and survive to breed.

One species that has received extensive radiotelemetric study throughout the annual cycle in several different locations and by several different investigators has been the meadow vole (Madison, 1980; Madison et al., 1984; McShea, 1985, 1990; Ostfeld et al., 1988; Webster and Brooks, 1981). To my knowledge, this species is the least fossorial among the many vole species studied (Wolff, 1985), and to this extent seems to be predisposed to be the least social based on the general association of burrow use and social group formation in voles. The data indicate a seasonal succession of social organizational modes (Madison and McShea, 1987). In the summer, there is a territorial system of solitary, breeding females with adult males moving opportunistically throughout larger, overlapping areas to gain access to receptive females. In the autumn, family groups form around each adult female. The groups consist of the female, one or more adult males, and the late summer-fall offspring of the female. In winter, more widely spaced groups of mixed lineage form as a result of what appears to be a merger of survivors from autumn groups that have experienced predation. In the spring, dyads of breeding females commonly occur initially, and these pairs tend to be monopolized by a larger male, which results in co-nesting groups of about three individuals (W. McShea, pers. comm.). Some females breed solitarily at this time, and by midspring all the females occur in individual breeding territories characteristic of the summer period.

The above sequence eventually may be shown to have a wider array of social modes, such as solitary females in the autumn, winter, and spring, and the modes may be shown to vary further with population density, food availability, shelter and weather factors, but statistical values for the population may not be indicative of events going on within and among all the social organizational modes. Clearly, the population must be socially partitioned during analysis before meaningful quantitative relationships between social behavior and population statistics can even begin to be considered.

Meadow voles also show many modal similarities to other species. For example, the autumn groups look in almost every way like the year-round social groups reported for pine voles (FitzGerald and Madison, 1983) and the spring, summer, and autumn groups of prairie voles (Getz and Hofmann, 1986). The winter groups look in most respects like those of the taiga vole *(Microtus xanthognathus:* Wolff and Lidicker, 1981). The spring dyads monopolized by a large reproductive male resemble the social behavior seen in the California vole *(Microtus californicus:* Ostfeld, 1986) and *M. arvalis* (Boyce and Boyce, 1988a). Clearly, the social organizational modes of the meadow vole appear at times to be similar to those observed in other species, but the collective social system can still be species-specific.

One last point in regard to the meadow vole sequence is that breeding occurs in three of the four seasonal modes described, the groups of mixed lineage in winter being the usual exception. Thus, there is more than one social organization of the meadow vole during the breeding season.

Another species that has been studied throughout the annual cycle is the pine vole (FitzGerald and Madison, 1983). This species lives almost entirely in burrow systems in social groups that are primarily monogamous. In these and other respects, pine voles appear to have social organizational modes similar to those reported by Getz and Hofmann (1986) for prairie voles. Intermediate in fossoriality and social complexity are several well-studied species including *M. montanus* (Jannett, 1978), *M. californicus* (Lidicker, 1980), *M. arvalis* (Boyce and Boyce, 1988a, 1988b), and *M. xanthognathus* (Wolff and Lidicker, 1981).

THE SOCIAL ORGANIZATIONAL MODE AND CYCLING THEORY

The organizational mode concept may lead to revision of the behavioral models that have been proposed to account for populating cycling in microtine rodents (Heske et al., 1988). Based on my experiences with microtines, some recommendations come quickly to mind.

The first involves the role of aggression in the behavioral models. An overview of the models reviewed by Heske et al. (1988) reveals that the stated or unstated assumption upon which most, if not all, of the models depend is that the incidence of aggression increases at high densities and that this results in declining birth rates and increased mortality. A review of the organizational modes of microtines, especially those modes during the late fall and winter when densities often peak, reveals wide-scale group living (Madison, 1984; West and Dublin, 1984). In species that are solitary during the summer, the formation of overwintering groups does not depend for its occurrence on the cessation of breeding or on high population densities, but rather appears to be associated with cold temperatures and huddling (nest cohabitation) for the purpose of heat conservation. Of course, group living during the winter may have other advantages, such as the collective protection of food caches in species that store food reserves (Boyce and Boyce, 1988b; Wolff and Lidicker, 1981).

Increased aggression among mammals is often followed by increased spacing, solitary existence, and in the case of group living animals, group fissioning. Increased aggression usually does not result in voluntary aggregation, increases in group living, or group fusion, yet these events often occur in microtines during the late fall and winter (Madison, 1984; West and Dublin, 1984). It may therefore be that increased social tolerance in autumn and winter has much more to do with predisposing a population to major declines in density than does social intolerance. At the very least, it is an idea worth investigating, especially in *M. pennsylvanicus.*

Understanding that populations consist of social organizational modes may also lead to the realization that modal diversity reflects behavioral plasticity or polymorphism, which may in turn lead to population stability. Individuals within different modes probably respond to different sets of selective pressures such that a shift in one selective agent is not likely to have as large an effect on a multimodal population as it may have on a unimodal population. Thus, populations that are unimodal, or in which one modal type makes up most of the population, at some time or place may be particularly susceptible to large density fluctuations. It may be productive to look at modal diversity for clues to population crashes, and especially to compare "noncyclic" and "cyclic" populations or species with respect to social modes.

One example in which the wide scale occurrence of one mode is associated with a population crash is reported for *M. arvalis* (Boyce and Boyce 1988b). In this species, virtually all the solitary breeding females perish during harsh winters, whereas the less fecund, communally breeding females survive. The solitary females make up the majority of the high density populations.

CONCLUSIONS

Microtine species are likely to be too socially diverse in time and space to compare in a simple way. Comparisons of modes of social organization within and among species are advocated. Studies of population processes may give statistics on rates of birth, death, and movement so unrelated to actual events going on between individuals that linkages between population variables and social events become weakened, if not invalid. The potential relationship between social complexity in organizational mode and noncyclicity needs to be examined. Finally, current theory on population cycles in microtine rodents needs to be reviewed in light of the possibility that social tolerance may be more important than social aggression in explaining population crashes.

ACKNOWLEDGMENTS

I thank Anne Clark and David Sloan Wilson for their critical reading of the manuscript. I also thank the National Science Foundation for their support of my research over the years.

LITERATURE CITED

Bernstein, I. S., and E. O. Smith. 1979. Primate Ecology and Human Origins, Garland Press, New York, 362 pp.

Boyce, C. C. K., and J. L. Boyce, III. 1988a. Population biology of *Microtus arvalis*. I. Lifetime reproductive success of solitary and grouped breeding females. Journal of Animal Ecology, 57:711-722.

———. 1988b. Population biology of *Microtus arvalis*. III. Regulation of numbers and breeding dispersion of females. Journal of Animal Ecology, 57:737-754.

Brown, J. L., and G. H. Orians. 1970. Spacing patterns in mobile animals. Annual Review of Ecology and Systematics, 1:239-262.

Crook, J. H. 1970. Social behaviour in birds and mammals. Academic Press, New York, 492 pp.

Dewsbury, D. A. 1988. The comparative psychology of monogamy. Nebraska Symposium on Motivation, 35:1-50.

Dunbar, R. I. N. 1979. Population demography, social organization, and mating strategies. Pp. 65-88, *in* Primate ecology and human origins (I. S. Bernstein and E. O. Smith, eds.). Garland Publishing Inc., New York, 362 pp.

FitzGerald, R., and D. M. Madison. 1983. Social organization of a free-ranging population of pine voles, *Microtus pinetorum*. Behavioral Ecology and Sociobiology, 13:183-187.

Getz, L. L., and J. E. Hofmann. 1986. Social organization in free-living prairie voles, *Microtus ochrogaster*. Behavioral Ecology and Sociobiology, 18:275-282.

Hansson, L. 1985. Geographic differences in bank voles *Clethrionomys glareolus* in relation to ecogeographical rules and possible demographic and nutritive strategies. Acta Zoologica Fennica, 22:319-328.

Heske, E. J., R. S. Ostfeld, and W. Z. Lidicker, Jr. 1988. Does social behavior drive vole cycles? An evaluation of competing models as they pertain to California voles. Canadian Journal of Zoology, 66:1153-1159.

Hinde, R. A. 1983. Primate Social Relationships. Sinauer Associates, Sunderland, Massachusetts, 384 pp.

Jannett, F. J., Jr. 1978. The density-dependent formation of extended maternal families of the montane vole, *Microtus montanus nanus*. Behavioral Ecology and Sociobiology, 3:245-263.

Kawata, M. 1985. Mating system and reproductive success in a spring population of the red-backed vole, *Clethrionomys rufocanus bedfordiae*. Oikos, 45:181-190.

Kummer, H. 1971. Primate Societies. Aldine Publishing Co., Chicago, 160 pp.

Lidicker, W. Z., Jr. 1980. The social biology of the California vole. The Biologist, 62:46-55.

Madison, D. M. 1980. Space use and social structure in meadow voles, *Microtus pennsylvanicus*. Behavioral Ecology and Sociobiology, 7:65-71.

————. 1984. Group nesting and its ecological and evolutionary significance in overwintering microtine rodents. Pp. 267-274, *in* Winter ecology of small mammals (J. F. Merritt, ed.). Carnegie Museum of Natural History, Special Publication, 10:1-380.

Madison, D. M., and W. J. McShea. 1987. Seasonal changes in reproductive tolerance, spacing, and social organization in meadow voles: a microtine model. American Zoologist, 27:899-908.

Madison, D. M., R. W. FitzGerald, and W. J. McShea. 1984. Dynamics of social nesting in overwintering meadow voles *Microtus pennsylvanicus:* possible consequences for population cycling. Behavioral Ecology and Sociobiology, 15:9-17.

McShea, W. J. 1985. Influences on the postpartum behavior of female meadow voles in a natural population. Ph.D. dissertation, State University of New York at Binghamton, Binghamton, New York, 113 pp.

————. 1990. Social tolerance and proximate mechanisms of dispersal among winter groups of meadow voles, *Microtus pennsylvanicus*. Animal Behaviour, 39:346-351.

Ostfeld, R. S. 1986. Territoriality and mating system of California voles. Journal of Animal Ecology, 55:691-706.

Ostfeld, R. S., S. R. Pugh, J. O. Seamon, and R. H. Tamarin. 1988. Space use and reproductive success in a population of meadow voles. Journal of Animal Ecology, 57:385-394.

Rowell, T. E. 1979. How would we know if social organization were *not* adaptive? Pp. 1-22, *in* Primate ecology and human origins (I. S. Bernstein and E. O. Smith, eds.). Garland Press, New York, 362 pp.

Sheridan, M., and R. H. Tamarin. 1986. Kinships in a natural meadow vole population. Behavioral Ecology and Sociobiology, 19:207-211.

Smuts, B. B., D. L. Cheney, R. M. Seyfarth, R. W. Wrangham, and T. T. Struhsaker. 1986. Primate societies, University of Chicago Press, Chicago, 578 pp.

Tamarin, R. H., M. Sheridan, and C. Levy. 1983. Determining matrilineal kinship in natural populations of rodents using radionuclides. Canadian Journal of Zoology, 61:271-274.

Webster, A. B., and R. J. Brooks. 1981. Social behavior of *Microtus pennsylvanicus* in relation to seasonal changes in demography. Journal of Mammalogy, 62:738-751.

West, S. D., and H. T. Dublin. 1984. Behavioral strategies of small mammals under winter conditions: solitary or social? Pp. 293-300, *in* Winter ecology of small mammals (J. F. Merritt, ed.). Carnegie Museum of Natural History, Special Publication, 10:1-380.

Wilson, D. S. 1975. A theory of group selection. Proceedings of the National Academy of Sciences (U.S.A.), 72:143-146.

Wilson, E. O. 1975. Sociobiology. Harvard University Press, Cambridge, Massachusetts, 697 pp.

Wolff, J. O. 1985. Behavior. Pp. 340-372, *in* Biology of New Work *Microtus* (R. H. Tamarin, ed.). American Society of Mammalogists, Special Publication, 8:1-893.

Wolff, J. O., and W. Z. Lidicker, Jr. 1981. Communal winter nesting and food sharing in taiga voles. Behavioral Ecology and Sociobiology, 9:237-240.

MICROTINE SOCIAL SYSTEMS, ADAPTATION,
AND THE COMPARATIVE METHOD

Richard S. Ostfeld and Lorrie L. Klosterman

Institute of Ecosystem Studies, New York Botanical Garden, Millbrook, NY 12545 U.S.A. (RSO),
and (formerly) Department of Biology, Boston University, Boston MA 02215 U.S.A. (RSO, LLK)

Summary.—Comparative methods have been the primary means of testing hypotheses regarding the adaptive function of social systems in voles. Most authors have assumed that species can be assigned accurately to a single social system. We assert that, due to phenotypic plasticity of individuals and interpopulational variation, such typological thinking often is not justified. The main implication of phenotypic plasticity is that it undermines current applications of the comparative method to the study of behavioral adaptation in microtine rodents. We suggest that the adaptive nature of the plasticity itself be analyzed using a comparative method.

INTRODUCTION

The purpose of this paper is to examine two questions: what are the ecological causes of social behavior, and how do we test hypotheses of adaptive significance? These questions arise from several decades of research demonstrating that social behavior influences population processes in microtine rodents. Their answers may help to expose the complex and variable ways in which behavior and population processes interact.

To approach these questions, we will employ a method commonly used by evolutionists to study adaptive traits: the comparative method. An adaptive trait is any feature of an organism that evolved because it improved performance of some function, and therefore fitness, of its bearers. Tactics of social behavior in microtine rodents are the ostensible adaptive traits that are pertinent to this discussion.

In what follows we will briefly describe the diversity of social systems among microtine rodents. We will then outline a general and a more specific version of the comparative method by which the ecological causes of this diversity may be explored. Both versions of the comparative method will then be applied to the relationship between food availability and social system in voles under the hypothesis that social systems are adaptive because they provide individuals increased access to dietary and other resources. In doing so we will expose an unstated assumption of the comparative method and show how violations of this assumption undermine the method's validity. Finally, we will recommend a more flexible and pluralistic approach to studying the adaptive function of social behavior in voles.

SOCIAL SYSTEMS IN MICROTINE RODENTS

Because voles are difficult or impossible to observe directly, studies of their social organization have relied on indirect techniques such as livetrapping and radiotelemetry. Due in part to the limitations inherent in these methods, most researchers have made inferences about social organization based on data that describe the use of space by individuals within a population. Systems of sex-specific territoriality, and to a lesser degree, of mating, have been scrutinized most intensely (Ostfeld, 1985; Wolff, 1985), whereas details of mate choice, intrasexual competition, infanticide, and other behaviors are almost wholly unstudied.

Recent research has revealed a remarkable social diversity among microtine species. In some species (e.g., *Microtus californicus:* Heske, 1987; Ostfeld, 1986) it appears that only adult males are territorial (i.e., their home ranges do not overlap), whereas in others *(M. pennsylvanicus:* Madison, 1980; Ostfeld et al., 1988; most or all species of *Clethrionomys:* Bondrup-Nielson and Karlsson, 1985; Gipps, 1985) only breeding females are territorial (Ostfeld, in press). Some species show polygynous mating patterns in which a single male appears to have exclusive access to more than one female (e.g., *M. xanthognathus:* Wolff and Lidicker, 1980); others mate monogamously *(M. ochrogaster:* Getz et al., 1981; *M. pinetorum:* FitzGerald and Madison, 1983), and in others both sexes seem to employ a promiscuous system in which members of both sexes probably mate with multiple partners (e.g., *M. pennsylvanicus:* Madison, 1980; *Clethrionomys* sp.: Gipps, 1985; Heske and Ostfeld, in press).

Although it may be that a given species tends to employ a particular type of territorial or mating system, evidence now indicates that these systems are not as rigid as has been assumed; several species adopt an alternative system under experimentally or naturally altered conditions (described below). This flexibility, though adding a new dimension to studies of the adaptive significance of various social systems, also is a critical source of difficulty in applying a comparative method.

A SIMPLIFIED COMPARATIVE METHOD

The comparative method was developed by Darwin (1859) for elucidating the adaptive function of morphological and behavioral features of organisms. In brief, we start by hypothesizing that a particular feature exists in a given species as a solution to a particular environmental "problem." Next, a comparison of diverse taxa is made to indicate whether the allegedly adaptive feature consistently coincides with the environmental factor. If other taxa faced with similar environmental problems regularly exhibit the same morphological or behavioral solution, then the hypothesis is supported.

Essentially, the investigator is looking for instances of convergent evolution, and the robustness of support for the hypothesis is proportional to the number of independent cases.

For example, one might hypothesize that hypsodont dentition in horses *(Equus caballus)* is adaptive for chewing coarse, abrasive vegetation. Using the comparative method to test this, the investigator examines other taxa that eat coarse vegetation. If they often have hypsodont teeth, whereas other taxa that exploit softer foods do not, then the hypothesis is supported. However, modern comparative methods recognize that the phylogenetic relatedness of those taxa that are being compared is critical (Ridley, 1983).

A MODERN COMPARATIVE METHOD

A problem recognized in modern versions of the comparative method is that not all taxa exhibiting a trait represent unique evolutionary events. Some instances that appear to be cases of convergent evolution may, in fact, have resulted from the inheritance of a trait from a common ancestor. If such taxa are included in a comparative analysis, the investigator will be using the same example repeatedly, artificially inflating sample size to give misleading results. It is necessary to know something of the phylogenetic relationships among taxa in order to ascertain whether the putative adaptive trait evolved independently.

For example, horses and zebras *(Equus burchelli)* both are browsers on abrasive vegetation, and both have hypsodont teeth, but outgroup comparison reveals that hypsodonty evolved in a common ancestor. In this case, hypsodont dentition is a shared ancestral character and not the result of convergent evolution; therefore, it is not valid to use these taxa as independent examples of adaptation. Comparing perissodactyls to herbivorous rodents, however, is a valid use of the comparative method, because their common ancestor almost certainly did not have hypsodont dentition. Most investigators employing modern versions of the comparative method use either a cladistic (Coddington, 1988; Felsenstein, 1985; Ridley, 1983) or statistical (analysis of variance) approach (Bell, 1989; Clutton-Brock and Harvey, 1984; Huey and Bennett, 1986; Pagel and Harvey, 1988) to determine which taxa can be considered independent evolutionary units, depending on whether the traits of interest are discrete or continuous.

A SPECIFIC CASE OF THE COMPARATIVE METHOD: RELATING DIET TO SOCIAL SYSTEM IN VOLES

Recently, one of us (Ostfeld, 1985) hypothesized that diet determines whether or not female voles defend territories, which determines whether males are territorial. It was predicted that voles whose diets consist mainly of forbs, fruits, and seeds would exhibit territoriality by females but not males, whereas those eating mostly grasses would show male but not female territoriality. To test this hypothesis, a comparative method was employed to identify co-occurrences of particular diets with the predicted territorial systems. As there were many cases of conformance to predictions, Ostfeld (1985) tentatively concluded that the hypothesis was supported, and called for more comparative and experimental data.

Ostfeld's (1985) conclusions were the subject of some criticism by Cockburn (1988) who agreed that the hypothesis was supported strongly by data from *Microtus* (in which there is considerable social diversity), but only weakly by *Clethrionomys* (Fig. 1). According to Cockburn (1988), because *Clethrionomys* is a monophyletic group in which all species show both territoriality by females and a diet of mostly fruits and seeds, it was incorrect to use several species of this genus as independent examples of conformance to predictions. Instead, the entire genus constitutes a single instance of conformance. The conformance of *Clethrionomys* is counterbalanced by *Arvicola terrestris,* which appears to have a social system inconsistent with predictions (Cockburn, 1988). However, more recent studies of *A. terrestris* support aspects of Ostfeld's (1985) model, although they reveal that resources other than food may influence strongly territorial behavior of females (Jeppsson, this volume). Cockburn's (1988) views reflect those of all modern versions of the comparative method, in which taxa of close phylogenetic relationship are assumed to represent nonindependent evolutionary units (Felsenstein, 1985; Pagel and Harvey, 1988; Ridley, 1983).

Cockburn's (1988) criticism is based on the assumption that, if a feature occurs in all members of a clade, it must have evolved only once in the common ancestor. Therefore, the trait occurs in descendent taxa because it was genetically fixed in the ancestor; it persists due to 'phylogenetic inertia.' Under this assumption, the comparative method cannot be used to determine whether or not the feature is adaptive in the descendent taxa. When the feature being studied is indeed genetically fixed, or nearly so, in any given species (as is almost certainly true for the case of tooth morphology in herbivorous mammals) then the assumption is valid, and the comparative method appropriate. However, whenever there is phenotypic plasticity in the expression of the trait, the assumption fails, and the comparative method should be modified.

There now exists substantial experimental and observational evidence that territorial systems in microtine rodents, including species of *Clethrionomys,* in fact are not genetically fixed, but respond to environmental or social variables. For example, experimental studies on *C. rufocanus* have revealed that males switch between nonterritorial and territorial tactics depending on intruder pressure and degree of spatial clumping of females (Ims, 1987, 1988). Supplemental feeding of a *C. glareolus* population resulted in a decrease in size and an increase in overlap among female home ranges (Andrzejewski and Mazurkiewicz, 1976). Observational studies by Viitala and Pusenius (this volume),

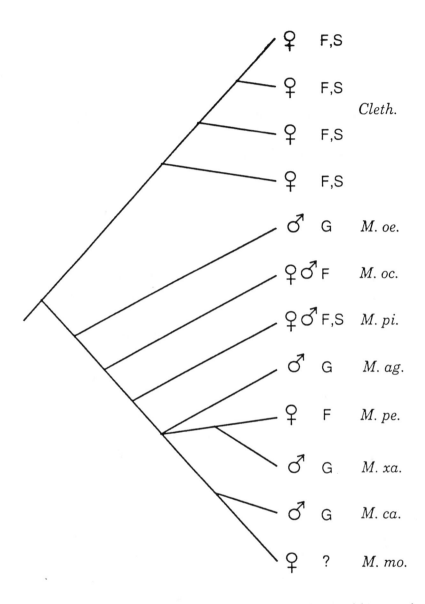

Fig. 1.—Cladogram of species of *Clethrionomys* and *Microtus* whose social systems have been described (Chaline, 1988). Also represented are the sex typically exhibiting territorial behavior and the predominant dietary items, where F, S = fruits and seeds, G = grasses, and F = forbs (Ostfeld, 1985). The relationships among *Clethrionomys* species are poorly understood, but it is accepted that they are a monophyletic group. *Microtus* species are abbreviated as: *M. oe., M. oeconomus; M. oc., M. ochrogaster; M. pi., M. pinetorum; M. ag., M. agrestis; M. pe., M. pennsylvanicus; M. xa., M. xanthognathus; M. ca., M. californicus;* and *M. mo., M. montanus.* We question the assumption that territoriality among females in *Clethrionomys* species is a symplesiomorphic character state because in at least two species it is phenotypically plastic.

Ylönen (this volume) and Ylönen et al. (1988) showed that female *C. glareolus* changed from territorial to grouping behavior as a result of improved food conditions or increased population density. Similar results have been observed in species of *Microtus*. In *M. californicus,* experimental clumping of food resources induced more extreme overlap in home ranges of females (Ostfeld, 1986). Populations of *M. agrestis,* appear to adopt fundamentally different social structures in different habitats (e.g., forest vs. grassland; Myllymäki, 1977; Viitala, 1977; Viitala and Pusenius, this volume). These examples, and others (Lott, 1984), expose a degree of intraspecific variability in social structure insufficiently recognized by small-mammal ecologists.

Intraspecific variability may result from variation among populations each fixed for a different trait, variation among populations the members of which show some flexibility, or phenotypic plasticity within individuals that swamps interpopulational variability. In the former case, the comparative method still may be employed provided the phylogenetic relationships among the populations are known (Cameron and McClure, 1988; Huey and Bennett, 1986; Lauder, 1986). It is the latter case, which appears to be supported by data on two species of *Clethrionomys,* that causes most severe problems for the comparative method.

The contention that *Clethrionomys* species employ a system based on territorial breeding females due to phylogenetic inertia is thus undermined. In fact, the evidence for intraspecific variability in social systems outlined above supports the view that each occurrence of territoriality in breeding females in a *Clethrionomys* species represents a response to an ecological factor that favors it.

Thus, we suggest that each species of *Clethrionomys* (and likely other voles as well) employs a modal social system around which there is considerable flexibility. (Madison, this volume, makes a similar argument.) The exact version of the modal system can be considered an independently adopted character state. Whether or not such a modal social system, with its flexibility, can be considered an adaptive trait in the evolutionary sense is debatable. If every species of *Clethrionomys* shows a similar degree of plasticity, and this is shown to have a strong heritable component, then the plasticity itself may be an evolved feature shared primitively within the genus. If our suggestions are correct, then it is more appropriate to use a comparative method to study the adaptive significance of behavioral plasticity than that of social systems per se.

DISCUSSION

Our understanding of microtine social systems has expanded rapidly. The belief that all vole species are socially uniform has been supplanted by the recognition of interspecific diversity (Ostfeld, 1985, in press; Wolff, 1985). In further explorations of the causes and consequences of social systems, researchers must address the extent of intraspecific variability expressed between populations and as phenotypic plasticity of individuals. As is often the case in scientific inquiry, a better understanding of the nature of social systems leads to ever greater complexity in our approaches to study them.

Before categorizing a particular species of vole by its social system, the degree of intraspecific variability must be explored via experimental and observational studies. If interpopulational variability comprises a significant portion of intraspecific variability, then a comparative approach using populations as taxonomic units may be warranted. If much of the intraspecific variability is due to phenotypic plasticity of individuals, however, comparative methods will be undermined. It is not yet clear whether the intraspecific variability in social systems of vertebrates is due mostly to interpopulational or intraindividual variability (Lott, 1984).

What has been shown provisionally in recent studies of voles is that: 1) territorial and mating systems usually are not based on genetically fixed behavioral adaptations, and therefore rigid comparative methods are inappropriate; 2) where distribution and renewal rate of resources are altered experimentally or naturally, territorial systems change; therefore, although a particular behavioral tactic may not be an adaptive trait in the strict sense, the ability of individuals to adopt tactics that maximize access to resources or mates under changing conditions (i.e., the plasticity itself) may be an adaptive trait. Thus, it may be appropriate to study the adaptive significance of phenotypic plasticity using a formal comparative method.

To our knowledge, the comparative method has not been applied formally to the evolution of reaction norms or adaptive phenotypic plasticity (Stearns, 1989; West-Eberhard, 1989). Because reaction norms tend to vary continuously (rather than discretely), a statistical comparative approach may be most fruitful. On the other hand, if thresholds of environmental variables elicit discrete switches in behavioral tactics, then a cladistic approach may be warranted.

Comparative methods must be used with extreme care in studying the adaptive nature of behavioral and other phenotypically plastic traits. Certainly the adaptive significance of behaviors that comprise social systems can be initially explored using a comparative method. However, before the degree of intraspecific variability is known, such a method should be used to refine hypotheses rather than to ascertain, based on a known phylogeny, how often the trait evolved independently. Hypotheses developed under the comparative method should be tested with experimental and observational studies, the purpose of which is twofold: to determine whether the trait is intraspecifically variable (and if so, the comparative method may require modification); and whether a particular behavioral tactic is a response to hypothesized environmental conditions.

The same environmental features ("problems") that give rise to adaptive evolutionary change ("solutions") in some taxa may also cause phenotypic change in other intraspecifically flexible species. The experimental approach to studying the adaptive function of traits often must be limited to those features that show reaction norms; less plastic traits often cannot be modified or abandoned even if they are maladaptive under experimentally altered conditions. If individuals vary their behavioral tactics under different experimental treatments in a manner consistent with predictions from evolutionary theory, then the change in expression of a trait is analogous, but not equivalent, to the process of evolutionary adaptation.

Despite some measure of intraspecific variability, most microtine species nevertheless seem to be predisposed to adopt a particular social system. For instance, independent studies of the same species under different environmental conditions often reveal quite similar social systems. Also, several species show suites of morphological and behavioral traits consistent with one primary mating system (Dewsbury, this volume; Heske and Ostfeld, in press). Thus, our admonition that social systems of voles are not rigidly fixed should not be interpreted as a belief in social chaos.

We hope that examples of phenotypic plasticity in individual behavior, and its influence on intraspecific variability in social systems, will continue to be sought in a diversity of mammalian orders. Cases in which species-specific or clade-specific social systems appear rigidly determined will likely prove as valuable to understanding behavioral variability as will cases of variability themselves.

ACKNOWLEDGMENTS

We thank Kurt Schwenk for helpful discussions and Andrew Cockburn and an anonymous referee for commenting on the manuscript. Ostfeld was supported by United States Public Health Service, National Institutes of Health grant HD06831. This is a contribution to the program of the Institute of Ecosystem Studies.

LITERATURE CITED

Andrzejewski, R., and M. Mazurkiewicz. 1976. Abundance of food supply and size of the bank vole home range. Acta Theriologica, 21:237-253.

Bell, G. 1989. A comparative method. The American Naturalist, 133:553-571.

Bondrup-Nielson, S., and F. Karlsson. 1985. Movements and spatial patterns in populations of *Clethrionomys* species: a review. Annales Zoologici Fennici, 22:385-392.

Cameron, G. N., and P. A. McClure. 1988. Geographic variation in life history traits of the Hispid cotton rat *(Sigmodon hispidus)*. Pp. 33-64, *in* Evolution of life history traits of mammals: theory and pattern (M. S. Boyce, ed.). Yale University Press, New Haven, Connecticut, 373 pp.

Chaline, J. 1988. Arvicolid data and evolutionary concepts. Pp. 237-310, *in* Evolutionary biology (M. K. Hecht, B. Wallace, and G. T. Prance, eds.). Plenum, New York, 21:1-434.

Clutton-Brock, T. H., and P. H. Harvey. 1984. Comparative approaches to investigating adaptation. Pp. 7-29, *in* Behavioural ecology: an evolutionary approach (J. R. Krebs and N. B. Davies, eds.). Sinauer Associates, Sunderland, Massachusetts, 493 pp.

Cockburn, A. 1988. Social behaviour in fluctuating populations. Croom Helm, London, 239 pp.

Coddington, J. A. 1988. Cladistic tests of adaptational hypotheses. Cladistics, 4:3-22.

Darwin, C. 1859. The origin of species by natural selection, or the preservation of favored races in the struggle for life. John Murray, London, 460 pp.

Felsenstein, J. 1985. Phylogenies and the comparative method. The American Naturalist, 125:1-15.

FitzGerald, R. W., and D. M. Madison. 1983. Social organization of a free-ranging population of pine voles, *Microtus pinetorum*. Behavioral Ecology and Sociobiology, 13:183-187.

Getz, L. L., C. S. Carter, and L. Gavish. 1981. The mating system of the prairie vole, *Microtus ochrogaster:* field and laboratory evidence for pair-bonding. Behavioral Ecology and Sociobiology, 8:189-194.

Gipps, J. H. W. 1985. Spacing behaviour and male reproductive ecology in voles of the genus *Clethrionomys*. Annales Zoologici Fennici, 22:343-351.

Heske, E. J. 1987. Spatial structuring and dispersal in a high density population of the California vole *Microtus californicus*. Holarctic Ecology, 10:137-148.

Heske, E. J., and R. S. Ostfeld. In press. Sexual dimorphism in size, relative size of testes, and mating systems in North American voles. Journal of Mammalogy.

Huey, R. B., and A. F. Bennett. 1986. A comparative approach to field and laboratory studies in evolutionary biology. Pp. 82-98, *in* Predator-prey relationships: perspectives and approaches from the study of lower vertebrates (M. E. Feder and G. V. Lauder, eds.). University of Chicago Press, Chicago, 198 pp.

Ims, R. A. 1987. Responses in spatial organization and behaviour to manipulation of the food resource in the vole *Clethrionomys rufocanus*. Journal of Animal Ecology, 56:585-596.

————. 1988. Spatial clumping of sexually receptive females induces space sharing among male voles. Nature, 335:541-543.

Lauder, G. F. 1986. Homology, analogy, and the evolution of behavior. Pp. 9-40, *in* Evolution of animal behavior: paleontological and field perspectives (M. H. Nitecki and J. A. Kitchell, eds.). Oxford University Press, Oxford, 184 pp.

Lott, D. F. 1984. Intraspecific variation in the social systems of wild vertebrates. Behaviour, 88:266-325.

Madison, D. M. 1980. Space use and social structure in meadow voles, *Microtus pennsylvanicus*. Behavioral Ecology and Sociobiology, 7:65-71.

Myllymäki, A. 1977. Intraspecific competition and home range dynamics in the field vole, *Microtus agrestis*. Oikos, 29:553-569.

Ostfeld, R. S. 1985. Limiting resources and territoriality in microtine rodents. The American Naturalist, 126:1-15.

―――. 1986. Territoriality and mating system of California voles. Journal of Animal Ecology, 55:691-706.

―――. in press. The ecology of territoriality in small mammals. Trends in Ecology and Evolution.

Ostfeld, R. S., S. R. Pugh, J. O. Seamon, and R. H. Tamarin. 1988. Space use and reproductive success in a population of meadow voles. Journal of Animal Ecology, 57:385-394.

Pagel, M. D., and P. H. Harvey. 1988. Recent developments in the analysis of comparative data. Quarterly Review of Biology, 63:413-440.

Ridley, M. 1983. The explanation of organic diversity: the comparative method and adaptations for mating. Clarendon Press, Oxford, 272 pp.

Stearns, S. C. 1989. The evolutionary significance of phenotypic plasticity. Bioscience, 39:436-445.

Viitala, J. 1977. Social organisation in cyclic subarctic populations of the voles *Clethrionomys rufocanus* (Sund.) and *Microtus agrestis* (L.). Annales Zoologici Fennici, 14:53-93.

West-Eberhard, M. J. 1989. Phenotypic plasticity and the origins of diversity. Annual Review of Ecology and Systematics, 20:249-278.

Wolff, J. O. 1985. Behavior. Pp. 126-137, *in* Biology of New World *Microtus* (R. H. Tamarin, ed.). Special Publication, American Society of Mammalogists, 8:1-893.

Wolff, J. O., and W. Z. Lidicker, Jr. 1980. Population ecology of the taiga vole *(Microtus xanthognathus)* in interior Alaska. Canadian Journal of Zoology, 58:1800-1812.

Ylönen, J., T. Kojola, and J. Viitala. 1988. Changing female spacing behaviour and demography in an enclosed breeding population of *Clethrionomys glareolus*. Holarctic Ecology, 11:286-292.

Social Systems and
Population Cycles in Voles
Advances in Life Sciences
© Birkhäuser Verlag Basel

SOCIAL ORGANIZATION AND POPULATION DYNAMICS
IN A *MICROTUS AGRESTIS* POPULATION

Sam Erlinge, Jep Agrell, Johan Nelson, and Mikael Sandell

Department of Ecology, Ecology Building, Lund University, S-223 62 Lund, Sweden (SE, JA, JN).

Department of Wildlife Ecology, Swedish University of Agricultural Sciences, S-901 83 Umeå, Sweden (MS).

Summary.—The relationship between spacing behavior and population dynamics of a noncyclic field vole *(Microtus agrestis)* population was examined in southern Sweden by mark-recapture and radiotracking. There was an annual decline in density over winter (nonbreeding season) to low densities in spring. During the nonbreeding period, home ranges overlapped greatly among both males and females, especially at high densities, and the level of intraspecific aggression was low. Interactions between individuals probably influence survival, but a field experiment in which predation was prevented showed that predation reduced vole numbers to a much lower level than that set by the spacing behavior of the voles. A continuous decline during the early breeding season was due primarily to predation and could not be ascribed to territorial behavior of females. Neither was the difference in annual peak densities related to between-year differences in spacing behavior. Peak densities were correlated with the number of litters produced by females that bred in the year they were born. Number of litters was not correlated with population density. Differences in food quantity or quality might have caused the variation in peak numbers between years. We conclude that spacing behavior is not a primary determinant of the pattern of population dynamics in this locality. Predation and probably food are of primary importance.

INTRODUCTION

There are close connections between social behavior and animal population dynamics. Interactions between individuals influence reproductive performance, survival, and dispersal patterns (Cohen et al., 1980; Sibly and Smith, 1985). In microtine populations that show cyclic fluctuations between years, it has been suggested that different behavioral genotypes are selected for and predominate during different phases of a cycle and that this phenomenon is the driving force of the cycles (Chitty, 1967; Krebs and Myers, 1974). Some other microtine populations do not show multiannual cycles but fluctuate seasonally with annual peak densities during some part of the breeding season. Such a noncyclic population of the field vole *(Microtus agrestis)* has been studied for several years in southern

Sweden (Erlinge et al., 1983; Hansson, 1971; Myllymäki et al., 1977). In the present paper we examine if the observed dynamic pattern in this population is determined primarily by the voles' spacing behavior.

STUDY AREA AND METHODS

The study was conducted in the Revinge area (55°42'N, 13°25'E) in southern Sweden. The study area consists of a homogenous wet meadow dominated by Poaceae sp. (primarily *Deschampsia caespitosa, Elymus repens,* and *Phleum pratense), Urtica dioica, Anthriscus sylvestris,* and *Circium arvense.* Trapping was conducted on three 0.5-ha grids separated from each other by 30 m. From the central grid all avian and mammalian predators except weasels *(Mustela nivalis)* were excluded by fencing. On each grid there were 7 by 13 trap stations with 7 m between stations. Two 'Ugglan' multiple-capture live traps were placed at each station. Throughout the year 5-day trapping sessions were conducted on each grid at 3-week intervals. One or two days before each trapping session, traps were prebaited with crushed oats. Traps were examined twice a day. At first capture, voles were marked individually by toe-clipping, and at each capture body weight, sex, reproductive status, and trap site were recorded. Data were collected between November 1983 and October 1985, covering two nonbreeding periods (November-March 1983-1984 and 1984-1985) and two breeding periods (April-October 1984 and 1985). Density is presented as average minimum number of animals known to be alive per 0.5 ha.

Home range overlap between individuals of the same sex was calculated from mapped home ranges. Overlap was considered to occur if any part of an individual's home range overlapped that of another individual. As the home ranges of some individuals could not be measured as areas, the degree of overlap was calculated as the proportion of individuals that had home ranges overlapping with one or more individuals of the same sex. For statistical tests the observed degree of overlap was compared to expected random overlaps. For each comparison one hundred overlaps were calculated by randomly distributing the observed ranges within the trapping grids; if the observed overlap was less than in all hundred, a significance level of $P < 0.01$ was assigned; if the observed overlap was less than all but four random overlaps, a significance level of $P < 0.05$ was assigned (Searcy, 1986).

Dyadic encounter tests were carried out to examine aggressive behavior. Adult animals were taken from the three grids of the study and were tested and released the same day they were captured. The tests were conducted indoors in a white-painted metallic arena with a glass front (150 by 75 by 50 cm). The arena was covered with saw dust and was thoroughly cleaned before each test. Animals were tested in pairs only with individuals of the same sex. Three main categories of behaviors were recorded: aggressive behavior (attack, counterattack, chase, boxing and wrestling), contact behaviors (approach, sniffing, grooming, and sitting together), and avoidance behavior (escape, jump, vocalizing, and sitting—modified from Colvin, 1973; Cranford and Derting, 1983). After a 10-min acclimation period, each test lasted for 20 min. Each animal was used only once and tests were performed both during the nonbreeding and the breeding seasons.

Radiotracking was conducted to complement capture-recapture data. In May and June 1984, seven adult males and eight adult females, all reproductively active, were radiotracked; in February 1985 during the nonbreeding season six adult males and four adult females were radiotracked. Collared transmitters weighed approximately 1.9 g, 5-8% of the voles' body mass. Batteries usually lasted for 7 days. Locations were taken every hour during both day and night. Individuals occupying adjacent or overlapping home ranges were tracked continuously for some hours to obtain detailed information on range overlap and behavior of animals when in close contact or in an area of overlap.

RESULTS AND DISCUSSION

Characteristics of population dynamics.—In autumn 1983, when the study started, vole density was high. The voles continued to reproduce into November and numbers peaked in December. A marked decline occurred during the nonbreeding period (December-March), and the number of voles further decreased during the early part of the breeding period (Fig. 1). In July 1984 there was a rapid increase

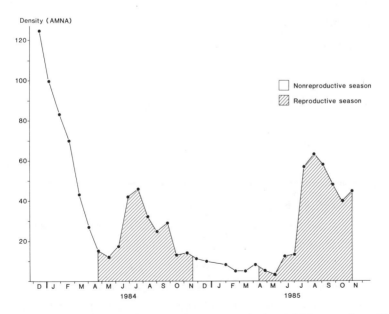

Fig. 1.—Changes in numbers of field voles in the unmanipulated 0.5-ha trapping grid during 1984 and 1985 in southern Sweden. The figures are average minimum number of animals known to be alive (AMNA).

to the annual peak. During the remaining part of the breeding period there was a continuous decline in density that continued throughout winter to a low in May 1985. Population density then increased rapidly to a peak in July. Peak density in 1985 was intermediate between those of the first and second years. The change in the numbers over these two years followed a pattern that has been observed in this area for several years (Erlinge et al., 1983; Hansson, 1971; Myllymäki et al., 1977). Thus, dynamics of this vole population had the following characteristics: a decline in density over winter (nonbreeding period) to low density in spring each year; continuing decrease in numbers during the early part of the subsequent breeding season (April and May); a between-year variation in recruitment success and peak densities during the breeding season.

Winter decline and spacing behavior.—Spacing patterns during the nonbreeding period (November-March) were characterized by overlapping home ranges among both males and females (Figs. 2, 3). In neither sex did the proportion of individuals with overlapping home ranges differ significantly from the calculated random distribution, that is, individuals were neither territorial nor aggregated. This was the case during both nonbreeding seasons, despite large differences in density (1983-1984: density = 56-166; 1984-1985: density = 8-31 individuals/0.5 ha). The proportion of home ranges of females that overlapped tended to be higher in 1983-1984 (high density: 83% overlap, $n = 69$) compared with 1984-1985 (low density: 36% overlap, $n = 11$), whereas home ranges of males overlapped to about the same extent during the nonbreeding season both at high and low density (83% overlap, $n = 54$ and 71% overlap, $n = 17$, respectively). In arena tests social tolerance of both sexes was high; no aggressive behavior was recorded during the 20 tests performed. Also, radiotracking revealed that some individuals repeatedly shared nests.

As aggression during the nonbreeding season was very low, it is unlikely that intraspecific behavior could be a direct cause of mortality during this period. Spacing behavior, however, can have a more subtle influence and dominance interactions might result in subordinate animals suffering higher mortality risk than dominant voles. In our vole population body weight was found to be a useful correlate of social dominance. Of 20 paired encounters between males during the breeding season, the dominant male was heavier in 16 cases, which was significantly more than expected if dominance was not influenced by body weight (Fisher exact test, $P < 0.01$). If social interactions resulted in disproportionate mortality in different categories, one would expect lighter (presumably subordinate) voles to have a shorter survival time than heavier (dominant) individuals. This was analyzed on animals present in the grids in January 1984 (high density). No significant influence of body weight on survival could be detected (analysis of covariance: males, $F_{1,123} = 1.82$; females, $F_{1,176} = 0.60$, $P > 0.10$ in both cases). Thus, social interactions do not seem to play a major role in selecting individuals that will be exposed to higher mortality; in all grids the disappearance of individuals was random in

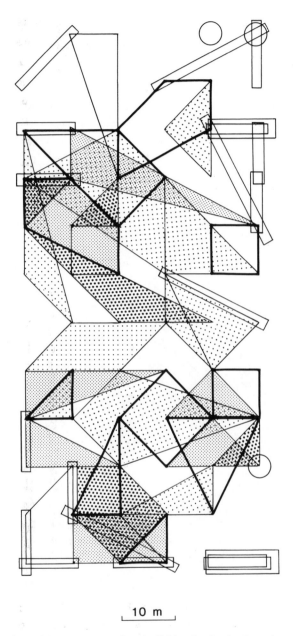

10 m

Fig. 2.—Distribution of home ranges of male field voles in the fenced trapping grid during the nonbreeding season at high density from December 1983 to January 1984 in southern Sweden. Number of males occurring simultaneously in the grid during this period was 54. Home range delineation is based on recapture locations (for each individual at least three captures during at least two subsequent trapping periods; $\overline{X}$ = 8.2 captures per individual). Geometric shapes are home ranges; overlaps are noted by dot patterns.

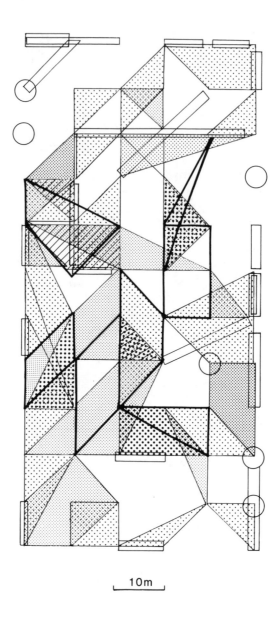

10m

Fig. 3.—Distribution of home ranges of female field voles during the nonbreeding season at high density from December 1983 to January 1984. Number of females was 69. Home range delineation is based on recapture locations (for each individual at least three captures during at least two subsequent trapping periods; $\bar{X}$ = 7.8 captures per individual). Geometric shapes are home ranges; overlaps are noted by dot patterns.

relation to body weight (social status).

Social interactions are suggested to be a basic factor underlying predation mortality (Errington, 1946; Jenkins et al., 1964). According to this view, predators play a secondary role removing a 'surplus' of individuals. Whether predation was a primary or secondary cause of mortality causing the decline in vole numbers in winter was tested experimentally. A 0.5-ha area was fenced to prevent avian and mammalian predators (except weasels) from preying on voles. Spacing behavior was unaffected; voles could move in and out and spacing pattern was the same in the fenced as in the unfenced grids (information from trapping and radiotracking). Changes in density in the predation-manipulated area were compared with two grids in which the voles were exposed to predation, one of which was provided with supplemental food. A typical decline over winter occurred in both grids exposed to predation although a delay of about one month was observed in the grid with supplemental food (Fig. 4). A similar but significantly smaller decline was observed in the fenced area (Fig. 4). This difference could not be ascribed to habitat differences; trapping data from April and July in 1988 after the fence had been removed showed similar densities on the grids (April, 16 and 13 individuals, and July, 47 and 52 individuals/0.5 ha, on previously fenced and unfenced grids, respectively; χ^2 = 0.469, and 0.532, respectively, P > 0.05 each). The decline in the fenced area may have been due partly to weasel predation, as we did not succeed in preventing this completely. Also, voles having their home ranges in the periphery of the fenced area had parts of their ranges outside the fence and so were exposed to predation. Individual survival during winter and spring, calculated as length of residence on the grids, was about twice as long in the fenced compared with the unfenced grids ($\bar{X} \pm SD$—males: 9.7 $\pm$ 6.6 and 5.4 $\pm$ 4.2 weeks, respectively; females: 12.2 $\pm$ 8.4 and 5.7 $\pm$ 5.4 weeks, respectively, P < 0.001 in both sexes, Mann-Whitney U-test). For individuals in the same grid there were no significant differences between survival of males and females.

If social interactions determine predation mortality, we would expect vole numbers to be the same in the fenced and the unmanipulated control grid. The decline over winter, however, was significantly less in the fenced than in the unfenced areas (Erlinge, 1987). Thus, we conclude that spacing behavior was not the primary cause of the high mortality and rapid decline during winter. Instead predation reduced densities to a lower level than that set by the spacing behavior of voles.

Decline in early breeding season and spacing behavior.—At the start of the breeding season in spring, overwintered females showed an overdispersed distribution, which suggested territorial behavior (Fig. 5). There was, however, no active defense of home ranges in terms of fighting and pursuing intruders. The boundaries between neighbors included overlapping zones that were regularly patrolled, but neighboring animals were seldom in close contact with each other; the distribution was maintained

52

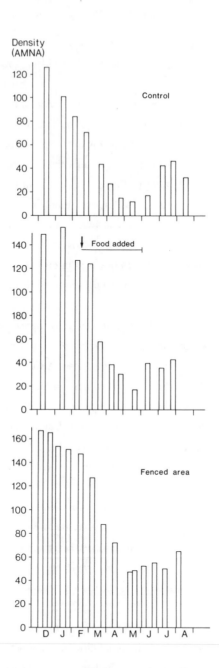

Fig. 4.—Changes in field vole numbers from winter 1983-1984 to summer 1984 on three grids in southern Sweden: one in which the voles were exposed to predation (control), another exposed to predation and provided supplemental food, and a grid in which predation was prevented by fencing (fenced area). Numbers are average minimum number of animals known to be alive.

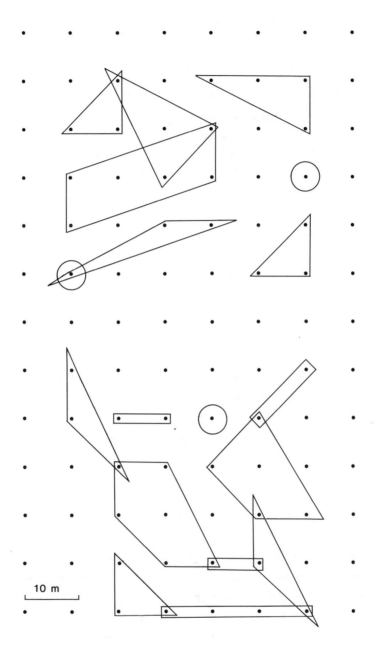

Fig. 5.—Distribution of home ranges of female field voles in southern Sweden during the breeding season (May 1984) in the predation-manipulated grid. Home range delineation is based on capture locations (for each individual at least three captures during two subsequent periods; $\bar{X} = 7.3$ captures per individual; $n = 18$). The dots denote trap sites.

through avoidance behavior (information from radiotracking). Also, in female-female encounter tests during the breeding season, females showed a low frequency of aggressive behaviors; contact and avoidance behaviors greatly dominated ($\bar{X} \pm SD$, $n = 15$—aggressive behaviors: 0.33 ± 0.72; contact behaviors: 5.87 ± 6.01; avoidance behaviors: 2.87 ± 3.54; Kruskal-Wallis test, $P = 0.001$).

Home ranges of overwintered males overlapped considerably in spring (Fig. 6) but also the males avoided close contact with each other (radiotracking data). Also, in encounter tests, avoidance and contact behaviors were more frequent than aggressive behaviors in males ($\bar{X} \pm SD$, $n = 19$—aggressive behaviors: 1.21 ± 3.42; contact behaviors: 4.63 ± 4.72; avoidance behaviors: 2.68 ± 4.68; Kruskal-Wallis test, $P = 0.01$). Each male had a home range that covered the ranges of several females; over a period of two months (April and May 1984), one male covered eight home ranges of females and the average number for each male ($n = 7$) was four females (trapping data).

Overwintered females started reproduction in the beginning of April. From this point on, we expect a time lag of about five weeks before young of the year enter the trappable population and potentially cause an increase in density. However, the increase in vole numbers in the breeding season starts in June, 3-4 weeks later than expected (Fig. 1). If the continuing decline in vole numbers was due to social dominance and suppression we would expect reproductive rate and recruitment of young to be correlated negatively with density of females. However, the calculated reproductive rate (percent of females pregnant or lactating), among overwintered females was the same in 1984 and 1985 (49 and 54%, respectively, $\chi^2 = 0.23$, $P > 0.5$) despite large between-year differences in density of females ($n = 39$ and 21, respectively). Further, the number of recruited juveniles from overwintered females was 25 in 1984 and 17 in 1985, which suggested no difference in per capita reproductive output of overwintered females between years ($\chi^2 = 0.32$, $P > 0.5$). Neither was there between-year difference in number of females born early in the breeding season (progeny of overwintered individuals) that reached reproductive age (10 and 6 females, respectively, $\chi^2 = 0.03$, $P > 0.8$). Thus, reproductive output in the early part of the breeding season seemed not to be inhibited by dominance among individuals in this population.

As was found from the experiment of predation manipulation, densities in spring were significantly lower on the control area than in the fenced area where predation was reduced (Fig. 4). In the area where the voles were exposed to predation, only a fraction of the suitable area was occupied in spring. Furthermore, the area protected from predators did not show a more pronounced decline, despite the higher density. Evidently the observed densities were well below the limit in which territorial behavior becomes the primary density-regulating factor.

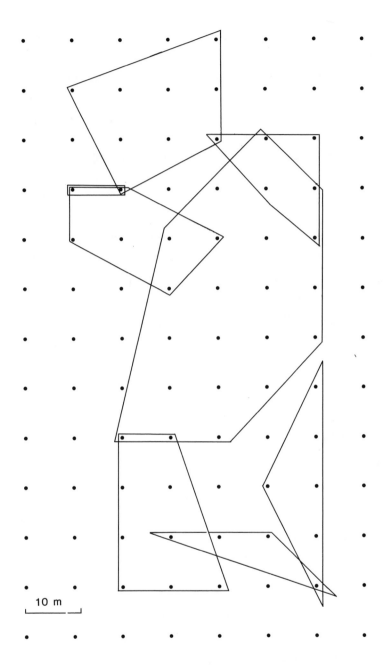

Fig. 6.—Distribution of home ranges of male field voles in southern Sweden during the breeding season in the predation-manipulated grid during May and June 1984. Home range delineation is based on recaptures (for each individual at least three captures during at least two subsequent periods; $\bar{X}$ = 6.3 captures per individual; n = 8). The dots denote trap sites.

Peak numbers and spacing behavior.—Peak densities during the breeding season reached different levels in different years and at different times of the breeding season (Fig. 1). In 1983 reproduction continued late in autumn, resulting in very high numbers in November and December. In 1984 and 1985 peak numbers occurred in July. Encounter tests in an arena and field observations connected with radiotracking showed that the voles displayed a low degree of intraspecific aggressive behavior. Signs of fighting such as wounds were observed very occasionally. More males than females had wounds, although the difference was not significant. Furthermore, the frequency of wounded individuals did not differ between years, neither in males (4 of 109 in 1984 and 10 of 136 in 1985; χ^2 = 1.36, $P > 0.10$ nor females (4 of 176 in 1984 and 3 of 121 in 1985; $\chi^2 = 0.013$, $P > 0.10$). Thus, this noncyclic population seems to lack the between-year differences in social behavior found in some cyclic populations of microtine rodents (Krebs, 1985). However, even if there is no difference between years in the way individuals behave towards each other, social behavior could influence population dynamics. A high density will cause each individual vole to engage in social interactions more frequently, which in turn could increase stress (Christian 1978, 1980). As shown above, the reproductive success of overwintered females does not seem to be affected by density. Furthermore, no relationship was found between reproductive output of individual females and density at the time they reproduced. Irrespective of density, reproductive output declined along with the reproductive season.

As no between-year differences in behavior and no influence of density on reproduction could be detected, it is unlikely that social behavior has a primary influence on peak densities. In several microtine species a close correlation between reproduction and food quality or quantity has been found (Batzli 1986; Ford and Pitelka, 1984). In our population, data from four years indicate that the food resource influences population growth during the reproductive season. An index for plant productivity, including species utilized by the field vole, showed a correlation with female survival, recruitment rate of juveniles, and population growth. Thus, between-year differences in peak density could not be ascribed to behavioral differences but seem to be due to variation in food supply. In conclusion, spacing behavior influences dynamics of this vole population in various ways, but it does not seem to be the primary determinant of the dynamic pattern; that seems to be determined by predation and probably food.

ACKNOWLEDGMENTS

We thank R. Ostfeld and two anonymous referees for constructive criticism, S. Douwes and K. Persson for preparing the illustrations, and G. Lindquist for typing the manuscript. Grants were received from the Swedish Natural Science Research Council (to Erlinge).

LITERATURE CITED

Batzli, G. O. 1986. Nutritional ecology of the California vole: Effects of food quality on reproduction. Ecology, 67:406-412.

Chitty, D. 1967. The natural selection of self-regulatory behaviour in animal populations. Proceedings of the Ecological Society of Australia, 2:51-78.

Christian, J. J. 1978. Neurobehavioural endocrine regulation in small populations. Pp. 143-158, *in* Populations of small mammals under natural conditions (D. P. Snyder, ed.). Pymatuning Laboratory of Ecology Special Publication, 5:1-237.

———. 1980. Endocrine factors in population regulation. Pp. 367-380, *in* Biosocial mechanisms of population regulation (M. N. Cohen, R. S. Malpass, and H. G. Klein, eds.). Yale University Press, New Haven, Connecticut, 406 pp.

Cohen, M.N., R. S. Malpass, and H. G. Klein, (eds.). 1980. Biosocial mechanisms of population regulation. Yale University Press, New Haven, 406 pp.

Colvin, D. V. 1973. Agonistic behaviour in males of five species of voles *Microtus*. Animal Behaviour, 21:471-480.

Cranford, J. A., and T. L. Derting. 1983. Intra and interspecific behavior of *Microtus pennsylvanicus* and *Microtus pinetorum*. Behavioral Ecology and Sociobiology, 13:7-11.

Erlinge, S. 1987. Predation and noncyclicity in a microtine population in southern Sweden. Oikos, 50:347-552.

Erlinge, S., I. Hoogenboom, J. Agrell, J. Nelson, and M. Sandell. In press. Density related home-range size and overlap in adult field voles *(Microtus agrestis)* in southern Sweden. Journal of Mammalogy.

Erlinge, S., et al. 1983. Predation as a regulating factor on small rodent populations in southern Sweden. Oikos, 40:36-52.

Errington, P. L. 1946. Predation and vertebrate population. Quarterly Review of Biology, 21:144-177.

Ford, R. G., and F. A. Pitelka. 1984. Resource limitation in populations of the California vole. Ecology, 65:122-136.

Hansson, L. 1971. Habitat, food and population dynamics of the field vole, *Microtus agrestis* (L.) in South Sweden. Viltrevy, 8:267-378.

Jenkins, D., A. Watson, and G. R. Miller. 1964. Predation and red grouse populations. Journal of Applied Ecology, 1:183-195.

Krebs, C. J. 1985. Do changes in spacing behaviour drive population cycles in small mammals? Pp. 295-312, *in* Behavioural ecology. Ecological consequences of adaptive behaviour (R. M. Snyder,

58

and R. H. Smith, eds.). Blackwell Scientific Publications, Oxford, 620 pp.

Krebs, C. J., and J. H. Myers. 1974. Population cycles in small mammals. Advances in Ecological Research, 8:267-399.

Myllymäki, A., E. Christiansen, and L. Hansson. 1977. Five-year surveillance of small mammal abundance in Scandinavia. EPPO Bulletin, 7:385-396.

Searcy, W. A. 1986. Are red-winged blackbirds territorial? Animal Behaviour, 34:1381-1391.

Sibly, R. M., and R. H. Smith (eds.). 1985. Behavioural ecology. Ecological consequences of adaptive behaviour. Blackwell Scientific Publications, Oxford, 620 pp.

Social Systems and
Population Cycles in Voles
Advances in Life Sciences
© Birkhäuser Verlag Basel

THE EFFECT OF AGGRESSION ON DISPERSAL AND RELATED STATISTICS IN *MICROTUS OCHROGASTER* POPULATIONS IN EASTERN KANSAS

Michael S. Gaines, Eisa M. Abdellatif, Michael L. Johnson, and Kenneth B. Armitage

Department of Systematics and Ecology, University of Kansas, Lawrence, KS 66045 U.S.A. (MSG, EMA, KBA)

Kansas Biological Survey, Foley Geohydrology Building, University of Kansas, Lawrence, KS 66045 U.S.A. (MLJ)

Present address of EMA: Department of Zoology, University of Khartoum, Khartoum, Sudan

Summary.—In this study we tested the hypothesis that aggression is a stimulus for dispersal in the prairie vole, *Microtus ochrogaster*. A population of prairie voles was established in each of two 1-ha enclosures equipped with exit traps; live trapping ensued for 20 months. Sixty percent of subadult males captured were implanted either with testosterone capsules to increase their aggressiveness (treatment enclosure) or with oil capsule shams (control enclosure). Wounding of males in the treatment enclosure was significantly higher than in the control enclosure. Dispersal rates from the treatment population were three times higher than in the control population, but these differences were not statistically significant. From these results we suggest that aggression by males is a proximate stimulus for dispersal.

INTRODUCTION

Dispersal can be investigated to determine either its ultimate or proximate causes. Investigations into ultimate causes involve questions couched in evolutionary terms; for example, what are the fitnesses of individuals with the dispersing and nondispersing phenotypes (Johnson and Gaines, 1985, 1987)? Investigations into proximate causes of dispersal focus on physiological and behavioral mechanisms that initiate dispersal in any one individual.

Numerous hypotheses exist that suggest different social, ecological, or ontogenetic factors as proximal causes of dispersal. Prominent among these is a hypothesis proposing that aggression between members of the population leads to dispersal (Armitage, 1974; Fairbairn, 1978; Savidge, 1974; Smith and Ivins, 1983). Most of these studies involve observations of aggressive behavior and dispersal, and hence are correlational in nature. Direct tests of hypotheses relating aggression to dispersal are difficult to perform.

An approach to test the role of aggression as a proximate stimulus for dispersal would be to monitor dispersal rates after manipulating the level of aggression in the population. Hormonal manipulation is an effective way of altering levels of aggressiveness. The hormone, testosterone, has a role in the expression of aggressive behavior by male rodents (Beeman, 1947; Davidson and Levine, 1972; Turner et al., 1980). A group of laboratory mice implanted with testosterone capsules was consistently more aggressive than the control group (Selmanoff et al., 1977). This relationship between aggressive behavior and testosterone was substantiated by castration and replacement experiments (Beeman, 1947; Yen et al., 1962). Castrated, free ranging males of *Microtus pennsylvanicus* were less active and less aggressive than intact males (Turner et al., 1980). Gipps (1982) was able to manipulate the levels of aggressive behavior by implanting silastic capsules containing either testosterone or scopolamine hydrobromide into male *M. townsendii* in the laboratory. Subadult males treated with testosterone fought more than sham animals, and adult males treated with scopolamine hydrobromide fought less than shams. In the laboratory, Gaines et al. (1985) were able to elevate levels of aggressive behavior of subadult male *M. ochrogaster* implanted with testosterone capsules.

In this study we attempt to answer two questions relating hormones to social behavior in the prairie vole, *M. ochrogaster*. First, do testosterone capsules implanted in subadult males in the field effectively elevate their aggressiveness? Second, does the level of aggression in a population change the rate of dispersal?

MATERIALS AND METHODS

Study area and trapping schedule.—This study was conducted at the Nelson Environmental Study Area 14 km NE Lawrence, Kansas. The vegetation in the study area consisted mainly of sand dropseed *(Sporobolus cryptandrus)*, smooth brome *(Bromus inermis)*, down brome *(B. tectorum)*, and Japanese brome *(B. japonicus)*. Other scattered vegetation included green foxtail *(Setaria sp.)*, ragweed *(Ambrosia sp.)*, golden rod *(Solidago sp.)*, sunflower *(Helianthus sp.)*, and poison ivy *(Toxicondendron radicans)*.

Two small-mammal enclosures, 1 ha each, were built in 1981 with 13 by 13 mm mesh welded wire. The wire extended 30 cm underground and 91 cm above ground. A Sherman live trap was inserted in a hole cut through the fence every 13.6 m to catch potential emigrants. A 1-m-wide strip on the inside periphery of each enclosure was kept mowed as a habitat barrier to prevent nearby residents from entering exit traps during their normal activities. Snap- and live-trapping outside the enclosures failed to detect any significant egress of voles from within the fences. A 10 by 10 trapping grid with traps spaced at 9.1-m intervals was established in each enclosure. Each trap was covered with a wooden board, and cotton was provided for nesting.

Twenty voles (10 males, 10 females) randomly chosen from a laboratory colony were introduced into each enclosure on 6 October 1982. Trapping was conducted biweekly from October 1982 until June 1984, when all animals were removed. During cool weather, traps were checked two consecutive mornings and the intervening afternoon. To prevent overheating of animals during warm weather, traps were closed after the first morning and opened that afternoon; consequently they were checked only twice.

At first capture, each animal was ear-tagged, sexed, weighed, and examined for external reproductive condition (males: testes scrotal or abdominal; females: vaginas perforate or not). All animals, except for young males, were released at the location of capture. Each time a vole was recaptured its tag number, location of capture, body weight, and reproductive condition were recorded. All animals caught in exit traps were recorded as dispersers. They were taken to the laboratory, sacrificed, and frozen to be examined later for wounding scars. Twenty-five young males weighing 18-34 g were taken to the laboratory for testosterone implantation and 15 males were used for sham implants.

Testosterone treatment.—Twenty-five subadult males (<34 g) from the treatment enclosure were implanted with testosterone capsules. Each capsule consisted of 15 mm of silastic medical-grade tubing (1.47 mm inner by 1.96 mm outer diameter), containing 15 μl of testosterone suspension and sealed on both ends by silastic medical adhesive. Testosterone was suspended in peanut oil to a concentration of 0.5 mg/μl. These capsules allow a release of testosterone by passive diffusion (Gaines et al., 1985). In that experiment, release rates from silastic capsules were measured in castrated males by radioimmuno-assay. Testosterone capsules effectively increased the testosterone titer in male voles for at least four weeks and increased their aggressiveness (Gaines et al., 1985). Young males from the control enclosure were implanted with sham capsules containing 15 μl of peanut oil. After being anesthetized with Metaphane (methyoxy flurane), a small incision was made in the loose skin between the shoulder blades of each male to be implanted. A testosterone or sham capsule was then inserted under the skin and the incision was sutured closed. Each implanted male was housed individually and provided with rat chow and water ad lib. until next morning when it was released at the location of capture.

During the last two trapping periods all captured animals were removed and taken to the laboratory. With the exception of 30 subadult males, all removed animals were sacrificed and frozen to be examined later for skin scars. The subadult males were divided randomly into two groups to collect supplemental behavioral data on the effect of testosterone implants on aggressiveness.

Behavioral assays.—All subadult males captured during the last two weeks and any implanted male captured two weeks or more after implantation were returned to the laboratory to determine their level of aggressiveness. Each testosterone-implanted male was paired with a sham-implanted male in a neutral arena, a medium size (35 by 50 cm) aquarium with a sliding glass door. The two voles to be tested in a paired encounter were placed in the arena at the same time. The arena was lighted from above with a table lamp directed away from the observer, while room lights were turned off. The behavior of each pair was observed for 10 minutes. To eliminate any bias of the observer, assayed males were assigned random numbers for pairing and their identity not known until the end of each encounter. Seven behavioral categories (Krebs, 1970) were recorded: approach; attack; avoidance; retaliation; threat; fleeing; and submission. Each male was assigned an index of aggressiveness by awarding 1 point for each approach or retaliation, 2 points for each attack, -1 point for each avoidance or fleeing, and -2 points for each submission.

Wounding index.—All sacrificed animals were skinned and examined for the presence of wounds. The skin was stretched and examined for wounding scars. A wounding index was assigned to each animal by awarding 1 point for each small scar (<2 mm diameter), 2 points for each medium scar (2-5 mm diameter), and 3 points for each large scar (>5 mm diameter).

RESULTS

Population statistics.—No differences were observed between the experimental and control populations with respect to any population statistic except dispersal. Abundances of the two populations were comparable, although generally the treatment population contained a few more animals. Densities varied from highs of 52 and 40 for the experimental and control populations respectively, to a low of 2 in both populations. There were no significant differences between the two populations in sex ratio ($\chi^2 < 1$) age structure ($\chi^2 = 1.94$), survival rates of males ($t = 0.44$) and females ($t = 0.40$), and reproductive activity of males ($\chi^2 < 1$) and females ($\chi^2 = 0.77$). The presence of subadult males with testosterone implants did not alter the statistics of the two populations, and any differences between the two populations in dispersal rates, levels of aggression, and patterns of movement do not appear to be related to the structure of the populations.

Levels of aggression.—As is often the case when measuring behavioral attributes, a great deal of individual variation was observed in the behavioral assays. This variation, coupled with small sample sizes made statistical significance difficult to achieve. Consequently, unless noted otherwise, all differences are statistically nonsignificant. However, it is instructive to examine the trends in each of the measures of aggression, as well as the dispersal rates and movement patterns in the treatment and control populations, because all of the results are consistent.

The mean ($\pm SE$) aggressive index of testosterone-implanted males was three times higher (10.7 $\pm$ 5.9, n = 19) than sham-implanted males (2.9 $\pm$ 2.5, n = 15) and more than ten times higher than unimplanted males (0.9 $\pm$ 0.1, n = 16) in dyadic encounters. In general, animals from the treatment population had an elevated wounding index compared to animals from the control population. Males dispersing from the treatment grid had a mean wounding index more than twice (8.0 $\pm$ 1.6, n = 16) that of males dispersing from the control population (3.3 $\pm$ 0.07, n = 9). The same was true for residents from the treatment (11.6 $\pm$ 2.9, n = 14) and control populations (4.8 $\pm$ 2.0, n = 13). Both of these differences are statistically significant (P = 0.05, Mann-Whitney U test). It is also interesting to note that the ratio of the wounding index between dispersers and residents from the two populations is identical (3.3:4.8 = 8.0:11.6 = 0.69:1.00). In both populations, residents had the higher wounding index compared with dispersers.

Thus animals implanted with testosterone capsules appeared more aggressive than sham-implanted or unimplanted animals. In populations with testosterone-implanted animals, both residents and dispersers were the recipient of absolutely more aggression as measured by the wounding index. However, neither dispersers nor residents in the treatment population received relatively more aggression than did the same groups in the control population.

Movement and dispersal.—The potential for dispersal can be reflected in the amount and distance of movements within the enclosures, as exploratory movement may be a precursor to dispersal (Johnson, 1989). The distance moved between successive trapping periods was calculated for animals in the treatment and control populations. In general, animals from the treatment population tended to move greater distances than animals from the control population (Fig. 1). The differences were statistically significant for subadults.

Over the entire experiment, 22 animals dispersed from the treatment population and 14 from the control population. Dispersal rate was calculated by dividing the number of animals leaving the population each trapping period by the resident population density during that period. The mean dispersal rate per two weeks was three times higher in the treatment population (8.41 $\pm$ 4.98) than in the control population (2.90 $\pm$ 0.92). However, of the 25 animals implanted with testosterone capsules, only one dispersed, and none of the 15 sham-implanted animals dispersed.

DISCUSSION

It appears that implanting subadult male voles with capsules containing testosterone increases their aggressiveness when compared to sham-implanted or unimplanted voles. Concomitant with this increase in aggression is an increased tendency to move and an increased dispersal rate in the treatment population. Whereas other factors may operate as proximal stimuli for dispersal, the evidence from this experiment supports the contention that aggression, mediated by testosterone levels, is a proximal cause of dispersal in the prairie vole.

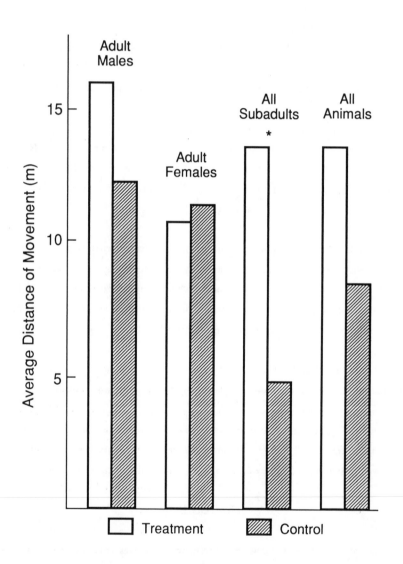

Fig. 1.—Average distances moved between trapping periods in testosterone implanted (open bar) and control (cross hatched) populations of *Microtus ochrogaster* ($^{*}P < 0.05$, *t*-test).

Ims (1989) proposed a similar mechanism for *Clethrionomys rufocanus* when he found that males dispersed in the absence of obvious external cues, indicating that there must be an internal physiological mechanism that initiates dispersal. His obvious candidate for this mechanism is a testosterone-mediated dispersal response. This idea was strengthened further as Ims also found that females from male-biased litters, and therefore females exposed prenatally to high levels of androgens (Vom Saal and Bronson 1980), tended to disperse, whereas females from female-biased litters tended to be philopatric. Holekamp (1986) tested the testosterone-dispersal hypothesis by injecting Belding's ground squirrels, *Spermophilus beldingi,* with testosterone soon after birth. She found higher dispersal rates in injected females than in uninjected females; in fact, injected females dispersed at rates similar to males. She concluded that early exposure (prenatal) to androgens was responsible for determining who dispersed, but that the exact trigger for dispersal is not well understood. Holekamp (1986) and Holekamp and Sherman (1989) proposed that an "ontogenetic switch" was set on the brain prenatally by androgenic steroids that are hypothesized to modify the morphology or behavior of neurons in the brain. The switch is triggered later in life, probably in response to accumulated body fat, and brings on a suite of behaviors culminating in dispersal.

In Belding's ground squirrels, the ontogenetic switch apparently was not related to aggressive behavior, as Holekamp (1986) could find no evidence of differential aggression directed at dispersers or nondispersers. What Holekamp did not consider is that the ontogenetic switch may be a differential response to aggression within the population. Higher levels of androgens prenatally may lower the "aggression threshold" such that the level of aggression that does not cause an unexposed animal to disperse, may cause an exposed animal to disperse. If this hypothesis is correct, increasing the level of aggression in the population would result in increased dispersal, as a greater number of animals would reach their aggression threshold (which would be set by the level of prenatal exposure). This mechanism appeared to function in our experiment. Implanting subadult males resulted in greater aggressiveness in the population, and therefore a greater dispersal rate. Dispersers exhibited a lower level of wounding, thus indicating a reduced aggression threshold.

Our conclusion that aggression may be a proximate stimulus for dispersal is tentative for several reasons. First, only 25 subadult males were implanted with testosterone capsules. The low sample sizes were due to poor trap responses of subadults in the population (Abdellatif, 1985). Second, because population densities in the treatment population were slightly higher than the control population, higher dispersal rates may have reflected a response to higher densities in the treatment population. However, dispersal rates usually decline as density increases (Gaines and McClenaghan, 1980).

What remains to be explored is what group of individuals within the population direct aggression at the dispersers. The social system of prairie voles is not well understood, having been described both as monogamous (Getz and Hofmann, 1986) and communal (Getz et al., this volume). One of the great challenges that lies ahead is to elucidate fully the social system and integrate information about physiology, population processes, and the social system to determine the proximal causes of dispersal.

A question that remains is why weren't there significant effects on other population statistics (e.g., survival and reproduction) when subadult males were implanted with testosterone capsules? One possible explanation is that we didn't consider the behavior of females. Taitt and Krebs (1982) implanted testosterone capsules in female *Microtus townsendii* to increase aggressiveness in one population and force-fed mestranol to females to reduce aggressiveness in another area. The testosterone treatment resulted in wounding among females, increased size of home ranges, and a reduction of female survival. Mestranol treatment had no effect on female population statistics, but males in this population survived better than control males. It is interesting that when Gipps et al. (1981) implanted testosterone capsules into males in a population of *M. townsendii*, there were no effects on population statistics. However, in another population where males were made less aggressive with implants of scopolamine hydrobromide, the rates of spring decline in male numbers were lower, female breeding started earlier, and more females bred compared to a control population. From these results we suggest that both females and males are sensitive to levels of aggression in the population. Females may have aggressive encounters with other females in defense of nest sites, whereas males may have aggressive encounters in mate acquisition. Also, females may be stressed more than males by increased population density because increased numbers may result in more challenges to site-specific individuals.

Historically, most research on behavior in microtines has been directed toward males. We agree with Taitt and Krebs (1985) that future research should be concentrated more on females. Manipulations should be performed in the field to increase and decrease aggression in both males and females using a factorial design. Results from such experiments will shed some light on the role of aggression in the population regulation of microtines.

ACKNOWLEDGMENTS

We thank Brent Danielson, Andrew Smith, and an anonymous reviewer for making critical comments on the manuscript. We are grateful to Scott Jackson and Scott Jamieson for their help with the trapping. The research was supported in part by National Science Foundation (U.S.A.) grant BSR-8314825 to MSG and the African Graduate Fellowship Program to EMA.

LITERATURE CITED

Abdellatif, E. M. 1985. The effect of aggression on dispersal and related parameters in microtine populations. Unpublished Ph.D. dissertation, University of Kansas, Lawrence, 72 pp.

Armitage, K. B. 1974. Male behavior and territoriality in the yellow-bellied marmot. Journal of Zoology (London), 172:233-265.

Beeman, E. A. 1947. The effect of male hormone on aggressive behavior in mice. Physiological Zoology, 20:373-405.

Davidson, T. M., and S. Levine. 1972. Endocrine regulation of Behavior. Annual Review of Physiology, 34:375-408.

Fairbairn, D. J. 1978. Behavior of dispersing deermice *(Peromyscus maniculatus)*. Behavioral Ecology and Sociobiology, 3:265-282.

Gaines, M. S., and L. R. McClenaghan, Jr. 1980. Dispersal in small mammals. Annual Review of Ecology and Systematics, 11:163-196.

Gaines, M. S., C. L. Fugate, M. L. Johnson, D. C. Johnson, J. R. Hisey, and D. M. Quadagno. 1985. Manipulation of aggressive behavior in male prairie voles *(Microtus ochrogaster)* implanted with testosterone in Silastic tubing. Canadian Journal of Zoology, 63:2525-2528.

Getz, L. L., and J. E. Hofmann. 1986. Social interaction in free living prairie voles, *Microtus ochrogaster.* Behavioral Ecology and Sociobiology, 8:189-194.

Gipps, J. H. W. 1982. The effects of testosterone and scopolamine HBr on the aggressive behavior of male voles, *Microtus townsendii.* Canadian Journal of Zoology, 60:946-950.

Gipps, J. H., M. J. Taitt, C. J. Krebs, and Z. Dundjerski. 1981. Aggression and the population dynamics of the vole *Microtus townsendii.* Canadian Journal of Zoology, 59:147-157.

Holekamp, K. E. 1986. Proximal causes of natal dispersal in Belding's ground squirrels *(Spermophilus beldingi).* Ecological Monographs, 56:365-391.

Holekamp, K. E., and P. W. Sherman. 1989. Why male ground squirrels disperse. American Scientist, 77:232-239.

Ims, R. A. 1989. Kinship and origin effects on dispersal and space sharing in *Clethrionomys rufocanus.* Ecology, 70:607-616.

Johnson, M. L. 1989. Exploratory behavior and dispersal: a graphical model. Canadian Journal of Zoology, 67:2325-2328.

Johnson, M. L., and M. S. Gaines. 1985. Selective basis for emigration of the prairie vole, *Microtus ochrogaster:* open field experiment. Journal of Animal Ecology, 54:399-410.

―――. 1987. The selective basis for dispersal of the prairie vole, *Microtus ochrogaster.* Ecology, 68:684-694.

Krebs, C. J. 1970. *Microtus* population biology: behavioral changes associated with the population cycle in *M. ochrogaster* and *M. pennsylvanicus.* Ecology, 51:34-52.

Savidge, I. R. 1974. Social factors in dispersal of deermice *(Peromyscus maniculatus)* from their

68

natal site. American Midland Naturalist, 91:395-405.

Selmanoff, M. K., E. Abreu, B. D. Goldman, and B. E. Ginsburg. 1977. Manipulation of aggressive behavior in adult DBA/2/Bg and C57BL/10/Bg male mice implanted with testosterone in silastic tubing. Hormones and Behavior, 8:377-390.

Smith, A. T., and B. L. Ivins. 1983. Colonization in a pika population: dispersal vs philopatry. Behavioral Ecology and Sociobiology, 13:37-47.

Taitt, M. J., and C. J. Krebs. 1982. Manipulation of female behavior in field populations of *Microtus townsendii*. Journal of Animal Ecology, 51:681-690.

———. 1985. Population Dynamics and Cycles. Pp. 567-620, *in* Biology of New World *Microtus* (R. H. Tamarin, ed.). Special Publication, The American Society of Mammalogists, 8:1-893.

Turner, B. N., S. L. Iverson, and K. L. Severson. 1980. Effects of castration on open field behavior and aggression in male meadow voles *(Microtus pennsylvanicus)*. Canadian Journal of Zoology, 58:1927-1932.

Vom Saal, F. S., and F. H. Bronson. 1980. Sexual characteristics of adult female mice are correlated with their blood testosterone levels during prenatal development. Science, 208:597-599.

Yen, H. C. Y., D. A. Day, and E. B. Sigg. 1962. Influence of endocrine factors on development of fighting behavior in rodents. Pharmacology, 4:173.

SOCIAL ORGANIZATION AND MATING SYSTEM OF THE PRAIRIE VOLE, *MICROTUS OCHROGASTER*

Lowell L. Getz, Betty McGuire, Joyce Hofmann, Theresa Pizzuto, and Barbara Frase

Department of Ecology, Ethology and Evolution, University of Illinois, Urbana, IL 61801 U.S.A.

Present address of BM: Department of Psychology, University of Massachusetts, Amherst, MA 01002 U.S.A.

Present address of JH: Illinois Natural History Survey, Champaign, IL 61820 U.S.A.

Present address of TP: Department of Entomology, Clemson University, Clemson, SC 29634 U.S.A.

Present address of BF: Department of Biology, Bradley University, Peoria, IL 61625 U.S.A.

Summary.—A communal nesting group, formed by additions to a monogamous pair breeding unit, is the basic year-round social unit of the prairie vole, *Microtus ochrogaster*. Before communal groups form, presumed monogamous pairs display traits normally associated with monogamy including cohabitation of a common nest, a shared home range, and dissolution of the pair primarily by mortality of one or both members. When juvenile nest mortality was reduced during late autumn-winter, extended-family groups formed. There was no difference in natal dispersal between summer and autumn-winter. Approximately 70% of the animals added to monogamous-pair breeding units were philopatric young. Unrelated adults (30% of the additions) joined extended-family groups in equal proportions in summer and late autumn-winter. Approximately half of the unrelated adults were reproductive when they joined an extended family group. During periods of winter reproduction most winter communal groups included at least one reproductive male and female, approximately half included two or more reproductive males and females (half of these were unrelated adults).

INTRODUCTION

The social organization of most species of microtine rodents is presumed to consist of adult males nesting separately from adult females with their young; mating systems appear to be polygynous or promiscuous (Ludwig, 1981; Madison, 1980a, b; Wolff, 1980, 1985). *Microtus californicus* and *M. montanus* may display facultative monogamy (Jannett, 1980; Lidicker, 1980). *M. pinetorum* appears to form extended family groups, and displays a variable mating system ranging from monogamy to promiscuity (FitzGerald and Madison, 1983). A social organization based on a pair-bonded monogamous mating system has been described for *M. ochrogaster* (Carter et al., 1986; Getz and

Hofmann, 1986; Getz et al. 1981; Thomas and Birney, 1979). However, communal nesting groups consisting of an extended family group and unrelated adults are commonly observed during the winter (Getz et al., 1987).

Communal nesting has been observed in a number of species of microtine rodents, including *M. pennsylvanicus* (Madison, 1984; Madison et al., 1984), *M. pinetorum* (FitzGerald and Madison, 1983), *M. xanthognathus* (Wolff and Lidicker, 1981) and *M. miurus* (Murie, 1961). In many species communal nesting is associated with winter or the nonreproductive period. Typically, communal nesting has been characterized as an adaptation for energy conservation (Beck and Anthony, 1971; Wiegert, 1961). Lesser aggressiveness associated with changed hormonal state of nonreproductive animals has been assumed to facilitate cohabitation of unrelated adults of otherwise noncommunal species (Madison et al., 1984; West and Dublin, 1984).

We now have evidence that the basic social organization of *M. ochrogaster* in all seasons consists of communal nesting groups derived from an original monogamous-pair breeding unit. These conclusions are derived from a six year study of a free-living population in east-central Illinois, described herein.

METHODS

Study areas.—The study was conducted in two adjacent 1-ha alfalfa *(Medicago sativa)* fields within the University of Illinois Biological Research Area (Phillips Tract), 6 km NE of Urbana, Illinois. The first area was planted with alfalfa in 1976 and used as a study site from October 1980 through July 1984. During the course of the study forbs other than alfalfa and grasses (e.g., ragweed, *Ambrosia* sp.; goldenrod, *Solidago* sp.; wild parsnip, *Pastinaca sativa;* and bluegrass, *Poa pratensis)* became major components of the vegetation. Alfalfa was planted in the second study area in the spring of 1982; the area was used June 1983-May 1987. The second field supported a relatively dense stand of alfalfa throughout the study. The two study areas were separated by a 10-m, closely mowed strip of bluegrass.

Field procedures.—In order to determine the mating system within the study populations we monitored nests used by adult females. Females to be located were identified on the basis of data from twice-monthly livetrapping with traps positioned in a 10-m grid pattern (Getz et al., 1979) and twice-weekly monitoring of nests (see below). The entire grid was trapped for three days each month; traps were set at 1500 h Tuesday, and checked at 2130, 0800 and 1500 h daily from Tuesday evening through Friday afternoon. Two weeks following the 3-day trapping session, those grid traps that were not located near known nests were set Wednesday afternoon and checked as above through Friday morning.

Nests of most females were located by use of ultraviolet reflective powder (Lemen and Freeman, 1985). Some were located by visual search or by placing radio transmitters on adult females. At any time the location of the nests of most or all of the breeding females in the study areas was known. After a nest was located, four or five multiple-capture live traps were placed near the burrow openings leading to underground nests or in runways leading to surface nests. Traps at each nest were set for two 28-h periods each week for as long as the nest was occupied; trapping at a nest continued for two weeks following the last capture of a resident to ensure the nest was no longer occupied. Cracked corn was used as bait and traps were covered with vegetation or aluminum-foil sunshields during the summer. We set the traps shortly after sunrise on Monday and checked them at 2-4 h intervals until midnight. Traps were checked twice on Tuesday morning, opened, and left in place. The nests were monitored at least seven times over the 28-h period. This trapping schedule was repeated Thursday morning through Friday morning. This regime of monitoring nests was maintained throughout the study except during the week of monthly grid-trapping when traps at nests were set only Monday through Tuesday.

When first captured, voles were marked individually by toe-clipping and weighed. At each capture, location, animal number, sex, and reproductive condition were recorded. For males, testes were recorded as either scrotal (reproductive) or abdominal (nonreproductive); for females, we determined if the vulva was closed (nonreproductive) or open, and if they were pregnant, lactating, or had recently lactated (reproductive). Weights of juveniles were used to estimate age at first capture (by reference to weights of animals of known age in a laboratory colony). Data are presented for the periods of late October-December 1980, mid May-December 1981, and late February 1982-May 1987.

Data analysis.—Only nests that were occupied for at least 14 days were included in the data analysis. Individuals had to be caught primarily at one nest for at least 10 days to be considered a resident of that nest. An animal caught more than one home range diameter (20 m) from the original nest following disappearance from that nest was considered to have dispersed. If an animal disappeared from a nest and was not caught again, we considered mortality to have occurred while the individual was still a resident of the nest. However, disappearance of an animal from a nest could also have involved dispersal from the nest, with mortality occurring before the animal was caught elsewhere. Such animals would be perceived to have died at the nest, leading to an underestimate of dispersal from the nest.

We conducted two analyses on known dispersal data from spring-autumn trapping in order to assess the validity of our estimates of dispersal and hence our definition of presumed mortality at nests. First, known dispersal of animals that disappeared from a nest immediately before a grid-trapping session was compared to known dispersal of animals that disappeared from a nest before another nest-trapping session. Dispersal data before nest trapping was compiled only for the week following that used for the before-grid-trapping analysis to reduce bias from temporal variation in dispersal. Grid traps were evenly spaced at a 10-m interval throughout the study areas and grid trapping started the same day the nest-trapping session ended. Nest traps were normally more widely spaced, and, there was a 2-day interval before the next nest trapping session began. Thus, animals dispersing from a nest before a grid trapping session would tend to encounter traps sooner than would dispersers before a nest trapping session. Further, the likelihood of dispersers being ejected from the vicinity of traps would be less likely at grid traps than at traps set directly at the nests of social groups (Getz and Hofmann, 1986). If many of the animals which we assumed to have died at the nest had actually dispersed before succumbing, we would expect known dispersal to be higher before a grid trapping session than before a nest trapping session.

Second, we compared known dispersal of animals that disappeared from a nest during periods when either more than 100 (100-220) or fewer than 25 nests were being trapped. The distance between traps was much greater in the latter group, thus allowing more time for mortality to occur before a disperser encountered a trap. Further, whereas up to 50% of the nests being trapped at high densities were actually unoccupied at the time, most nests being trapped at low densities were occupied. Thus, at high densities not only would dispersers have a greater probability of encountering traps before succumbing, but there would be no repulsion of dispersers from traps at unoccupied nests.

Three apparent social groups were identified in the free-living population: male-female (monogamous) pairs, single female units, and communal nesting groups. Monogamous pairs included only one reproductive adult male and female and sometimes young that remained at the natal nest; however, if young remained until adult (≥ 30 days of age), the group was considered to be communal. Single-female groups included only one reproductive adult female and no resident adult males. Young were occasionally present at the nest of single females; if the young remained until adulthood, the group was considered communal. Males were trapped at 17.5% of the 166 single-female groups when we first began monitoring the nest, but disappeared before meeting the 10-day criterion for residence. These groups most likely represented monogamous pairs, the nest of which we began monitoring just before the male disappeared. In addition, 33.9% ($n = 61$) of the female survivors of monogamous pairs remained at the original nest for more than 14 days without acquiring a new mate. Thus, a large proportion of the apparent single-female breeding units may also have been survivors of monogamous pairs, the male of which disappeared before our monitoring the nest. We conclude that single-female breeding units were comprised of survivors of monogamous pairs that had not remated; thus, single female units do not represent a basic breeding unit. Most communal nesting groups formed from a breeding unit to which young born to the reproductive female remained to adult age thus forming an extended family group. Communal groups usually included presumed unrelated adults that joined the extended family group. A few communal groups formed by the joining together of unrelated adult males and females.

Although we did not determine degree of relatedness among adults, wandering adults or those from different social groups were assumed to be unrelated. Young that weighed ≤20 grams when first captured at a nest were presumed to be offspring of a female living at that nest.

RESULTS

Validity of dispersal estimates.—There was no significant difference in the subsequent capture of animals that disappeared from a nest before a grid trapping session (29.9%; $n = 137$) and before another nest trapping session (27.6%; $n = 116$). Although not statistically significant, known dispersal was actually higher (33.3%; $n = 39$) when fewer than 25 nests were trapped than when more than 100 traps were in operation (20.6%; $n = 92$). When 26-99 nests were being trapped known dispersal was 30.9% $(n = 42)$.

It is also possible that dispersers from a nest may have left the entire study area without being caught at grid or other nest traps. However, all suitable *Microtus* habitat to the north and west of the study areas was livetrapped at monthly intervals as part of a concurrent population study. An agricultural field unsuitable for *Microtus* was located to the south, whereas tall-grass prairie habitat to the east was separated from the study areas by a macadam road that acted as an ecological barrier to dispersal; part of this latter area was also trapped monthly. In short, opportunities for undetected dispersal out of the study areas were limited; less than 3.3% of the individuals disappearing from our study areas were caught elsewhere. Most voles that disappeared from the study areas were presumed to have died within the study area.

Although indirect, the above evidence suggests that our estimates of dispersal from the nest are reasonably accurate. Accordingly, our assumption of mortality at the nest for animals that disappeared from a nest, never to be captured elsewhere, is supported.

Social group size and type.—Mean monthly social group size *(±SE)* throughout the study varied as follows *(n* in parentheses): January, 4.51 ± 0.24 (148); February, 3.36 ± 0.17 (125); March, 2.67 ± 0.14 (108); April, 2.19 ± 0.12 (77); May, 1.75 ± 0.09 (68); June, 1.86 ± 0.97 (93); July, 1.71 ± 0.08 (92); August, 1.80 ± 0.07 (127); September, 1.96 ± 0.08 (154); October, 2.90 ± 0.13 (184); November, 4.66 ± 0.19 (215); December, 5.05 ± 0.21 (204). Group size was correlated positively with population density (Kendal τ [B] correlation coefficient, 0.37; $P < 0.0001$; $n = 84$).

March-October, 73.1% of 386 social groups were monogamous-pair or single-female (i.e., survivor of monogamous pair) breeding units. Communal nesting groups comprised 26.9% of the social groups during this time; mean size of the spring-early autumn communal groups was 3.5 ± 0.10 (maximum of 6) individuals. From November through February, 68.6% of 325 social groups were communal; mean communal group size was 8.4 ± 0.34 (maximum of 21) individuals. The remaining 31.4% of the winter social groups were monogamous-pair (24.0%) or single-female (7.4%) groups.

Fate of monogamous pairs.—Only 26.5% of the 249 monogamous pair dissolutions resulted from dispersal of one or both individuals from the nest (both male and female, 13.2%; male only 10.9%; female only, 2.4%). The remaining 73.5% of the monogamous pairs broke up by presumed mortality of one or both individuals (both, 18.9%; male only, 26.9%; female only, 27.7%). There was no difference in the overall mortality of males and females at the nest; 45.8 and 46.6% of the males and females, respectively, of monogamous pairs disappeared from the nest through mortality.

Males and females were present at the nest an average of 17.2 ± 2.6 and 22.4 ± 2.3 days, respectively, following disappearance of their mate; this difference was significant at the 0.001 level (Mann-Whitney *U*-test, *Z* corrected for ties = -4.412). Most (60.3% of 59) male survivors of monogamous pairs dispersed from the nest, an average of 8.4 ± 2.0 days following loss of mate. Those males that did not disperse survived at the original nest an average of 19.1 ± 4.8 days (*n* = 24). Fewer female survivors (36.6% of 92) dispersed from the nest; those that did disperse (*n* = 35) remained at the nest for an average of 16.0 ± 2.8 days before leaving. The 57 females that did not disperse survived at the nest for an average of 26.3 ± 3.2 days. Presence of young at the nest had no influence on the length of time either male or female survivors remained at the nest before dispersing.

Only 19.1 and 19.4% of the male and female survivors, respectively, of monogamous pairs formed a new breeding unit. Less than half (48.2%) of the 27 male survivors that dispersed from the nest and did not form a new pair visited another breeding unit within the population. Of those that did visit breeding-unit nests, 57.9% visited single female nests and 42.1% monogamous-pair nests. Such males were each observed to visit only slightly more than one breeding unit nest (1.2 and 1.4 monogamous pair and single female breeding units, respectively) before disappearing.

Communal groups.—Most winter communal groups formed mid October-November. Of the 223 winter communal groups, 46.5 and 23.5% formed from monogamous-pair and single-female breeding units, respectively. Only 30.0% involved unrelated adults joining together to form a communal group. All communal groups observed in the spring and summer formed by additions to monogamous-pair or single-female breeding units.

Young born into late autumn-winter breeding units constituted 69.5% of the additions to the breeding unit (Table 1). Twice as many unrelated adult males as females joined the extended family groups. Young born into the breeding unit constituted 74.7% of the additions involved in formation

Table 1.—Number of groups and individuals and percent philopatric young and unrelated adults added to monogamous-pair and single-female breeding units of *M. ochrogaster* to form communal nesting groups in east-central Illinois.

Season	Groups (n)	Individuals (n)	Philopatric Young (%)	Unrelated Adults Males (%)	Unrelated Adults Females (%)
Autumn–Winter	229	1,288	69.5	20.3	10.2
Spring–Summer	104	194	74.7	8.3	17.0
Total	333	1,482	70.2	18.7	11.1

of spring-summer communal groups. Unlike late autumn-winter, approximately twice as many unrelated adult females as males joined the spring-summer extended family communal groups. Owing to the small sample size, this difference may not be biologically significant.

At the time of joining an extended-family communal group in winter, 62.1 and 41.7% of the 356 males and 240 females, respectively, were reproductive; 74.0% of the 96 reproductive females were pregnant. Although *M. ochrogaster* is normally nonreproductive during winter in east-central Illinois, reproduction was relatively high during the winters of 1982-1983 and 1986-1987 when communal groups are the predominant social group. During these two winters there was at least one reproductive male or female in 93.0 and 80.0%, respectively, of the 80 communal groups present; 47.4 and 52.5% had two or more reproductive males and females, respectively. Of the 42 winter communal groups with more than one reproductive female, 45.2% involved unrelated females; 47.6% included mothers with daughters and 7.1%, sisters. Unrelated males were in 55.5% of the 27 winter communal groups with more than one reproductive male; fathers with sons were present in 33.3% and brothers in 18.5% of these groups. All adults joining spring-summer communal groups were reproductive and remained so while residents of the group.

Reasons for increase in social group size.—There was essentially no difference in natal dispersal between spring-summer and early autumn-winter. During late autumn and winter 27.0% of 211 individuals dispersed from the natal nest; 28.2% of 376 young dispersed from the natal nest the rest of the year. Slightly fewer females dispersed from the natal nest in late autumn-winter than the rest of the year (21.1 and 27.0% of 90 and 167 individuals, respectively). Natal dispersal of males during the same periods was 31.4% (*n* = 121) and 29.2% (*n* = 209), respectively.

Survival of young until 30 days of age, the age at which we considered them to have become adults (and to have become members of an extended family group), was estimated for spring-summer and autumn-winter periods. Survival was calculated in terms of number per litter. The number of litters produced was estimated by totaling the number of days reproductively active females (pregnant or lactating) were present and dividing by the approximate gestation period (22 days). At the end of the breeding season, females were considered to have ceased reproduction with birth of the last litter, even though continuing to lactate for at least 20 days. In this method of estimating juvenile survival we assume no significant seasonal difference in litter size; it is thus only a crude estimate.

The average number of young per litter that survived to ≥ 30 days of age, the age at which individuals were considered to have become members of a communal group, for the period March-November (number of litters in parentheses) are as follow: March, 0.52 (88); April, 0.19 (89); May, 0.45 (92); June, 0.21 (122); July, 0.17 (82); August, 0.35 (138); September, 0.52 (181); October, 1.58 (216); and November, 0.97 (194). Survival to 30 days of age was 0.34 individuals per litter April-September and 1.29 per litter in October and November, when most communal groups formed.

DISCUSSION

There is considerable field and laboratory evidence for monogamy in *M. ochrogaster* (Carter et al., 1986; Dewsbury, 1985; Getz et al., 1981; Getz and Hofmann, 1986; Gruder-Adams and Getz, 1985; Oliveras and Novak, 1986; Thomas and Birney, 1979; Wilson, 1982). Members of breeding pairs display the following traits normally associated with monogamy (Kleiman, 1977): nest cohabitation and shared home ranges, paternal care of young, suppression of reproductive activation of young remaining within the family group, and mating essentially for life (relatively few survivors of monogamous pairs remate).

Three types of breeding units were observed in field populations of *M. ochrogaster:* monogamous-pair, single-female, and communal-nesting. The former two types constituted 73.1% of the breeding units observed during spring, summer, and early autumn. Single-female breeding units appear to represent female survivors of monogamous pairs, the males of which have disappeared and the females of which have not remated. Communal nesting groups comprised of extended family groups and unrelated adults were present primarily during the winter. However, during the present study a total of 104 communal groups, 14.6% of the total 711 breeding units monitored, were observed during the spring and summer. Although somewhat smaller, composition of these spring-summer communal groups was essentially the same as that of the winter communal groups.

All unrelated adults that joined summer communal groups, and approximately half of those that joined winter groups, were reproductive. All spring-summer communal groups included reproductive males and females. During two winters when the population remained reproductive, 93 and 80% of the communal groups included reproductive males and females, respectively. Approximately half of the communal groups these two winters included two or more reproductive males and females. Furthermore, in at least 45% of those communal groups with more than one reproductive male or female, unrelated adults were involved. Thus, cessation of reproduction and changes in hormonal state do not appear to be requirements for formation and maintenance of communal groups in *M. ochrogaster.*

Most (69.5%) of the additions to the basic breeding unit from which a communal group formed were young born into the group. Extended-family social groups were seldom observed during the spring-early autumn period. Differences in natal dispersal between spring-early autumn and late autumn-winter (only 1.2% lower during the latter period) are not sufficient to account for increased social group size in winter. Increased juvenile survival to ≥30 days of age during October and November (3.8 times that during spring and summer) appears to be the primary factor responsible for development of extended-family communal groups in winter.

We must address why there is increased juvenile survival at the nest in late autumn and winter. The only predators in the region capable of entering underground nests (none of the nests were observed to have been dug up) are snakes (primarily the fox snake, *Elaphe vulpina,* and prairie king snake, *Lampropeltis calligaster)* and weasels (*Mustela frenata* and *M. nivalis).* The former are active only during the period of presumed high nest mortality; snakes in east-central Illinois emerge in early spring and enter hibernation in mid October. Both species of weasels are active throughout the year.

When snakes, but not other predators, were excluded from a portion of the study area July-September 1985, communal nesting groups similar in size and composition to those normally occurring in winter formed in August and September (Getz et al., 1990). Average breeding unit size within the snake exclosure was 4.1 and 6.6 voles in August and September, respectively, as compared to 2.2 and 2.5 for the same months in the open population. Philopatric young born into the original breeding units within the exclosure constituted 71.1% of the additions to the breeding unit. The remaining 28.9% of the additions were unrelated adults that joined the breeding unit. Juvenile survival during July-September (number surviving until old enough to leave the nest) was 0.98 and 0.65 young per litter inside the exclosure and in the open population, respectively.

In summary it appears the basic, year round social organization of *M. ochrogaster* consists of communal groups that form from a monogamous breeding pair by the addition of philopatric young and a few unrelated adults. During spring-early autumn juvenile nestling mortality (from snake predation) is so high few social groups become communal. During these periods most social groups consist of monogamous pairs or single-female breeding units; the latter appear to be survivors of monogamous pairs that have not remated. When present as monogamous pairs the male-female breeding units display many of the characteristics of monogamy: cohabitation of a common nest, a shared home range, paternal care of young, dissolution primarily by mortality, persistence of survivors at the original nest, and low incidence of remating of survivors.

During late autumn and winter, when snakes are in hibernation, juvenile survival increases and the predominate social group is communal. We suggest that communal groups are prevented from forming in spring-early autumn as a result of high levels of snake predation on juveniles in the nest.

Detailed analyses of causative factors involved in formation and maintenance of communal nesting groups are now in progress. Results of these analyses will allow us to propose hypotheses regarding selective advantages of communal breeding groups in *M. ochrogaster.*

ACKNOWLEDGMENTS

This study was supported by grants from the National Science Foundation (DEB 78-25864), National Institutes of Health (HDO9328), and the University of Illinois Research Board to LLG. We express our appreciation to the following individuals for assistance with the field work: Kathryn Gubista, Phil Mankin, Wendy Holmgren, Patti Malmborg, Sandra Edwards, Cindy Triebold, Sheri Gruder-Adams, Bob Berk, Leah Gavish, Brian Klatt, Margaret Welke, Pamela Sutherland, Connie Rinaldo, and Sheila Vanthournout. We are especially indebted to Maria Snarski not only for assistance with the field work, but for her invaluable help in preparing the field data for analysis.

LITERATURE CITED

Beck, L. R., and R. G. Anthony. 1971. Metabolic and behavioral thermoregulation in the long-tailed vole, *Microtus longicaudus.* Journal of Mammalogy, 52:404-412.

Carter, C. S., L. L. Getz, and M. Cohen-Parsons. 1986. Relationships between social organization and behavioral endocrinology in a monogamous mammal. Advances in the Study of Behavior, 16:109-145.

Dewsbury, D. A. 1985. Paternal behavior in rodents. American Zoologist, 25:841-852.

FitzGerald, R. W., and D. M. Madison. 1983. Social organization of a free-ranging population of pine voles, *Microtus pinetorum.* Behavioral Ecology and Sociobiology, 13:183-187.

Getz, L. L., and J. E. Hofmann. 1986. Social organization in free-living prairie voles, *Microtus ochrogaster.* Behavioral Ecology and Sociobiology, 18:275-282.

Getz, L. L., C. S. Carter, and L. Gavish. 1981. The mating system of the prairie vole, *Microtus ochrogaster:* Field and laboratory evidence of pair-bonding. Behavioral Ecology and Sociobiology, 8:189-194.

Getz, L. L., J. E. Hofmann, and C. S. Carter. 1987. Mating system and population fluctuations of the prairie vole, *Microtus ochrogaster.* American Zoologist, 27:909-920.

Getz, L. L., N. G. Solomon, and T. M. Pizzuto. 1990. Suspected snake predation and social organization of the prairie vole, *Microtus ochrogaster.* The American Midland Naturalist, 123:365-371.

Getz, L. L., L. Verner, F. R. Cole, J. E. Hofmann, and D. Avalos. 1979. Comparisons of population demography of *Microtus ochrogaster* and *M. pennsylvanicus.* Acta Theriologica, 24:319-349.

Gruder-Adams, S., and L. L. Getz. 1985. Comparison of the mating system and paternal behavior in *Microtus ochrogaster* and *M. pennsylvanicus.* Journal of Mammalogy, 66:165-167.

Jannett, F. J., Jr. 1980. Social dynamics of the montane vole, *Microtus montanus,* as a paradigm. The Biologist, 62:3-19.

Kleiman, D. 1977. Monogamy in mammals. Quarterly Review of Biology, 52:39-69.

Lemen, C. A., and C. A. Freeman. 1985. Tracking mammals with fluorescent pigments: a new technique. Journal of Mammalogy, 66:134-136.

Lidicker, W. Z., Jr. 1980. The social biology of the California vole. The Biologist, 62:46-55.

Ludwig, D. R. 1981. The population biology and life-history of the water vole *(Microtus richardsoni).* Ph.D. dissertation, University of Calgary, Alberta, 274 pp.

Madison, D. M. 1980a. Space use and social structure in meadow voles, *Microtus pennsylvanicus.* Behavioral Ecology and Sociobiology, 7:65-71.

———. 1980b. An integrated view of the social biology of *Microtus pennsylvanicus.* The Biologist, 62:20-33.

———. 1984. Group nesting and its ecological and evolutionary significance in overwintering microtine rodents. Pp. 267-274, *in* Winter ecology of small mammals (J. F. Merritt, ed.). Special Publication, Carnegie Museum of Natural History, 10:1-380.

Madison, D. M., R. FitzGerald, and W. McShea. 1984. Dynamics of social nesting in overwintering meadow voles *(Microtus pennsylvanicus):* possible consequences for population cycles. Behavioral Ecology and Sociobiology, 15:9-17.

Murie, A. 1961. A naturalist in Alaska. Devin-Adair, Old Greenwich, Connecticut, 302 pp.

Oliveras, D., and M. Novak. 1986. A comparison of paternal behaviour in the meadow vole, *Microtus pennsylvanicus,* the pine vole, *M. pinetorum,* and the prairie vole, *M. ochrogaster.* Animal Behaviour, 34:519-526.

Thomas, J. A., and E. C. Birney. 1979. Parental care and mating system of the prairie vole, *Microtus ochrogaster.* Behavioral Ecology and Sociobiology, 5:171-186.

West, S. D., and H. T. Dublin. 1984. Behavioral strategies of small mammals under winter conditions: solitary or social? Pp. 293-299, *in* Winter ecology of small mammals (J. F. Merritt, ed.). Special Publication, Carnegie Museum of Natural History, 10:1-380.

Wiegert, R. G. 1961. Respiratory energy loss and activity patterns in the meadow vole, *Microtus pennsylvanicus pennsylvanicus.* Ecology, 42:245-253.

Wilson, S. C. 1982. Parent-young contact in prairie and meadow voles. Journal of Mammalogy, 63:300-305.

Wolff, J. O. 1980. Social organization of the taiga vole *(Microtus xanthognathus).* The Biologist, 62:34-45.

———. 1985. Behavior. Pp. 340-372, *in* Biology of New World *Microtus* (R. H. Tamarin, ed.). Special Publication, American Society Mammalogists, 8:1-893.

Wolff, J. O., and W. Z. Lidicker, Jr. 1981. Communal winter nesting and food sharing in taiga voles. Behavioral Ecology and Sociobiology, 9:237-240.

Social Systems and
Population Cycles in Voles
Advances in Life Sciences
© Birkhäuser Verlag Basel

POPULATION CONSTANCY OF THE ROCK VOLE, *MICROTUS CHROTORRHINUS*, IN NORTHEASTERN MINNESOTA.

Frederick J. Jannett, Jr.

Department of Biology, Science Museum of Minnesota, 30 East 10th Street, St. Paul, MN 55101 U.S.A.

Summary.—Each of nineteen populations of rock voles, *Microtus chrotorrhinus,* was monitored for 6 or 7 years by annual sampling. Voles were relatively uncommon the first year (8 sites), a result I attribute to artifacts of sampling. Numbers were constant in following years (all 19 sites). The standard deviation of the base-10 logarithm of population size, s, was 0.06 for 10 populations over 6 years, lower than all 45 values of s for 14 species of *Microtus* and *Clethrionomys,* and lower than 17 of 18 values for species of *Peromyscus* and *Apodemus* reported by Ostfeld (1988), indicating population constancy from year to year.

INTRODUCTION

Fluctuations in numbers exhibited by some *Microtus* populations are most dramatic in expansive open fields of graminoids with which most species of *Microtus* are primarily associated (Frank, 1957). In a literature survey of North American *Microtus,* Getz (1985) concluded that only three vole species *(M. chrotorrhinus, M. longicaudus,* and *M. oregoni)* were associated with forbs as opposed to graminoids.

The rock vole, *Microtus chrotorrhinus* was not described until 1894 (Miller, 1894), and there has been no long-term population study of the species. In a review of the literature on its natural history, Kirkland and Jannett (1982) concluded that it is found in a variety of forest types, and it is most commonly associated with rocks or talus, water in surface or subsurface streams, and mosses and forbs. It eats forbs primarily (Whitaker and Martin, 1977). Martin (1971) considered the rock vole one of the rarest in North America and, in reviewing its biology, found only 564 specimens in museum collections. The present study was undertaken to ascertain if populations of this species show multiannual fluctuations in numbers.

MATERIALS AND METHODS

The study was undertaken in Cook County in northeastern Minnesota at the extreme western edge of the range of the species (Kirkland and Jannett, 1982). A rock vole was caught in this area in

1921, but not again until the 1970's (Timm, 1974). The region was heavily logged around the turn of the century, but none of the sites in the present study showed evidence of recent cutting. All sites were forested. The dominant canopy species were black spruce *(Picea mariana)*, paper birch *(Betula papyrifera)*, and quaking aspen *(Populus tremuloides)*. The most common shrub understory species were alder *(Alnus* sp.), willow *(Salix* sp.), and beaked hazel *(Corylus cornuta)*. Low shrubs and herbs included Labrador tea *(Ledum groenlandicum)*, blueberry *(Vaccinium* sp.), bunchberry *(Cornus canadensis)*, and Clinton's lily *(Clintonia borealis)*. Mosses and lichens were abundant. Sixteen of the 19 sites were found originally by Christian and Daniels (1985) by looking for openings in the canopy associated with boulder patches. Most of these sites appeared to be glacial boulder streams, rather than talus outcroppings typical of many sites associated with the species in the eastern United States. The three additional sites were eskers identified by Sharp (1953).

I found in preliminary studies that rock voles could be more easily caught with Museum Special break-back traps (Woodstream Corporation, Lititz, Pennsylvania) than with small, nonfolding aluminum live traps (H. B. Sherman, Tallahassee, Florida); pit traps are not feasible in this habitat.

To obtain sufficient numbers for analysis of population trends, rock voles were sampled at 19 sites. Sampling was done in September when populations may be at their annual peak in numbers. Snow precludes efficient trapping in October.

Trap lines were standardized, except for some aspects in 1983 (see below). Each line had 50 Museum Special traps (new style with plastic treadle) set one per station for two consecutive 24-h periods. They were baited with peanut butter and, in front of the treadle, rolled oats and small apple chips. I set all traps, and examined them with another person. Traps were set, examined, and removed at approximately 24-h intervals between 0900 and 1800 h, with rare exceptions.

Each trap line was set at a boulder field. The configuration of the trap lines could not be standardized because the boulder fields, with which the voles are associated, were variable in size and shape. The smallest boulder field was a single patch covered by traps in a grid pattern having maximum linear distances 36 by 23 m. The longest boulder field was about 126 m long and 20 m at its widest; half of the traps were set on one side and half on the other. An attempt was made to sample all microhabitats at each site with respect to cover, water, and canopy closure, but trapping was most intensive along edges. The location of trap stations remained constant throughout the study. A trap was set within 1 m of the respective station marker. When possible, traps were placed next to fresh sign such as plant clippings or scat. At many stations the position of the trap was exactly the same each year. The traps were used only for this study and to sample a similar small-mammal community elsewhere in northern Minnesota in 1989.

The sampling regime for the eight sites in September 1983 differed from that described above for the entire suite of 19 sites in 1984-1989 in the following aspects. Either of two other individuals set half of each of some of these lines. Old style (wooden treadle) Museum Special traps were used along with new style traps in a ratio of about 1:3.7, respectively. The new style traps had previously been used only in August 1983 and in succeeding years they too accumulated a patina reflecting past use.

These eight sites also constituted a subset among the sites with respect to previous trapping success. They included one site where Christian and Daniels (1985) caught one or more rock voles in 1982 but where none was caught in preliminary trapping by the author in August 1983, and seven where they caught no rock voles; each of these sites had one or more in September 1983. At each of eight other sites, at least one rock vole was caught in 1982 by Christian and Daniels (1985) and by the author in August 1983. The last group of sites was that of three eskers where sampling was first undertaken in 1984.

Three lines were left set for a third day because >25 traps were sprung and empty on one of the first two days. For this criterion, a missing trap was counted as two sprung empty traps. There were 11 trap lines with large numbers of sprung, empty traps caused by rain, martens *(Martes americana)*, beavers *(Castor canadensis)*, or bears *(Ursus americanus)*. If bears disturbed a line on two consecutive days, no further effort was made at that site that year.

To test the null hypothesis that the numbers of rock voles did not fluctuate, two-tailed Wilcoxon matched-pairs signed-ranks tests (Siegel, 1956) were used. There were four series of year-by-year comparisons. In the first series of tests, I compared rock vole numbers caught at the subset of eight sites studied in 1983, and in the second series I compared numbers at all 19 sites. Thirteen samples were not included in the analyses: three were only 1-day samples due to rain; in each of eight others the total number of sprung empty traps was >50 in the standard 2-day period; lastly, data were also excluded for one site in 1988 and 1989 because an immediately adjacent area, including some of the marginal trap stations, was clearcut earlier in 1988. Data from a third day available for three sites were not analyzed.

Trapping effort may affect the numbers caught, so in another two series of tests I analyzed the numbers per 100 trap nights, wherein one trap night is one trap left open for approximately 24 h. To indicate the traps available for rock voles more accurately, the following were subtracted from the maximum 100 or 150 trap nights: one-half trap night for each trap that was sprung and empty, nonfunctional, or contained another species, and one trap night for each trap not found. Two such series of comparisons (1983 subset and all sites combined) were made, based on the same data sets as those yielding absolute numbers, but additionally data were included from the eight samples not previously analyzed because of excessive numbers of sprung empty traps, and from the third day of trapping for three of these eight lines.

The same data sets of rock voles per 100 trap nights were tested by analysis of variance after a square root transformation. The 1983 subset of sites was tested separately. All 19 sites were tested

84

over 1984-1989. Where appropriate, a Duncan's multiple-range test was applied.

For a comparison of the temporal variability of these populations with that reported for other species, I calculated the standard deviation of the base-10 logarithm of population size $(s;$ Connell and Sousa, 1983). I followed the procedure of Ostfeld (1988) and got a single number of voles for the year by combining all samples. Two values were calculated: for the 1983 subset of sites and for all sites. Data from four sites in the 1983 subset over seven years were used in the calculation; each of the other four sites in the subset had one or two samples with excessive numbers of empty sprung traps, and was therefore not included. In the 6 years of data from all 19 sites, there were 10 complete series used in the calculations.

Specimens reported here are in the collection of the Science Museum of Minnesota. The most common and widespread small mammals at these sites were *Microtus chrotorrhinus, Clethrionomys gapperi, Peromyscus maniculatus, Blarina brevicauda,* and *Sorex cinereus.* Other species present were *M. pennsylvanicus, Synaptomys cooperi, Zapus hudsonius, Napaeozapus insignis, Tamias striatus, Eutamias minimus, Glaucomys sabrinus, Condylura cristata, S. palustris, S. arcticus,* and *Microsorex hoyi.*

RESULTS

At least one rock vole was caught at each site each year (Fig. 1). There was an average of 7.3 $(\pm 0.4$ *SE)* rock voles in the 109 samples included in the first two series of tests. In 1983, there were significantly fewer voles than in each subsequent year at the 1983 subset of eight sites $(P < 0.05)$. The following are the N and T values, respectively, for 1983 versus each subsequent year (1984-1989): 7, 1; 7, 2; 7, 1; 7, 0; 8, 0; and 6, 0. There was no other significant difference $(P < 0.05)$ in pair-wise comparisons of years based on the 1983 subset of sites, nor was there any based on all 19 sites (1984-1989).

The number of rock voles per 100 trap nights in a sample averaged 10.2 $(\pm 0.6$ *SE).* The number of rock voles per 100 trap nights was again significantly smaller in 1983 than in each subsequent year for this subset $(P < 0.05)$. The following are the N and T values, respectively, for 1983 versus each subsequent year (1984-1989): 7, 1; 8, 3; 8, 1; 8, 0; 8, 0; and 8, 0. There was only one other pair-wise comparison that showed significantly different numbers (1986 versus 1989 for all 19 sites, $N = 17$, $T = -32$, $P < 0.05$). These years were, respectively, those with the highest and lowest numbers of rock voles per 100 trap nights.

The analysis of variance of rock voles per 100 trap nights in the 1983 subset of sites showed a significant difference between years $(F = 6.23,$ $d.f. = 6$, $P < 0.0001)$ and the Duncan test indicated that 1983 was the only year outside the grouping of all others. In the analysis of sites sampled in 1984-1989, there was no significant difference $(F = 1.09,$ $d.f. = 5$, $P = 0.374)$.

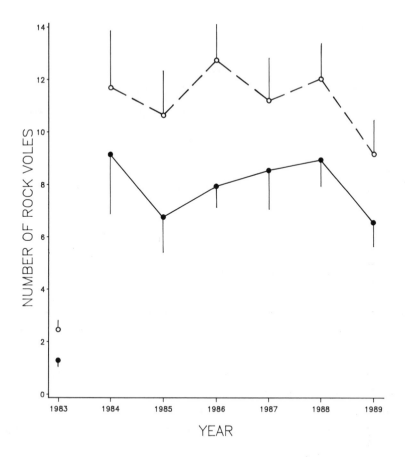

Fig. 1.—Average number of rock voles per sample *(-SE;* dots and solid line) based on four samples in 1983, 10 in 1984-1989), and average number of rock voles per 100 trap night sample *(+SE;* circles and dashed line) based on seven samples in 1983, 15 in 1984-1989.

For the 1983 subset of four samples over seven years, s (the standard deviation of base-10 logarithms of population size) was 0.28. For the 10 samples over six years, s was 0.06.

DISCUSSION

The data indicate that numbers of rock voles in northeastern Minnesota are relatively constant and do not fluctuate as do many other populations of voles (Krebs and Myers, 1974). I accept the simplest explanation for the relative scarcity of rock voles in 1983, that it was an artifact of trapping procedure. The trap effort differed in several ways. Most of the traps were new that year and therefore may not have been as attractive to voles as they were when "aged." Three people set traps, none of whom had experience trapping in the area. And, lastly, some of the traps were old style Museum Specials that may have been less appropriate for this species (less sensitive). West (1985) compared the numbers of small mammals of 10 species taken in old and new style Museum Specials. There was a difference in numbers caught for three species, albeit in both directions. Additionally, for *Clethrionomys californicus* and three species of *Sorex,* more specimens were obtained in new style traps, although not with statistical significance.

A second explanation for low numbers of rock voles in 1983 is that these sites, where either Christian and Daniels (1985) did not catch rock voles in 1982 or where I did not in August 1983, are more susceptible to short-term fluctuations in numbers, perhaps by flooding. I think this unlikely because from 1984 through 1989 the subset showed no detectable fluctuation.

A third explanation for the numbers of rock voles in 1983 is that they reflect the end of a period of very low numbers (D. Christian, pers. comm.). Only continued monitoring of some or all of these *M. chrotorrhinus* populations could address this hypothesis.

The s of 0.06 for the 10 populations of rock voles over 6 years is lower than each of the 45 individual and composite values calculated by Ostfeld (1988) for 14 species of *Clethrionomys* and *Microtus* (range: 0.09-0.95). It is also smaller than each of the 12 calculated by Ostfeld (1988) for *Peromyscus maniculatus* and *P. leucopus* (range: 0.07-0.56), and smaller than all but one of the six calculated for *Apodemus flavicollis* and *A. sylvaticus* (range: 0.05-0.21). Rock voles in northeastern Minnesota exhibit a pattern of constancy. The ecological determinants of this pattern may provide tests for hypotheses of population regulation and adaptive significance of the social systems of voles.

ACKNOWLEDGMENTS

This work was supported each year by the Minnesota Department of Natural Resources, the Science Museum of Minnesota, and the author. I particularly thank the staff of the Nongame Program of the Minnesota Department of Natural Resources for their research perspective, and the National Forest Service for access to a field cabin 1986-present. I thank M. Candee, J. Davies, J. Jannett, J. Moodie, R. A. Stehn, and particularly R. Oehlenschlager for help in the field. J. Jannett helped with the work at many stages and S. Nowland typed the manuscript.

LITERATURE CITED

Christian, D. P., and J. M. Daniels. 1985. Distributional records of rock voles, *Microtus chrotorrhinus,* in northeastern Minnesota. Canadian Field-Naturalist, 99:356-359.

Connell, J. H., and W. P. Sousa. 1983. On the evidence needed to judge ecological stability or persistence. The American Naturalist, 121:789-824.

Frank, F. 1957. The causality of microtine cycles in Germany. Journal of Wildlife Management, 21:113-121.

Getz, L. L. 1985. Habitats. Pp. 286-309, *in* Biology of New World *Microtus* (R. H. Tamarin, ed.). American Society of Mammalogists, Special Publication, 8:1-893.

Kirkland, G. L., Jr., and F. J. Jannett, Jr. 1982. *Microtus chrotorrhinus.* Mammalian Species, 180:1-5.

Krebs, C. J., and J. H. Myers. 1974. Population cycles in small mammals. Advances in Ecological Research, 8:267-399.

Martin, R. E. 1971. The natural history and taxonomy of the rock vole, *Microtus chrotorrhinus.* Unpublished Ph.D. dissertation, University of Connecticut, Storrs, 123 pp.

Miller, G. S., Jr. 1894. On a collection of small mammals from the New Hampshire mountains. Proceedings of the Boston Society of Natural History, 26:177-197.

Ostfeld, R. S. 1988. Fluctuations and constancy in populations of small rodents. The American Naturalist, 131:445-452.

Sharp, R. P. 1953. Glacial features of Cook Co., Minnesota. American Journal of Science, 251:855-883.

Siegel, S. 1956. Nonparametric statistics for the behavioral sciences. McGraw-Hill, New York, 312 pp.

Timm, R. M. 1974. Rediscovery of the rock vole *(Microtus chrotorrhinus)* in Minnesota. Canadian Field-Naturalist, 88:82.

West, S. D. 1985. Differential capture between old and new models of the Museum Special snap trap. Journal of Mammalogy, 66:798-800.

Whitaker, J. O., Jr., and R. E. Martin. 1977. Food habits of *Microtus chrotorrhinus* from New Hampshire, New York, Labrador and Quebec. Journal of Mammalogy, 58:99-100.

Social Systems and
Population Cycles in Voles
Advances in Life Sciences
© Birkhäuser Verlag Basel

PATTERNS OF VISITATION IN PRAIRIE VOLES
(*MICROTUS OCHROGASTER*) REVEAL A ROLE FOR MALES
IN POPULATION REGULATION

B. McGuire, T. Pizzuto, and L. L. Getz

Department of Ecology, Ethology, and Evolution, University of Illinois, Champaign, IL 61820 U.S.A.

Present address of BM: Department of Psychology, University of Massachusetts, Amherst, MA 01003 U.S.A.

Present address of TP: Department of Entomology, Clemson University, Clemson, SC 29631 U.S.A.

Summary.—Spacing behavior appears to play a role in population regulation of microtine rodents. We used information gathered from livetrapping at nests and the periphery of home ranges of prairie voles (*Microtus ochrogaster*) to continue our examination of the role of spacing behavior in population regulation. Resident and nonresident adult males captured at the outskirts of home ranges were reproductive rather than nonreproductive and did not differ in body weight. Although the majority of adult females were reproductive, the pattern was more pronounced for residents. The presence of adult males in a resident group deterred visits by nonresident males. By excluding nonresident males from the home range, resident males appeared to influence the reproductive condition of their daughters; if females became reproductive while living at home, they did so at an earlier age when living in groups where resident males were absent than where resident males were present. From these results we suggest that adult males play a role in setting breeding density in natural populations of prairie voles.

INTRODUCTION

Spacing behavior appears to be a potent force in population dynamics of microtine rodents (Krebs, 1985). Many field researchers have examined the possible existence in voles of gender-specific roles in population regulation. Despite variation in experimental technique, from sex-specific removal experiments in species that exhibit polygyny and female territoriality we infer a general tendency for females to influence recruitment, survival, and sexual maturation of other females (*Microtus pennsylvanicus*, Boonstra and Rodd, 1983; *Clethrionomys gapperi*, Bondrup-Nielsen, 1986; *C. rutilus*, Gilbert et al., 1986; *C. glareolus*, Gipps et al., 1985). The effects of male removal on the population processes of these species were typically less obvious and less consistent. In *M. townsendii* (Redfield et al., 1978a), but not *M. oregoni* (Redfield et al., 1978b), adult females also exerted a greater influence on population parameters than did adult males. However, interpretation of these findings is difficult due to lack of information on the mating and territorial systems of these two species. Nevertheless, the pattern that emerges from removal experiments in species characterized by polygyny and female territoriality is that females, through their spacing behavior, set breeding density within populations.

Prairie voles *(Microtus ochrogaster)* differ from the above-mentioned species in that they exhibit male-female territoriality (Hofmann et al., 1984) and a social organization based on the addition of philopatric young to a stable breeding pair (Getz et al., this volume). Typically, 70 and 75% of male and female offspring, respectively, remain at the natal nest past weaning, and apparently unrelated adults often join these extended families and form communal groups. Although a variety of social groupings occurs in natural populations, male-female pairs and single-female units (apparent female survivors of male-female pairs) together comprise approximately 73% of social groups that occur during the breeding season; during the nonbreeding season, communal groups are most common (Getz et al., this volume). Based on patterns of association between reproductive males and females in the field and an assortment of laboratory data on behavior and reproduction (Dewsbury, 1981), prairie voles have generally been described as monogamous; genetic analyses are necessary, however, to confirm mating exclusivity in natural populations.

Estrus in virgin prairie voles is induced by exposure to unfamiliar males; a young female that sniffs the genital area of an unfamiliar male ingests a urinary chemosignal that initiates reproductive activation (Carter et al., 1980). Although this substance is present in the urine of male family members, young females typically do not sniff their father or brothers and therefore do not pick up the estrus-inducing chemosignal. Family members not only fail to stimulate young females, but also appear to inhibit their growth and reproductive maturation (Batzli et al., 1977; Carter et al., 1986; McGuire and Getz, 1981). High levels of interaction with nonresident males are necessary to overcome the suppression typically experienced by young females living in family groups (Hofmann and Getz, 1988). Opportunities for young females to interact with nonresident males occur in natural populations of prairie voles. We have found that the most common intruders into the home ranges of family groups are adult males from neighboring nests; such males may be paired or single at time of capture (McGuire et al., 1990).

Rather than manipulating patterns of social interaction within the population by large scale removal of males or females as done by other investigators, we examined spacing behavior through intensive livetrapping at nests and at the periphery of home ranges of family groups. We first add to our recent characterization of participants in potential social interactions (McGuire et al., 1990) by providing new information on reproductive condition and body weight of resident and nonresident animals. We then focus on whether resident males, through their spacing behavior, limit interactions between their daughters and nonresident males and thereby influence the proportion of breeding females within the population.

METHODS

Data pertaining to trapping at the periphery of home ranges were collected simultaneously with those presented in McGuire et al. (1990), and thus the methods are the same. Data pertaining to trapping at nests derive from a companion study conducted in the same and in an adjacent field over an approximately 5-year period (Getz and Hofmann, 1986).

The study sites were two adjacent 1-ha alfalfa *(Medicago sativa)* fields on the University of Illinois Biological Research Area, Urbana, Illinois. The first area was used from October, 1980 through July, 1984, the second area from June, 1983 through May, 1987. The two fields were separated by a 10-m closely mowed strip of bluegrass *(Poa pratensis).*

Three trapping regimes were used. Analysis of social interactions involved trapping at burrows leading to underground nests (nest trapping: Getz and Hofmann, 1986) and at the periphery of home ranges of social groups (peripheral trapping: McGuire et al., 1990). Population fluctuations were monitored by grid trapping throughout the study (Getz et al., 1987). In all three trapping regimes we used multiple-capture live traps baited with cracked corn. At each capture, location, animal number (from toe clip), sex, weight, wounds, and reproductive condition were recorded. We used body weight to classify each individual as adult (>30 g for males; >28 g for females), subadult (20-30 g for males; 20-28 g for females), or juvenile (<20 g for males and females). Males were classified as reproductive if testes were scrotal; females were considered reproductive when pregnant or lactating.

We located nests of prairie voles by visual search and by dusting animals with ultraviolet reflective powder (Lemen and Freeman, 1985). Once a nest was located, four or five live traps were placed in runways leading to it. Traps were set for two 28-h periods each week and monitoring continued for as long as the nest was occupied. Shortly after sunrise on Monday, traps were set and examined at from 2- to 4-h intervals until midnight. On Tuesday morning the traps were examined twice and locked open. The same schedule was followed Thursday through Friday. With the exception of weeks during which grid trapping was conducted (see below), we trapped at nests on a twice weekly schedule. During the one week of grid trapping each month, nest traps were set on Monday and Tuesday only. We monitored nests of all individuals known to be alive in each of the study areas and present data for the period of February 1982 through May 1987.

We used monthly grid trapping to monitor changes in population densities of prairie voles in the two study fields. Traps were set, one per station, at 10-m grid intervals for a 3-day period each month. We set grid traps Tuesday afternoon and checked them daily through Friday afternoon at 2130, 0800, and 1500 h.

Peripheral trapping, conducted from March, 1986 through April, 1987, was used to monitor presence of resident and nonresident animals at the outskirts of home ranges of social groups. We encircled the nest of a social group (focal group) with five to eight traps about 5 m from the nest (5-10 m represented the typical distance from the nest to the outer boundaries of home ranges of social groups in the alfalfa habitat: Getz et al., 1986; Hofmann et al., 1984). We set peripheral traps on Tuesday, after the nest traps were locked open, and checked them at 1500 and 2100 h. On Wednesday, traps were checked at 0700, 1500, and 2100 h, and locked open. Each month we trapped at the periphery of home ranges for 3 weeks; peripheral traps were not set during the week of grid trapping.

We defined four social groups (male-female pair, communal group, single-female unit, or single-male unit; McGuire et al., 1990). Male-female pairs included a pair of reproductive adults, with or without offspring. Communal groups contained at least two adults (not a male-female pair) and any young present. Single-female units consisted of an adult female and any young; resident males were not present in these groups. Adult males, with or without older offspring, comprised the final group. In order to be included in the analysis, nests had to be occupied for at least 14 days.

Individuals captured in peripheral traps were classified according to status of residence (McGuire et al., 1990). Briefly, whereas we assigned the classification "resident" to those animals that were consistently caught at the focal nest both the week before and the week after their capture in its peripheral traps, we assigned the classification "resident-moving" to individuals that were caught at the focal nest the week before but not the week after their capture in its peripheral traps. Animals in the latter category were known to have changed nest sites because they were subsequently caught at new locations in the study fields. Whereas neighbors lived within 20 m of the focal nest, nonneighbors lived more than 20 m from the focal nest. Finally, "unknown" individuals were captured for the first time in peripheral traps and then disappeared from the study areas.

RESULTS

Over the course of approximately 5 years of trapping at nests, 711 social groups were monitored. We trapped at the periphery of home ranges of 74 of these groups; of the 583 captures of prairie voles in peripheral traps, 23 were classified as unknown with respect to category of residence and were not included in analyses.

Further Characterization of Participants in Potential Social Interactions
at the Periphery of Home Ranges: Reproductive Condition and Body Weight

Adult males captured at the periphery of home ranges tended to be reproductive rather than nonreproductive and this pattern did not differ among categories of residence (Table 1; χ^2 = 4.2, *d.f.* = 3, *P* < 0.24). In contrast, distribution of captures of reproductive and nonreproductive adult females differed among the four residence categories (Table 1; χ^2 = 14.3, *d.f.* = 3, *P* < 0.005). Whereas most resident females that were captured were reproductive rather than nonreproductive, the pattern was less pronounced for neighbors and reversed for nonneighbors. Resident and nonresident adult males did not differ in body weight $(\bar{X} \pm SE$ = 39.6 ± 0.6 g and 38.7 ± 0.4 g, respectively; t = 1.4, *d.f.* = 359, *P* < 0.17). Female body weights were not analyzed due to variation as a result of pregnancy.

Influence of Resident Males on Visitation by Nonresidents
to the Periphery and Nest

Type of social group and visitation by nonresidents (between-group comparison).—We recently reported that nonresident males visited the periphery of home ranges of single female groups more frequently than they visited male-female, communal, or single-male groups (McGuire et al., 1990). Below we describe a similar between-group comparison for captures that occurred directly at nests rather than at the outskirts of home ranges.

Table 1.—Captures of reproductive and nonreproductive adult male and female prairie voles, *Microtus ochrogaster,* in each category of residence in Illinois. Captures occurred at the periphery of home ranges of social groups.

Sex	Residence	Reproductive condition			
		Reproductive		Nonreproductive	
		n	%	n	%
Male	Resident	81	87.1	12	12.9
	Resident-moving	34	97.1	1	2.9
	Neighbor	114	92.7	9	7.3
	Nonneighbor	31	93.9	2	6.1
Female	Resident	69	77.5	20	22.5
	Resident-moving	33	84.6	6	15.4
	Neighbor	39	60.0	26	40.0
	Nonneighbor	0	0.0	2	100.0

We summarized nonresident captures directly at nests over the 5-year study period and found patterns of visitation similar to those noted at the periphery of home ranges. Nonresident males visited nests of single females more frequently than they visited nests of male-female pairs (3.7 and 1.5 times per week, respectively) and frequency of visitation by nonresident females did not vary as a function of type of social group. Although data from nests and the periphery of home ranges yielded qualitatively similar results, the magnitude of differences in visitation to different types of social groups varied with location within the home range. Whereas nonresident males visited nests of single females approximately 2.5 times as frequently as they visited nests of male-female pairs, they visited the periphery of home ranges of single females four times as frequently as they visited the periphery of home ranges of male-female pairs (single female, $\bar{X} \pm SE = 8.0 \pm 1.4$ visits per week; male-female pair, 2.0 ± 0.6 visits per week; McGuire et al., 1990).

Change in group composition and visitation by nonresidents (within-group comparison).—Fourteen of the 74 social groups monitored during the period of trapping at the periphery changed adult composition and persisted long enough for us to track changes in rate of visitation by adult males and females. In most cases, composition changed as a result of disappearance of mate (eight groups changed from male-female pairs to single-female units; two groups changed from communal groups to single-female units; two groups changed from male-female pairs to single-male units). In only two instances did composition change as a result of mate acquisition (two groups changed from single-female units to male-female pairs). We analyzed whether, within these groups, visitation changed as a function of presence or absence of the resident male; our analysis was limited to those groups that changed from male-female pairs to single-female units or vice versa $(n = 10)$. The number of visits per week by nonresident males was greater when resident males were absent from these groups $(\bar{X} \pm SE = 10.0 \pm 2.3)$ than when they were present $(1.5 \pm 1.0; F = 22.7, d.f. = 1, 9, P < 0.001)$. Although captures per week of nonresident females followed a similar pattern, the difference was not statistically significant (resident males absent, 2.2 ± 0.8; resident males present, $0.8 \pm 0.4; F = 2.8, d.f. = 1, 9, P < 0.15$).

We summarized data obtained from trapping directly at nests of 57 social groups that either lost or acquired resident males and found changes in visitation by nonresident males similar to those noted at the periphery of home ranges. Whereas nonresident males visited these groups approximately 2.8 times per week when resident males were absent, they visited 1.9 times per week when resident males were present. These data again indicate that although results from nest and peripheral trapping are qualitatively similar, differences in visitation by nonresident males as a function of presence or absence of resident males in the focal group are more pronounced at the periphery of home ranges than at nests.

Impact of Territorial Behavior of Resident Males on Reproductive Condition
of Young Females Living at Focal Nests

Only 10-15% of female prairie voles born at focal nests survived to the age at which they could become reproductive. Of those females that survived to 30 days of age, whether or not an adult male (presumably their father—relationship is inferred from patterns of association at the nest and not from genetic analyses) was present in the social group tended to influence their reproductive condition. Whereas 75.0% (12/16) of females that survived to 30 days of age became reproductive while living in single female groups, only 51.7% (15/29) of similarly aged females showed signs of reproduction while living in male-female groups (χ^2 = 1.5, $d.f.$ = 1, P < 0.23). Furthermore, if females became reproductive while living at home, they did so at an earlier age when living in single-female groups ($\overline{X}$ ± SE = 33.7 ± 2.8 days, n = 12) than when living in male-female units (43.9 ± 2.4 days, n = 24; Wilcoxon 2-sample test, U = 440, P < 0.02).

When young females from all types of social groups were considered, reproductive condition had a tendency to influence the likelihood of dispersal from the natal nest. Whereas 31.7% (33/104) of females that became reproductive while living at home dispersed, 20.4% (31/152) of nonreproductive females left home (χ^2 = 3.6, $d.f.$ = 1, P < 0.06). In addition, the likelihood of reproductive females dispersing tended to vary according to composition of the natal group. Whereas 33.3% (5/15) and 44.4% (4/9) of reproductive females dispersed from male-female pairs and single-female units, respectively, only 17.2% (22/128) of reproductive females left communal groups (χ^2 = 5.6, $d.f.$ = 2, P < 0.06). The relatively low proportion of reproductive females dispersing from communal groups probably reflects the fact that such groups are most common during the winter months when vegetative cover is sparse and voles appear to restrict their movements (McGuire et al., 1990).

DISCUSSION

Gaulin and FitzGerald (1986, 1989) used laboratory and field techniques to examine the relationship between mating system and sex differences in spatial ability in microtine rodents. They compared maze performance and size of home range as determined by radiotelemetry of males and females of a polygynous species, the meadow vole *(Microtus pennsylvanicus),* with those of males and females of apparently monogamous species, the pine vole *(M. pinetorum)* and prairie vole. Male and female meadow voles differed in home range size and performance on spatial ability tasks. Male meadow voles had larger home ranges and higher scores in maze performance than did females. Differences in size of home ranges of male and female meadow voles were apparent only during the breeding season. In contrast, irrespective of season, sex differences in pattern of ranging and maze performance were absent in pine and prairie voles. Gaulin and FitzGerald (1986, 1989) suggested that sex differences in ranging patterns were shaped by sexual selection; males of polygynous species presumably range more widely than do females to increase access to potential mates. Furthermore, if range expansion is a male reproductive tactic, then sex differences in ranging should be apparent only during the breeding season. In the case of monogamous species, males, regardless of reproductive status, should be similar to females in their pattern of movement; wandering by monogamous males would most likely lead to encounters with paired females.

Our findings from intensive livetrapping of a population of prairie voles indicate that sex differences in pattern of movement occur even in an apparently monogamous species. Although male and female residents of focal groups were captured with approximately equal frequency at the periphery of their home range, males ranged further than females and were frequently captured at the outskirts of home ranges of neighboring groups (McGuire et al., 1990). Males also showed a greater tendency than did females to move through the home range of a focal group and visit the nest. Our finding of more extensive movement by male, as compared to female, prairie voles is consistent with a recent report of sex differences in size of home range in this species (Swihart and Slade, 1989). In addition to apparent sex differences in ranging in prairie voles, patterns of visitation by males also appeared more sensitive than those of females to composition of the social group. Nonresident males adjusted their frequency of visitation to specific groups as a function of loss or acquisition of a resident male in those groups.

Presence of adult males in the focal group deterred visits by nonresident males to the nest and to the periphery of the home range. In our between-group comparison we found that male intruders were captured less frequently at social groups where adult males were present than at groups where adult males were absent. Similar results were obtained in our within-group comparison; rate of visitation by nonresident males to a specific group changed in response to the addition or loss of a resident male at that group. Whereas transitions from male-female pairs to single-female units were typically followed by increased rate of intrusion by nonresident males, changes from single-female units to male-female pairs were characterized by subsequent decreases in visitation by nonresident males. We suggested that mate guarding is a likely component of territorial defense by male residents (McGuire et al., 1990). Male prairie voles display extensive paternal care in the form of brooding, grooming, and retrieving of pups (Gruder-Adams and Getz, 1985; Hartung and Dewsbury, 1979; McGuire and Novak, 1984; Oliveras and Novak, 1986; Thomas and Birney, 1979), and may protect their investment by preventing insemination of their mate by nonresident males.

Ejection of nonresident males from the home range of the family group appeared to influence the reproductive condition of young females at focal nests. Although not statistically different, a larger proportion of females living in groups where resident males were absent (75.0%) than where they were present (51.7%) showed signs of reproduction. Additionally, if females became reproductive while living at home, they did so at an earlier age when living in groups without resident males than when living in groups with resident males. From these results we suggest that adult male prairie voles, through their territorial behavior, influence the proportion of breeding females within the population. In other species of microtine rodents studied to date, adult females, rather than males, appear to set breeding density *(Microtus pennsylvanicus,* Boonstra and Rodd, 1983; *Clethrionomys gapperi,* Bondrup-Nielsen, 1986; *C. rutilus,* Gilbert et al., 1986; *C. glareolus,* Gipps et al., 1985). Large-scale removal of adult females from these populations typically resulted in increased survival, recruitment, and rate of maturation of the young females that remained. In prairie voles studied under laboratory conditions, lactating females behaved aggressively toward male and female intruders, but chased nonresidents less than did their mates (Getz and Carter, 1980). The role of the breeding female in territorial defense may be reduced relative to that of the male as a result of time and energy constraints of lactation. Nevertheless, the probable constraints associated with reproduction and the apparent role of adult males in setting breeding density do not preclude a role for adult females in population regulation. Exposure to female prairie voles or their urine has been shown to inhibit growth and sexual maturation (Batzli et al., 1977; Getz et al., 1983), raising the possibility that the primary influence of prairie vole females on population density occurs through pheromonal rather than direct behavioral channels.

The enhanced role of the male in regulating breeding density in prairie voles appears consistent with the predominantly monogamous mating system and male-female territoriality described for this species. In order to understand the effect of female prairie voles on population parameters, it may be necessary to examine whether production or effectiveness of the inhibitory chemosignal in their urine varies as a function of factors such as population density and season. Performance of sex-specific removal experiments would also be helpful in further defining the roles of male and female prairie voles in population regulation. Because experiments involving perturbation of the sex ratio have been restricted largely to species that exhibit polygyny and female territoriality, results from species with different social systems are necessary to test the generality of current hypotheses on the effects of male and female behavior on population processes in microtine rodents.

ACKNOWLEDGMENTS

This research was supported by National Institutes of Health grant HD09328 to L. L. Getz. We thank E. Sorenson, P. Gronemeyer, P. Klatt, L. Clay, K. Torney, G. Milani, and P. Mankin for assistance with fieldwork. We are grateful to M. Snarski for her help with fieldwork and data entry.

LITERATURE CITED

Batzli, G. O., L. L. Getz, and S. S. Hurley. 1977. Suppression of growth and reproduction of microtine rodents by social factors. Journal of Mammalogy, 58:583-591.

Bondrup-Nielsen, S. 1986. Investigation of spacing behaviour of *Clethrionomys gapperi* by experimentation. Journal of Animal Ecology, 55:269-279.

Boonstra, R., and F. H. Rodd. 1983. Regulation of breeding density in *Microtus pennsylvanicus*. Journal of Animal Ecology, 52:757-780.

Carter, C. S., L. L. Getz, and M. Cohen-Parsons. 1986. Relationships between social organization and behavioral endocrinology in a monogamous mammal. Pp. 109-145, *in* Advances in the study of behavior, volume 16. (J. S. Rosenblatt, C. Beer, M. C. Busnel, and P. J. B. Slater, eds.) Academic Press, Inc., New York, 343 pp.

Carter, C. S., L. L. Getz, L. Gavish, J. L. McDermott, and P. Arnold. 1980. Male-related pheromones and the activation of female reproduction in the prairie vole *(Microtus ochrogaster)*. Biology of Reproduction, 23:1038-1045.

Dewsbury, D. A. 1981. An exercise in the prediction of monogamy in the field from laboratory data on 42 species of muroid rodents. Biologist, 63:138-162.

Gaulin, S. J. C., and R. W. FitzGerald. 1986. Sex differences in spatial ability: an evolutionary hypothesis and test. The American Naturalist, 127:74-88.

———. 1989. Sexual selection for spatial-learning ability. Animal Behaviour, 37:322-331.

Getz, L. L., and C. S. Carter. 1980. Social organization in *Microtus ochrogaster* populations. Biologist, 62:56-69.

Getz, L. L., and J. E. Hofmann. 1986. Social organization in free-living prairie voles, *Microtus ochrogaster*. Behavioral Ecology and Sociobiology, 18:275-282.

Getz, L. L., D. Dluzen, and J. L. McDermott. 1983. Suppression of reproductive maturation in male-stimulated virgin female *Microtus* by a female urinary chemosignal. Behavioural Processes, 8:59-64.

Getz, L. L., J. E. Hofmann, and L. Jike. 1986. Relationship between social organization, mating system, and habitats of microtine rodents. Acta Theriologica Sinica, 6:273-285.

Getz, L. L., J. E. Hofmann, B. J. Klatt, L. Verner, F. R. Cole, and R. L. Lindroth. 1987. Fourteen years of population fluctuations of *Microtus ochrogaster* and *M. pennsylvanicus* in east central Illinois. Canadian Journal of Zoology, 65:1317-1325.

Gilbert, B. S., C. J. Krebs, D. Talarico, and D. B. Cichowski. 1986. Do *Clethrionomys rutilus* females suppress maturation of juvenile females? Journal of Animal Ecology, 55:543-552.

Gipps, J. H. W., M. P. Flynn, J. Gurnell, and T. D. Healing. 1985. The spring decline in populations of the bank vole, *Clethrionomys glareolus,* and the role of female density. Journal of Animal Ecology, 54:351-358.

Gruder-Adams, S., and L. L. Getz. 1985. Comparison of the mating system and paternal behavior in *Microtus ochrogaster* and *M. pennsylvanicus.* Journal of Mammalogy, 66:165-167.

Hartung, T. G., and D. A. Dewsbury. 1979. Paternal behavior in six species of muroid rodents. Behavioral and Neural Biology, 26:466-478.

Hofmann, J. E., and L. L. Getz. 1988. Multiple exposures to adult males and reproductive activation of virgin female *Microtus ochrogaster.* Behavioural Processes, 17:57-61.

Hofmann, J. E., L. L. Getz, and L. Gavish. 1984. Home range overlap and nest cohabitation of male and female prairie voles. American Midland Naturalist, 112:314-319.

Krebs, C. J. 1985. Do changes in spacing behaviour drive population cycles in small mammals? Pp. 295-312, *in* Behavioural ecology: ecological consequences of adaptive behaviour (R. M. Sibly and R. H. Smith, eds.). Blackwell Scientific Publications, Oxford, 620 pp.

Lemen, C. A., and P. W. Freeman. 1985. Tracking mammals with fluorescent pigments: a new technique. Journal of Mammalogy, 66:134-136.

McGuire, B., and M. Novak. 1984. A comparison of maternal behaviour in the meadow vole *(Microtus pennsylvanicus),* prairie vole *(M. ochrogaster)* and pine vole *(M. pinetorum).* Animal Behaviour, 32:1132-1141.

McGuire, B., T. Pizzuto, and L. L. Getz. 1990. Potential for social interaction in a natural population of prairie voles *(Microtus ochrogaster).* Canadian Journal of Zoology, 68:391-398.

McGuire, M. R., and L. L. Getz. 1981. Incest taboo between sibling *Microtus ochrogaster.* Journal of Mammalogy, 62:213-215.

Oliveras, D., and M. Novak. 1986. A comparison of paternal behaviour in the meadow vole *(Microtus pennsylvanicus),* the pine vole *(M. pinetorum),* and the prairie vole *(M. ochrogaster).* Animal Behaviour, 34:519-526.

Redfield, J. A., M. J. Taitt, and C. J. Krebs. 1978a. Experimental alteration of sex ratios in populations of *Microtus townsendii,* a field vole. Canadian Journal of Zoology, 56:17-27.

———. 1978b. Experimental alterations of sex-ratios in populations of *Microtus oregoni,* the creeping vole. Journal of Animal Ecology, 47:55-69.

Swihart, R. K., and N. A. Slade. 1989. Differences in home-range size between sexes of *Microtus ochrogaster.* Journal of Mammalogy, 70:816-820.

Thomas, J. A., and E. C. Birney. 1979. Parental care and mating system of the prairie vole, *Microtus ochrogaster.* Behavioral Ecology and Sociobiology, 5:171-186.

PREDATION AND ITS POTENTIAL IMPACT ON
THE BEHAVIOR OF MICROTINE RODENTS

William J. McShea

Department of Conservation, National Zoological Park, Conservation and Research Center, Front Royal, VA 22630 U.S.A.

Summary.—I examined three separate studies of meadow voles for rates and patterns of predation. Predation losses were highest during the winter and lowest during the autumn. For lactating females, predation losses were highest during the first week postpartum. Litters had higher losses to predation in spring than autumn. The proportion of predation losses to specialist predators was highest in the spring. Response to specialist predators may influence the behavior and dispersal characteristics of microtine rodents.

INTRODUCTION

Predation can influence the population processes of microtine populations. Population fluctuations in microtines may be enhanced by the functional and numerical response of predators (Pearson, 1985). Predation on several species of microtines *(Microtus californicus,* Pearson, 1971; *Microtus ochrogaster,* Martin, 1956; *Lemmus,* Pitelka et al., 1955) has been postulated to accentuate population fluctuations through increased predation pressure during periods of decreasing density. The composition of the predator community also may influence the stability of population densities (Andersson and Erlinge, 1977; Erlinge, 1987; Erlinge et al., 1983). Populations of *Clethrionomys glareolus* and *Microtus agrestis* that are prey for rodent-specialist predators (e.g., weasels) experienced greater fluctuations in density than populations that were preyed upon by more generalist predators (e.g., feral cats, foxes, *Vulpes vulpes:* Hansson, 1987; Hansson and Henttonen, 1985).

Not only may predation influence prey population dynamics, but the behavior of prey species has a significant impact on predator populations. The distribution of least weasels *(Mustela nivalis)* is correlated with the density and distribution of *Microtus agrestis* (Erlinge, 1974), and, in general, mustelids are dependent on the abundance of microtine prey (King, 1985). Henttonen (1987) suggested that the social organization of prey can determine the success of mustelid reproduction. Henttonen (1987) presented evidence that mustelid populations in Scandinavia more closely track *Microtus* population densities, which are usually higher than *Clethrionomys* densities. The degree of territoriality shown by females within microtine populations could determine the density of voles and thereby the ability of female mustelids to support litters.

With coevolution of mustelid-microtine systems, each species should be sensitive to changes in the behavior of the other. If predation is a significant source of mortality in microtines, it may exert strong selective force on behaviors such as social organization and dispersal, which influence a vole's probability of being preyed upon. Patterns of predation examined at the individual level may explain behavioral traits in microtines. In this paper I will examine losses due to predation within populations of meadow voles *(Microtus pennsylvanicus)* and discuss their potential impact on the distribution and movements of individuals.

METHODS

The data on predation were taken from three separate studies on meadow voles. Two studies were conducted near Binghamton, New York: the first on an enclosed population during autumn and winter, 1981-1982 (Madison et al., 1984), and the second on an unenclosed population during spring and autumn of 1983 and 1984 (McShea and Madison, 1987, 1989). The third study was conducted on a natural population near Front Royal, Virginia during the winters of 1987 and 1988 (McShea, 1990). All studies included only adults (>28 g), with the second study in Binghamton, New York, limited to adult females. The populations were livetrapped at least once a month, and between 15 and 38 individuals were radiotracked.

In all studies, the animals were implanted with radiotransmitters (Madison et al., 1985). An estimate of which predator was responsible for the death of the animal was possible by the placement of the transmitter (e.g., in a mustelid nest), tooth impressions in the wax used to coat the transmitter, and tracks and signs near the transmitter. The time of death was taken as the last date of capture, or the last time the animal was determined alive through radiotracking, whichever was later. All mustelids were considered specialist predators, and feral cats, foxes, dogs and raptors were considered generalist predators (Erlinge et al., 1983; Hansson, 1987, 1988). Dispersal was considered movement ≥30 m from a nest or trap site without return for at least a week.

Percent losses due to predation are given as a range, with the lower value assuming all disappearances are due to dispersal and the upper value assuming all disappearances are due to predation. For the enclosed population the upper value is probably a true estimate of predation, due to the probable absence of dispersal. For the study in Virginia, the known dispersals were not used to calculate the upper range. The focus of the second study was not predation and the known losses to predation are probably an underestimate.

For litters located during the second study (McShea and Madison, 1987, 1989), loss was assumed to occur if none of the pups entered the trappable population. All litters with only partial mortality of pups were not considered predation losses because of the possibility that mortality resulted from maternal care patterns (McShea and Madison, 1987); eight litters born less then 30 days before the last trapping date of the season were excluded. The 123 litters used to examine predation were from 53 females.

The synchrony of losses within each study was examined by dividing the studies into 20-day periods and recording the number of disappearances per period. For the study of the enclosed population (Madison et al., 1984) the radiotracking schedule did not allow examination of a 20-day period, so the periods are variable ($\bar{X}$ = 26 days, range 17-46, r between number of losses and length of period = 0.08, P > 0.05). In order to estimate the synchrony of predation losses within the population, a coefficient of dispersion ($s^2/\bar{X}$: Sokal and Rohlf, 1981) was calculated from the total number of disappearances, as opposed to the known deaths. This was done to increase sample size within each period, with the assumption that not all disappearances were due to predation, but rather that death and dispersal are positively correlated (McShea, 1990).

RESULTS

Percent losses due to predation were highest within the enclosed population (48-78%), with considerable overlap of the Virginia and second Binghamton study (ranges 19-77% and 11-89%, respectively; Table 1). The loss of animals due to predation was not evenly distributed across the three study seasons (χ^2 = 8.66, $d.f.$ = 2; P < 0.05; Table 1), with the lowest predation losses in autumn. There was no significant difference in the percentage of prey taken by specialist predators (χ^2 = 5.13; P > 0.05), but the trend was toward specialist predators in the spring and generalist predators in the autumn (Table 1). Only during the winter was there any notable synchrony in population losses (coefficient of dispersion values >1.0; Table 1).

The disappearance of mothers during lactation occurred in 20% of the litters observed in 1983 and 1984, whereas 31% of the litters disappeared without loss of the mother (Table 2). Of the disappearing mothers, the known predation losses were concentrated within the first week postpartum (7, 2, and 1 losses, respectively, for the three weeks after parturition). The remaining disappearances, which include dispersal, are not concentrated during early lactation (3, 6, and 5 losses, respectively). As with adult losses, litter losses were higher in spring than autumn (59 and 41%, respectively; χ^2 = 4.25, $d.f.$ = 1; P < 0.05).

During 1983 and 1984, of the 131 litters examined, all females moved their nests after disturbance by the researcher. Of the 31 females that produced more than one litter, all moved their nest between parturitions. Home ranges of females usually contained several old and partially completed nests in addition to the nest with pups.

Table 1.—Loss of meadow voles due to predation and disappearance for each period of study. The percent loss due to predation is given as a range, with the low value assuming all disappearances were due to dispersal and the high value assuming all disappearances were due to predation. The coefficient of dispersion is a measure of synchrony for population losses (predation and disappearances), with values significantly >1 indicating synchrony.

| | | Losses of Animals | | | | |
| | Radio-tracked | Predation | | | Loss to predation | Coefficient of |
Season	(n)	Specialist	Generalist	Disappeared[a]	(%)	dispersion
Autumn						
1981[b]	20	0	4	8	20-60	1.5
1983[c]	24	1	2	5	12-33	1.1
1984[c]	19	1	1	1	11-16	0.6
Total	63	2	7	14	14-37	
Winter						
1982[b]	26	11	7	6	69-92	6.1
1987	31	0	6	11(5)	19-39	3.2
1988	30	8	4	13(2)	40-77	3.0
Total	87	19	17	31(7)	41-69	
Spring						
1983[c]	38	4	4	16	21-89	0.4
1984[c]	27	7	1	5	30-48	1.1
Total	65	11	5	21	25-57	

[a]Numbers in parentheses are known dispersers.
[b]Enclosed population.
[c]All adult females.

Table 2.—The fate of mothers and litters (meadow voles) between the times the litter is located and the pups are recruited. A litter was considered to have disappeared if no members were captured within 30 days of birth.

Season	n	Litter and mother disappeared	Litter disappeared and mother alive	Litter and mother alive
Spring				
1983	42	9(6)[a]	14	19
1984	22	7(3)	8	7
Autumn				
1983	36	4(1)	11	21
1984	23	4(0)	5	14
Total (%)		20	31	50

[a]Numbers in parentheses are cases in which the mother was killed by a predator.

DISCUSSION

Measurements of predation of microtines are potentially flawed because they rely on direct observation of conspicuous predators (Craighead and Craighead, 1956), location and analysis of predator scats (Southern and Lowe, 1982), or location of discarded transmitters (Madison, 1979; present study). These techniques tend to underestimate the degree of predation within the population and each is biased toward specific types of predators. However, the problems of estimating predation losses are comparable to the problems of estimating population density and dispersal, and we should not attribute all disappearances from a population to dispersal (Hilborn and Krebs, 1976), but to attempt to delineate the categories of death and dispersal.

Most studies of meadow voles focus on specific predator types, and estimates of 16% population losses due to semi-feral cats (Christian, 1975), 17% due to snakes (Madison, 1978), and 19% (Baker and Brooks, 1981) to 25% (Craighead and Craighead, 1956) due to raptors are, as would be expected, significantly lower than the overall losses reported here. Madison (1979) estimated losses due to predation at 32-44% for radiotracked voles during three summer studies. The predation losses reported here are comparable and show those summer losses to be intermediate to winter and autumn losses. Although snow cover probably renders voles less susceptible to some predators, winter was the period of highest mortality within these studies. A possible explanation for the high mortality was the intermittent snow cover experienced during winters in Virginia. The low predation losses in autumn are in agreement with data on *Microtus agrestis* populations in Sweden (Erlinge et al., 1983) in which increased population density, and the abundance of juveniles, reduced the percentage of the adult population preyed upon. Lower predation losses for adults in autumn may allow an increase in "predation-prone" activities, such as lactation and foraging.

High losses due to predation within the enclosed population may be a unique case, or point to a problem with enclosure studies. Desy and Batzli (1989) suggest that enclosures disrupt not only dispersal but predation. How disruptive enclosures are to predation may depend on the type of enclosure constructed; predation should be taken into account when designing enclosures.

Eventually, most, if not all, microtines succumb to predation. Attributing death to predation is not as important as determining what type of predator is responsible for the death (e.g., generalist or specialist predator) and during what life stage the predation occurs. The impact of predation is usually measured at the population level (Desy and Batzli, 1989; Erlinge et al., 1983; King, 1985; Pearson, 1985), but, as pointed out by Pearson (1985), information is needed on how selective predation is and if this selection is constant.

It is unclear if predation is a selective process. Semi-feral cats do not appear to select prey based on sex, age (Christian, 1975; George, 1974), or time of activity (George, 1974), but may take animals from suboptimal areas (Madison, 1979). Snakes may prey selectively on lactating females and large males (Madison, 1978) and the results presented here indicate that predation on lactating females occurs most often during the first week postpartum. The frequent shifting of nests and the abundance of abandoned nests may be a response to predation pressures on lactating females. Specialist predators may be selective by searching for nests and "odoriferous individuals" (Madison, 1978), whereas generalist predators are nonselective; however, the present data are not complete enough to address this issue.

The type of predator attributed to each kill did vary among seasons, with predation by specialists being highest in winter and spring. The predation by specialists in spring may be due not only to the exposure of nest sites and runways in the melting snow, but also shifts in the hunting behavior of mustelids. Female mustelids concentrate movements within smaller areas and specialize in rodent prey with the onset of reproduction (Erlinge, 1974, 1977). The breakup of meadow vole communal nests is due to increased aggression and the loss of nestmates through predation (McShea, 1990). Variability in the predation losses could regulate the occurrence of communal nests within spring populations of meadow voles (McShea and Madison, 1984).

At the population level it has been shown that predators can be effective controls on microtine population densities (Desy and Batzli, 1989; Erlinge et al., 1983). Little is known about how individual voles respond to predation. Voles can detect the presence of mustelids (Stoddart, 1976) and there is evidence that voles alter their behavior in response to predator scents. *Clethrionomys glareolus* will disperse from sections of enclosures that are visited by weasels (Jędrzejewski and Jędrzejewska, 1990) and *M. pennsylvanicus* avoids areas used by *Blarina brevicauda* (Fulk, 1972). However, beyond avoidance of areas with minimal cover, the response of voles to predators may be minimal, particularly if predation is nonselective. As opposed to predation by generalists, predation by specialists may be selective and would provoke specific responses. The area temporarily exploited by female stoats *(Mustela erminea)* during the spring is less then 100 m across (Erlinge, 1977), a distance voles can easily disperse beyond. Most generalist predators occupy home ranges several km across (King, 1985), a distance beyond effective dispersal by voles.

Dispersal in response to predation would be a viable response to female mustelids and not to most generalist predators. In an enclosed population of *Clethrionomys glareolus,* sub-adults, nonreproductive adults, and reproductively active males shifted their home ranges in response to mustelid scent (Jędrzejewski and Jędrzejewska, 1990). Adult females and juveniles less then 30 days old do not shift their home ranges, reflecting age and sex class differences in site tenacity. During the winter, dispersal in meadow voles coincides with the loss of nestmates (McShea, 1990), and again males are more likely to disperse than females.

Microtine populations exposed to only specialist predators exhibit wider population fluctuations than populations exposed to generalist and specialist predators (Hansson, 1987; Hansson and Henttonen, 1985). These population differences are probably correlated with predator-prey dynamics (Erlinge, 1987), but may also reflect differences in the dispersal characteristics of the populations. Dispersal biased toward subadults and nonreproductive adults (Lidicker, 1985) may be triggered by the actions of specialist predators. I predict that microtine populations exposed to specialist predators would exhibit higher dispersal rates, and produce a different dispersal population, than populations exposed to generalist predators. Individual differences in the response of voles to predators may determine the characteristics of the dispersal population and the spacing within microtine populations.

ACKNOWLEDGMENTS

Preparation of this manuscript was supported by the Department of Conservation, National Zoological Park and by the Friends of the National Zoo. D. M. Madison provided unpublished data and helpful comments, and excellent suggestions were provided by two anonymous reviewers.

LITERATURE CITED

Andersson, M., and S. Erlinge. 1977. Influence of predation on rodent populations. Oikos, 29:591-597.

Baker, J. A., and R. J. Brooks. 1982. Impact of raptor predation on a declining vole population. Journal of Mammalogy, 63:297-300.

Christian, D. P. 1975. The vulnerability of meadow voles, *Microtus pennsylvanicus,* to predation by domestic cats. American Midland Naturalist, 93:524-526.

Craighead, J. J., and F. C. Craighead, Jr. 1956. Hawks, owls and wildlife. Wildlife Management Institute, Washington, D.C., 443 pp.

Desy, E. A., and G. O. Batzli. 1989. Effects of food availability and predation on prairie vole demography: a field experiment. Ecology, 70:411-421.

Erlinge, S. 1974. Distribution, territoriality and numbers of weasels *Mustela nivalis* in relation to prey abundance. Oikos, 25:308-314.

———. 1977. Spacing strategy in stoat *Mustela erminea.* Oikos, 28:32-42.

———. 1987. Predation and noncyclicity in a microtine population in southern Sweden. Oikos, 50:347-352.

Erlinge, S., et al. 1983. Predation as a regulating factor in small rodent populations in southern Sweden. Oikos, 40:36-52.

Fulk, G. W. 1972. The effect of shrews on the space utilization of voles. Journal of Mammalogy,

53:461-478.

George, W. G. 1974. Domestic cats as predators and factors in winter shortages of raptor prey. Wilson Bulletin, 86:384-396.

Hansson, L. 1987. An interpretation of rodent dynamics as due to trophic interactions. Oikos, 50:308-318.

———. 1988. The domestic cat as a possible modifier of vole dynamics. Mammalia, 52:159-164.

Hansson, L., and H. Henttonen. 1985. Gradients in density variations of small rodents: the importance of latitude and snow cover. Oecologia (Berlin), 67:394-402.

Henttonen, H. 1987. The impact of spacing behavior in microtine rodents on the dynamics of least weasels *Mustela nivalis* - a hypothesis. Oikos, 50:366-370.

Hilborn, R., and C. J. Krebs. 1976. Fates of disappearing individuals in fluctuating population of *Microtus townsendii*. Canadian Journal of Zoology, 54:1507-1518.

Jędrzejewski, W., and B. Jędrzejewska. 1990. Effect of a predator's visit on the spatial distribution of bank voles: experiments with weasels. Canadian Journal of Zoology, 68:660-666.

King, C. M. 1985. Interactions between woodland rodents and their predators. Pp. 219-248, *in* The ecology of woodland rodents, bank voles and wood mice (D. R. Flowerdew, J. Gurnell, and J. H. W. Gipps, eds.). Oxford University Press, Oxford, 418 pp.

Lidicker, W. Z., Jr. 1985. Dispersal. Pp. 420-454, *in* Biology of New World *Microtus* (R. H. Tamarin, ed.). Special Publication, The American Society of Mammalogists, 8:1-893.

Madison, D. M. 1978. Behavioral and sociochemical susceptibility of meadow voles *(Microtus pennsylvanicus)* to snake predators. American Midland Naturalist, 100:23-28.

———. 1979. Impact of spacing behavior and predation on population growth in meadow voles. Pp. 20-29, *in* Proceedings of the third eastern pine and meadow vole symposium (R. E. Byers, ed.). New Paltz, New York, 86 pp.

Madison, D. M., R. W. FitzGerald, and W. J. McShea. 1984. Dynamics of social nesting in over-wintering meadow voles *(Microtus pennsylvanicus):* Possible consequences for population cycling. Behavioral Ecology and Sociobiology, 15:9-17.

———. 1985. A user's guide to the successful radiotracking of small mammals in the field. Pp. 28-39, *in* Proceedings of the fifth international conference on wildlife biotelemetry (R. W. Weeks and F. M. Long, eds.). University of Wyoming Press, Laramie, Wyoming, 118 pp.

Martin, E. P. 1956. A population study of the prairie vole *(Microtus ochrogaster)* in northeastern Kansas. University of Kansas Publications, Museum of Natural History, 8:361-416.

McShea, W. J. 1990. Social tolerance and proximate mechanisms of dispersal among winter groups of meadow voles *Microtus pennsylvanicus*. Animal Behaviour, 39:346-351.

McShea, W. J., and D. M. Madison. 1984. Communal nesting between reproductively active females within a spring population of *Microtus pennsylvanicus*. Canadian Journal of Zoology, 62:344-346.

———. 1987. Partial mortality of nestling meadow voles. Animal Behaviour, 35:1253-1255.

———. 1989. Measurements of reproductive traits in a field population of meadow voles. Journal of Mammalogy, 70:132-141.

Pearson, O. P. 1971. Additional measurements of the impact of carnivores on California voles *(Microtus californicus)*. Journal of Mammalogy, 52:41-49.

———. 1985. Predation. Pp. 535-566, *in* Biology of New World *Microtus* (R. H. Tamarin ed.). Special Publication, The American Society of Mammalogists, 8:1-893.

Pitelka, F. A., P. Q. Tomich, and G. W. Treichel. 1955. Ecological relations of jaegers and owls as lemming predators near Barrow, Alaska. Ecological Monographs, 25:85-117.

Southern, H. N., and V. P. W. Lowe. 1982. Predation of tawny owls *(Strix aluco)* on bank voles *(Clethrionomys glareolus)* and wood mice *(Apodemus sylvaticus)*. Journal of Zoology (London), 198:83-102.

Sokal, R. R., and F. J. Rohlf. 1981. Biometry: the principles and practice of statistics in biological research. Second ed. W. H. Freedman and Company, San Francisco, California, 859 pp.

Stoddart, D. M. 1976. Effects of the odour of weasels *(Mustela nivalis* L.) on trapped samples of their prey. Oecologia (Berlin), 22:439-441.

A TEST OF THE CHARNOV AND FINERTY HYPOTHESIS OF POPULATION REGULATION IN MEADOW VOLES

Stephen R. Pugh and Robert H. Tamarin

Department of Biology, Boston University, Boston, MA 02215 U.S.A.

Present address of SRP: College of Basic Studies, Boston University, Boston, MA 02215 U.S.A.

Summary.—Charnov and Finerty (1980) hypothesized that the relatedness of individuals may influence their behavioral interactions and thus could play a role in regulating the density of microtine rodent populations. They predicted that the level of relatedness among neighboring voles should be high at low density and should decrease rapidly as density increases. We tested this prediction by determining the patterns of relatedness and dispersion among individual meadow voles, *Microtus pennsylvanicus,* using a radionuclide-electrophoresis technique. We did not find a consistently high level of relatedness among adult residents at low density nor did we find a consistent reduction in relatedness among neighbors as density increased. These results do not support the Charnov and Finerty hypothesis.

INTRODUCTION

Despite over 30 years of intensive research, a satisfactory explanation for the 3-5 year fluctuations in density among some populations of microtine rodents remains elusive. Much research effort in recent years has been concentrated on the role of social behavior in regulating microtine density (Krebs, 1985). Charnov and Finerty (1980) hypothesized that the relatedness of individuals may influence their behavioral interactions and thus could play an important role in population regulation. Although this hypothesis has received attention from theorists (Warkowska-Dratnal and Stenseth, 1985) and experimentalists (Boonstra and Hogg, 1988; Ylönen et al., 1990), it has not been tested directly on natural populations of voles. This is primarily due to the difficulty in determining patterns of relatedness in a small secretive mammal like a vole.

Charnov and Finerty (1980) proposed that at low density the average level of relatedness of neighboring voles should be high, and therefore individual voles interact primarily with relatives. When density increases the average level of relatedness among neighbors should rapidly decline as dispersal causes individuals to come into contact more frequently with unrelated individuals. Charnov and Finerty (1980) further suggested that aggressive interactions among individuals are influenced by their relatedness: interactions among nonrelatives should be much more aggressive than interactions among relatives. Therefore, at high densities, when the average level of relatedness is low, there should be a high frequency of aggressive interactions that could precipitate a population decline. As density drops, dispersal rates decrease. When density reaches a low phase, the average level of relatedness among neighbors should begin to increase and the cycle can begin anew. In this paper we test the hypothesis that there is a relationship between population density and the relatedness of neighbors in a population of meadow voles, *Microtus pennsylvanicus.*

METHODS

Study area and trapping.—This study was conducted on three 0.7-ha grids in South Natick, Massachusetts, U.S.A., that have been the site of long-term studies of the population ecology of meadow voles (Ostfeld et al., 1988; Pugh and Tamarin, 1988; Tamarin et al., 1984). Two of the grids (K and L) were surrounded on all sides by a vole-proof fence made of corrugated metal. A 0.2-ha area of woodland was included within each fenced grid to create a dispersal area or sink (Lidicker, 1975). Tamarin et al. (1984) showed that this design permitted normal population processes within the enclosed population. We chose this design because by controlling animal movements we could increase the probability of successfully determining relatedness of voles in the population. The third grid (M) was open on three sides and served as a control. The populations were founded in July, 1985. After all individuals were removed from each grid by trapping, 13 to 15 adult (≥32g) and subadult (<32g) voles were released on each grid (grid K: five subadult females, two subadult males, two adult females, four adult males; grid L: two subadult females, six subadult males, four adult females, one adult male; grid M: three subadult females, two subadult males, four adult females, six adult males). Genotypes of all individuals at five polymorphic loci were determined by electrophoresis prior to their release. Individuals were released in such a way that each allele was represented on all three grids and electrophoretic heterozygosity was maximized.

One hundred Ketch-all multiple-capture live traps were baited with oats, supplied with cotton bedding, and set in each area in a grid pattern with 7.6 m between trap stations. Except for midwinter nonbreeding periods, trapping was conducted biweekly from August 1985 to December 1988. Traps were set late in the afternoon on the first day of each trapping period and checked on the following two mornings. Upon capture, each vole was given an individually numbered ear tag, and standard data on reproductive condition and weight were recorded. All animals were removed to a nearby field site for further processing and returned to their capture location within 3 h. Six pitfall and 21 Ketch-all traps were set continuously in each dispersal sink during the 1986 trapping season only (pitfall trapping was discontinued after the 1986 season because of low numbers of captures) and checked at 2 to 3 day intervals. All voles captured in the dispersal sinks were removed permanently.

Determining relatedness.—Relatedness was determined by a radionuclide-electrophoresis technique (Pugh and Tamarin, 1988; Sheridan and Tamarin, 1986; Tamarin et al., 1983). Briefly, it involved injecting all pregnant and lactating females with a unique combination of two gamma-emitting radionuclides. Maternity was determined by the transfer of radionuclides from mother to offspring via the placenta or through milk. Upon initial capture, all voles were checked for radionuclide burden with a portable whole-body counter. The presence of a particular unique combination of isotopes in a new recruit identified its mother. Paternity was estimated using electrophoresis. Genotypes of all individuals on the grid were determined at five presumptive loci from blood and saliva (Gaines and Krebs, 1971; Selander et al., 1971; Sheridan and Tamarin, 1985, 1986). Paternity was determined by a log-likelihood model based on the genetic similarity of the mother, offspring, and putative father (Foltz and Hoogland, 1981).

Pedigrees were drawn showing the patterns of relatedness (Pugh and Tamarin, 1988). From these pedigrees, Wright's coefficient of relationship (Hamilton, 1964) was calculated for all pairwise combinations of voles that were caught on the same day.

Two methods of analysis were used to determine what association, if any, existed between the relatedness of animals and their pattern of dispersion, and whether this association varied with density. First, average coefficients of relationship were calculated for each grid for both the entire population and among neighbors. Neighbors were defined as animals caught within two trap stations on the same day. This distance approximates the diameter of a typical home range for meadow voles in our populations (Ostfeld et al., 1988). We also calculated average coefficients of relationship among neighbors for low and moderate density populations, and among groups divided according to the age class and sex of the pair of voles. Density was considered moderate if the minimum number known alive was >36. Second, a correlation analysis was conducted between the coefficient of relationship and the intertrap distance between all pairs of animals caught on the same day. A significant negative correlation should exist if individual voles are associating preferentially with relatives. For animals caught twice in one trapping period, only the first trap location was used. Spearman rank correlation coefficients were calculated between the coefficient of relationship and the distance between a pair of voles on each grid, at both low and moderate density. Individuals of unknown relatedness (recruits with no radionuclide label at first capture that did not sire or recruit any offspring of their own) were eliminated from the data set.

RESULTS

The density of voles on all three grids was low to moderate over the four years of the study (Fig. 1). The highest densities occurred in 1986 and the lowest in 1987 and early 1988. Although some variation in density did occur between years, these populations did not appear to undergo the 3-5 year fluctuations in density typically reported for this species. When trapping was stopped in late 1988, all three populations were expanding, indicating that they could reach peak densities (typically over 100/ha: Tamarin, 1984) in 1989 or 1990. Relatedness was determined for 207 of 301 (68.8%) voles trapped on grid K, 173 of 220 (78.8%) voles on grid L, and 143 of 355 (40.3%) voles on grid M.

The average coefficient of relationship among neighbors approximated that of half siblings $(r = 0.25)$ on grids K and L, and first cousins $(r = 0.13)$ on grid M. The average coefficient of relationship was greater on the two fenced grids (K and L) than on the unfenced control grid (M), both among neighbors (Kruskal-Wallis test, $H = 183.9$, $P < 0.001$) and on the entire grid $(H = 1080.2, P < 0.001)$. In all three grids it was higher among neighbors than on the entire grid (Table 1). There was a significant negative correlation between the coefficient of relationship and the distance between pairs of voles on all three grids (Grid K: $r = -0.27$, $P < 0.001$; Grid L: $r = -0.14$, $P < 0.001$; Grid M: $r = -0.26$, $P < 0.001$).

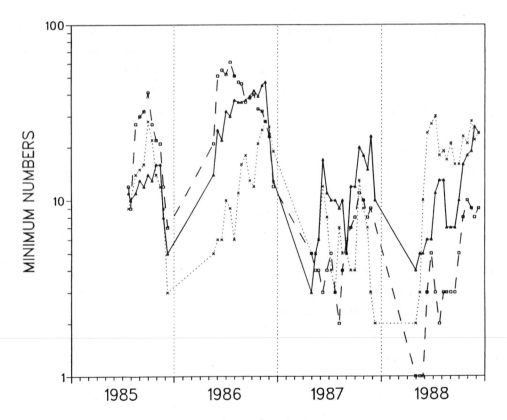

Fig. 1.— Density (minimum numbers alive) of meadow voles on the three grids, 1985-1988, in South Natick, MA. (Grid K, solid line; Grid L, dotted line; Grid M, dashed line.)

Table 1.—Average coefficient of relationship of meadow voles on the three grids (K, L, M) according to neighbor status and density.

Relationship	Grid K			Grid L			Grid M		
	$\bar{X}$ ±	SD	n	$\bar{X}$ ±	SD	n	$\bar{X}$ ±	SD	n
Throughout study									
Neighbors	0.27	0.25	1075	0.25	0.23	876	0.12	0.21	685
Total	0.16	0.21	4538	0.18	0.20	3464	0.05	0.15	2856
Among neighbors									
Low density	0.32	0.25	684	0.25	0.23	876	0.09	0.19	253
Moderate density	0.17	0.22	391				0.14	0.22	432

When the analysis was done separately in low and moderate density populations, the results were somewhat contradictory. On grid K the average coefficient of relationship among neighbors was significantly greater at low density (Mann-Whitney, $U = 89{,}008$, $P < 0.001$), whereas on grid M the average coefficient of relationship was significantly greater at moderate density $(U = 49{,}056$, $P = 0.003$; Table 2). There was a significant negative correlation between the coefficient of relationship and the distance between pairs of voles at both low and moderate densities on Grids K and M. However, the negative correlation was stronger at low density on grid K and stronger at moderate density on grid M; grid L never achieved moderate density (grid K: low density, $r = -0.27$, $n = 2{,}471$, moderate density, $r = -0.21$, $n = 2{,}067$; grid L: low density, $r = -0.14$, $n = 3{,}464$; grid M: low density, $r = -0.18$, $n = 1{,}095$, moderate density, $r = -0.31$, $n = 1{,}761$; $P < 0.001$ in all cases).

The greatest degree of association of relatives occurred among subadults (Figs. 2, 3, 4); there was very little association between adult relatives. This is most apparent on grid M where the average coefficient of relationship was consistently low among adults in all sex combinations. However, there were some exceptions to this trend on grids K and L. On grid L, a significant association among relatives was maintained between adult females at low density. On grid K, a reasonably high average coefficient of relationship was maintained among adults in all sex combinations at low density. This decreased markedly at moderate density.

116

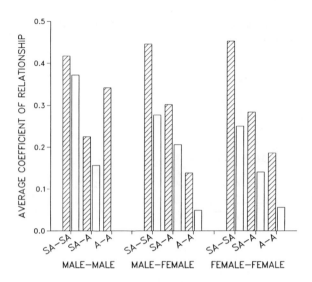

Fig. 2.—Average coefficients of relationship of neighboring meadow voles at low (striped bars) and moderate (open bars) densities according to the sex and age class of the pair (SA = subadult, A = adult) on grid K.

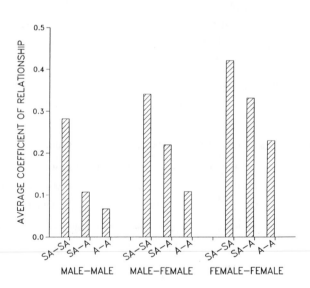

Fig. 3.—Average coefficients of relationship of neighboring meadow voles at low density according to the sex and age class of the pair (SA = subadult, A = adult) on grid L.

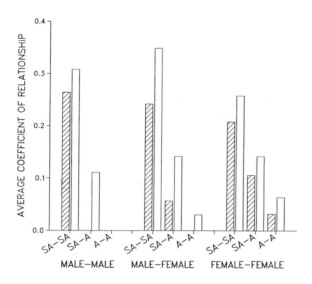

Fig. 4.—Average coefficients of relationship of neighboring meadow voles at low (striped bars) and moderate (open bars) densities according to the sex and age class of the pair (SA = subadult, A = adult) on grid M.

DISCUSSION

The results of this study do not provide strong support for the Charnov and Finerty (1980) hypothesis, which predicts that as density increases average relatedness among neighbors should decrease. When all sex and age class combinations were pooled, this prediction was met only on one fenced grid (K); the predicted decrease in relatedness among neighbors did not occur on the open grid (M). This conclusion must be qualified somewhat because these populations did not appear to cycle during the period of study, only reaching moderate densities. It is possible that at true peak densities a decrease in relatedness could occur. However, grid M reached the highest density of the three grids, and a decrease in relatedness among neighbors did not occur. Also, the only decline in relatedness of neighbors with increased density occurred on grid K, in which the fence, limiting immigration, may have played a role.

Further evidence against the Charnov and Finerty hypothesis is seen when the populations are subdivided according to the sex and age class of pairs of voles. The hypothesis predicts that the decline in density is precipitated by an increase in aggression among unrelated individuals that limits survival and reproduction. This aggression would most likely occur either between adults or between adult-subadult pairs (primarily lactating females and unrelated subadults: Ferkin, 1989; Rodd and Boonstra,

1988). A high average coefficient of relationship among subadults simply indicates that littermates remain together on the home range of their parents before natal dispersal. On all three grids the highest degree of association among relatives occurred among subadults. On grid M, even at low density, the average coefficient of relationship between adults and between adult-subadult pairs was relatively low (Fig. 5). On the fenced grids the results were equivocal. On grid L, there was evidence of association of related adults and adult-subadult pairs only among females, whereas on grid K there was a relatively high average coefficient of relationship among adults at low density that decreased as density increased.

There have been two recent attempts to test the Charnov and Finerty hypothesis. Boonstra and Hogg (1988), in a study on meadow voles, *M. pennsylvanicus,* also found a lack of support for the hypothesis. They released groups of related or unrelated females onto small fenced grids and monitored their population statistics over a 3-month period. They found no differences in the numerical responses of related and unrelated populations. However, Ylönen et al. (1990) conducted a similar study with the bank vole, *Clethrionomys glareolus.* Populations of familiar, related individuals ("friends") reached densities twice as high as those of unfamiliar, unrelated "strangers" and had higher rates of recruitment and survival. They attributed these conflicting results to the differences between *Microtus* and *Clethrionomys* in the importance of social interactions in regulating population density.

Other predictions of the Charnov and Finerty hypothesis (e.g., a relationship between relatedness and aggressive behavior) have not been tested yet. However, a major prediction—a decrease in the relatedness of neighbors with increasing density—is not supported by our results. Although densities in this study did not reach a level typical of a peak population, the fact that there was not a consistently high level of relatedness among adult neighbors even at low density fails to support this hypothesis.

ACKNOWLEDGMENTS

We appreciate the cooperation of Elissa Landre, director of the Broadmoor Audubon Sanctuary, in South Natick, Massachusetts. Michael Ferkin, Rick Ostfeld, Joshua Seamon, and Donna Zanelli helped with fieldwork. Michael Ferkin read and commented on an earlier copy of this manuscrip. This research was supported by National Institutes of Health grant HD18620 to RHT.

LITERATURE CITED

Boonstra, R., and I. Hogg. 1988. Friends and strangers: a test of the Charnov-Finerty hypothesis. Oecologia (Berlin), 77:95-100.

Charnov, E. L., and J. P. Finerty. 1980. Vole population cycles: a case for kin-selection?

Oecologia (Berlin), 45:1-2.

Ferkin, M. H. 1989. Adult-weanling recognition among captive meadow voles *(Microtus pennsylvanicus)*. Behaviour, 108:114-124.

Foltz, D., and J. Hoogland. 1981. Analysis of the mating system in the black-tailed prairie dog *(Cynomys ludovicianus)* by likelihood of paternity. Journal of Mammalogy, 62:706-712.

Gaines, M. S., and C. J. Krebs. 1971. Genetic changes in fluctuating vole populations. Evolution, 25:702-723.

Hamilton, W. D. 1964. The genetical evolution of social behavior. I and II. Journal of Theoretical Biology, 7:1-52.

Krebs, C. J. 1985. Do changes in spacing behavior drive population cycles in small mammals? Pp. 243-256, *in* Behavioural ecology: ecological consequences of adaptive behaviour (R. M. Sibly and R. H. Smith, eds.). Symposium of the British Ecological Society, Blackwell Scientific Publications, Oxford, 25:1-620.

Lidicker, W. Z., Jr. 1975. The role of dispersal in the demography of small mammals. Pp. 103-128, *in* Small mammals: their productivity and population dynamics (F. B. Golley, K. Petrusewicz, and L. Ryszkowski, eds.). Cambridge University Press, London, 451 pp.

Ostfeld, R. S., S. R. Pugh, J. O. Seamon, and R. H. Tamarin. 1988. Space use and reproductive success in a population of meadow voles. Journal of Animal Ecology, 57:385-394.

Pugh, S. R., and R. H. Tamarin. 1988. Inbreeding in a population of meadow voles, *Microtus pennsylvanicus*. Canadian Journal of Zoology, 66:1831-1834.

Rodd, F. H., and R. Boonstra. 1988. Effects of adult meadow voles, *Microtus pennsylvanicus,* on young conspecifics in field populations. Journal of Animal Ecology, 57:755-770.

Selander, R., M. H. Smith, S. Y. Yang, W. E. Johnson, and J. B. Gentry. 1971. Biochemical polymorphism and systematics in the genus *Peromyscus*. I. Variation in the oldfield mouse *(Peromyscus polionotus)*. Studies in Genetics, 6:49-90.

Sheridan, M., and R. H. Tamarin. 1985. Genetic variation of salivary amylase in meadow voles. Journal of Mammalogy, 66:821-823.

―――. 1986. Kinships in a natural meadow vole population. Behavioral Ecology and Socio-biology, 19:206-211.

Tamarin, R. H., L. M. Reich, and C. A. Moyer. 1984. Meadow vole cycles within fences. Canadian Journal of Zoology, 62:1796-1804.

Tamarin, R. H., M. Sheridan, and C. K. Levy. 1983. Determining matrilineal kinship in natural populations of rodents using radionuclides. Canadian Journal of Zoology, 61:271-274.

Warkowska-Dratnal, H., and N. C. Stenseth. 1985. Dispersal and the microtine cycle: comparison of two hypotheses. Oecologia (Berlin), 65:468-477.

Ylönen, H., T. Mappes, and J. Viitala. 1990. Different demography of friends and strangers: an experiment on the impact of kinship and familiarity in *Clethrionomys glareolus*. Oecologia (Berlin), 83:333-337.

Social Systems and
Population Cycles in Voles
Advances in Life Sciences
© Birkhäuser Verlag Basel

121

SOCIAL ORGANIZATION AND POPULATION CONTROL IN THE PINE VOLE, *MICROTUS PINETORUM*

Margaret H. Schadler

Department of Biological Sciences, Union College, Schenectady, NY 12308 U.S.A.

Summary.—Pine voles, *Microtus pinetorum*, reared in large enclosures in the laboratory exhibited social constraints that controlled population density. In a 14-year study of 23 parental groups, populations were self limiting at a mean of 16 animals per population. Birth of litters was limited largely to the single founding female. Reproduction ceased in 15 groups when populations grew and litter survival dropped to zero, and in the remaining groups when the founding mother (six groups) or father (two groups) died. Stimulation of estrus in nonreproducing females by exogenous injection of sex hormones did not result in production of litters. Mature, parous females suppressed reproduction in young females. In the parental groups, nonreproductive females did not breed with introduced strange males in the presence of mature females. In a separate experiment weanling females housed in small groups with mature parous females showed suppressed reproduction when, at chronological maturity, they were introduced to strange males. In 75% of these groups only the mature female gave birth and in an additional 19% the mature female and one young gave birth. Nonreproductive animals in parental groups and in small groups were capable of breeding when paired with strange animals of the opposite sex.

INTRODUCTION

Pine voles, *Microtus pinetorum,* living in the wild maintain stable populations from year to year with only seasonal changes, a condition unusual for most microtine rodents (Horsfall et al., 1973; Paul, 1970). Mechanisms that allow for this stability depend little on external environmental forces but instead reside largely in the structured social system of pine voles. In this chapter I report social constraints that control breeding in the laboratory in this animal.

We have studied the social organization of freely reproducing colonies of pine voles in our laboratory since the mid 1970s using large enclosures that mimic conditions in the field. According to Paul (1970) and FitzGerald and Madison (1983) wild pine voles live in colonial territories in burrow systems in which members occupy overlapping ranges. In New York State, researchers reported that colonies consisted of family groups of five or more with two adults and several juveniles and subadults (Benton, 1955) or two to nine adults and young (FitzGerald and Madison, 1983), or occasionally in groups having as many as 16 members (Gourley and Richmond, 1972.) The fossorial habitat provides protection from the elements and predators and at the same time fosters close social encounters.

These rodents are indigenous to the United States east of the Mississippi River, an area of temperate climate and abundant rainfall. In their natural environment, they are trapped in small numbers (1-3/ha depending on latitude) in deciduous forests or at the edge of the woods. Apple *(Malus* sp.) horticulture provides an ideal habitat for these animals for they occur in larger numbers in maintained orchards. Maximum number of animals in an orchard differs in different latitudes. Paul (1970) found 16-20/ha in North Carolina; Horsfall et al. (1973) repeatedly trapped 35/ha or fewer in Virginia; and Benton (1955) reported that a trapper had found 85/ha in New York. In abandoned orchards, populations drop to the low numbers found in natural environments (Forbes, 1972).

Reproductive potential of pine voles was reported by us to be low (Schadler and Butterstein, 1979), a condition uncommon for most voles. Litter size was small with a mean at weaning of 2.6 pups in the laboratory and 2.2 in the wild compared to 5.5 for meadow voles, *Microtus pennsylvanicus,* a sympatric species, (Colvin and Colvin, 1970). Gestation was long for a microtine rodent, 24 days versus 20-21 days (Morrison et al., 1976) or 20-22 days (Batzli et al., 1977) in other voles. Maturity occurred late. No periods of estrus took place in the absence of males. Unfamiliar (strange) males induced estrus followed by copulation which in turn induced ovulation and conception (Schadler and Butterstein, 1987). Strange males induced abortion followed by estrus and copulation in females throughout at least 15 days of pregnancy (Schadler, 1981).

The favorable orchard habitat provides an abundance of food and nest sites, resources that could support large numbers of animals even at a low rate of reproduction. Horsfall (1953), based on vole grazing potential, estimated that a maintained apple orchard could easily supply food and shelter to support a minimum of 400 voles per hectare, a number many times higher than the largest reported population. Clearly, populations of voles stabilize at a number well below the carrying capacity of the environment, a characteristic that made them an attractive animal for studying social systems that control population density.

METHODS

I initiated the laboratory colony with animals I trapped in Ulster County, New York in 1974 and 1975. The breeding colony was outbred in 1980 with animals collected from the same source.

Laboratory conditions.—Laboratory housing was designed to mimic as closely as possible conditions in burrows in the field. Voles lived in family groups in large metal enclosures, 1 by 1 by 0.4 m with constant temperature of 16-18°C and photoperiod of 12L:12D. Wood shavings covered floors to a depth of 8-12 cm. Two metal trays 35 by 20 cm placed on wood blocks 5 by 10 cm provided darkness and shelter. Animals received rat lab blocks, rabbit pellets, apples, and water ad lib.

Families began with a single breeding pair and continued as freely growing colonies until a minimum of 60 days passed following the successful rearing of the last surviving litter. Some colonies remained together for 250-300 days before they were disbanded. During that time, offspring remained with the family. The criterion for reproductive status was production of offspring. Animals were toe clipped for identification. Colonies were observed a minimum of three times weekly and a log kept of births, deaths, and behavior of residents. Laboratory space limitations decreed that a maximum of three colonies could be maintained simultaneously; experiments ran successively and continuously from 1975 until 1989.

By experimental manipulations of family groups we tested various parameters of social control of population. When these tests required small cages, animals were placed in metal mouse cages 18.5 by 26 by 14.5 cm with heavy wire mesh covers fitted with food hoppers that served both to deliver food and to provide cover. Food, water, and laboratory environment were the same.

Experimental manipulations.—Three family groups that had ceased reproducing had 30-50% of offspring removed. In all cases founding parents remained.

In experiment 1, founding males from three reproducing family groups with a founding female were removed and replaced with strange males. Males from an additional four groups that had no living founding female were removed and replaced with strange males. Births of litters and identities of reproducing females were noted.

In experiment 2, the effect of mature, parous females on fertility of young females housed with them during maturation of the young was tested. In a separate experiment young females were reared in small single-sex cages from birth with their mothers or from weaning with mature, parous females (*n* = 34 groups with three to four females per cage). Young females were allowed to mature in the absence of males. When young animals reached full chronological maturity at 12 weeks of age, an unrelated male was introduced to each cage. Males remained in the cages throughout the remainder of this experiment. Birth of litters was noted. All litters born in the experimental cages were removed at weaning.

In experiment 3, the effect of removal of reproducing females was tested. Following weaning of one or at the most two litters, the older, reproducing female was removed from each of 11 cages from experiment 2 leaving the nonreproductive but chronologically mature cagemates housed with the introduced (strange) male.

Nonreproductive females from four parental groups received intraperitoneal injections of 1 μg estradiol and 20 μg progesterone on each of three days. Estrus was checked daily via vaginal smears.

124

Presence of cornified epithelial cells is diagnostic of estrus in pine voles (Schadler and Butterstein, 1979, 1987).

Females from five family groups were checked for perforate vaginas and males for scrotal testes. Animals from three groups were killed and their gonads examined histologically. When colonies were disbanded, representative voles from nine surviving groups (*n* = 63) were paired in small cages with mature animals of the opposite sex from the breeding colony.

Two siblings or a parent and offspring from nonreproducing families were placed in mixed sex pairs in small cages to check for reproduction by family members caged together.

RESULTS

Self-limitation of populations.—In the 18 families that produced five or more litters, reproduction ceased and numbers remained stable at a mean of about 16 animals (range 12-23; Fig. 1). In 15 of 18 groups, only the founding female bore litters. In three groups, a first-generation daughter gave birth to one or two litters. In two of these three families, the founding female was over 1 year of age when the daughter delivered her first litter.

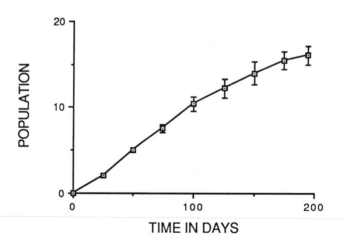

Fig. 1.—Mean population size of 18 freely growing parental groups of pine voles that produced five or more successive litters in 200 days in the laboratory.

Populations stabilized in the 15 colonies in which the founding parents survived when infant mortality reached 100%. Most colonies suffered minimal adult mortality but infant survival fell to zero when population density rose. Reproduction ceased in the remaining three colonies that produced five or more litters and in five additional groups when the founding mother (six groups) or father (two groups) died with no unrelated vole to replace the missing parent.

Behavior of family members affected infant mortality in crowded groups. Fathers and brothers as well as female relatives huddled with infants and retrieved them when necessary. The highly social pine voles tended to huddle or cluster together under a single shelter. Although all enclosures had two shelters voles always congregated for at least part of the day under one. As numbers of voles increased, animals became crowded. Juveniles as well as adults carried infants not attached to the mother's nipples or huddled with them without interference from the mother. As crowding increased, activity also increased. Animals moved outside the shelter more frequently often carrying newborns with them. Infants were seen being passed from one vole to another or dropped outside the shelter. At low densities, infants were rarely observed detached from the mother's nipples but crowding changed this behavior. Nursing was disrupted and newborns were observed scattered throughout the cluster. Infants grew thin and usually died by the age of 7-10 days. Infanticide was rare; pups had no wounds and wood shavings were not bloody.

Reducing density triggered increase in population growth.—Populations that had stopped reproducing because infant mortality reached 100% resumed growing when crowding was alleviated. Removal of 30 to 50% of offspring from three of these nonreproducing family groups resulted in immediate revival of growth as long as founding parents remained. In all cases, newborns survived and numbers steadily climbed. No colony manipulated in this manner returned to its former size but the founding females were all growing old.

Status of reproductive females with new males.—In experiment 1, removal of males from parental groups and replacing them with strange, mature males did not change the reproductive status of mothers and daughters. In three families with a single breeding female (the founding female), it alone bred with the new male. In four families without a founding female, one or two daughters bred with the new male.

In experiment 2, mature, parous females suppressed reproduction in young females caged with them (Table 1). Strange males introduced to 25 groups of females of mixed ages sired litters in 24 groups. Of these, mature females delivered litters in 23 groups (96%). In six cages (25%) young females also gave birth. However, litters were born to young females in all nine groups with only young females.

Table 1.—Number of laboratory cages of pine voles and number of litters within the cages following the introduction of unrelated mature males. Each cage in which mature and young females produced litters had only two breeding females.

			Mothers of litters in cage		
Cage occupants	Number of cages	Cages with litters	Mature female only	Mature and young females	Young female only
Mothers with daughters	8	8	7	1	1
Strange females with young females	17	16	16	4	0
Young females only	9	9			9[a]

[a]Four cages had two or more breeding females.

In experiment 3, suppression of reproduction was temporary because removal of mature reproducing females from 11 cages of experiment 2 resulted in reproduction by younger cagemates in nine of the 11 cages. One young female in seven groups and two females in two additional groups successfully bred.

Sex steroids.—Nonreproductive daughters that received injections of hormones exhibited estrous vaginal smears but failed to produce litters.

Nonfertile voles had the capacity to breed.—Examination for reproductive maturity showed that just over half of females showed vaginal opening and most males had scrotal testes. Histological examination of gonads of animals showed tertiary or Graafian ovarian follicles in all females and mature sperm in 80% of males. About 20% of males, however, had small testes with tightly packed seminiferous tubules of small diameter with little spermatogenesis.

Voles that had ceased reproducing and then were paired in small cages with unfamiliar animals of the opposite sex bred (91% of females and 80% of males). In all but three cases, conception occurred within 2-5 days of pairing. However, voles remained infertile when paired as siblings or parent and offspring of the opposite sex in small cages. None of these pairs produced offspring.

DISCUSSION

Our laboratory findings on social organization of freely reproducing pine voles were supported by FitzGerald and Madison (1983) in field studies in a New York State orchard; they used livetrapping and radiotelemetry. Several investigators have reported field studies on pine voles but only FitzGerald and Madison (1983) with their telemetry provided more than circumstantial evidence for pine vole social organization. Our long term study constitutes the only laboratory examination of some aspects of pine vole society.

Field data from telemetry on animals living in an apple orchard confirmed our findings that pine voles tolerated life in cohesive and exclusive family groups in which mature males and females lived together and offspring grew to maturity. Wild voles lived in family territories in which members occupied overlapping ranges and one or occasionally two common nest sites (FitzGerald and Madison, 1983). Size of reproducing groups was limited to two to nine animals and no breeding occurred outside of family territories.

In laboratory colonies, all family members clustered at various times during the day under a single chosen shelter mimicking nesting behavior in the wild. This behavior appears to be uncommon for most voles. Of seven species of *Microtus* reported in a review by Wolff (1985) only individuals of *M. pinetorum* continuously occupied communal family territories. McGuire and Novak (1984) noted that individuals of *M. pinetorum* continuously shared a single nest whereas *M. ochrogaster* individuals often split the family between two alternative nests. *M. pennsylvanicus* males and females never shared a single nest.

Laboratory groups attained a greater population density than that reported in telemetry studies but not on average greater than the 16 individuals noted by Gourley and Richmond (1972) in livetrapping studies. Alleviation of crowding in laboratory colonies resulted in resumption of survival of litters and consequent increase in residents.

Restriction of breeding to the founding female in our parental groups could have been a laboratory artifact. However, we previously reported that sibling-sibling inhibition occurred (Schadler, 1983). Also, FitzGerald and Madison (1983) monitored 20 social groups in the field and found that 16 had a single reproductive female. Only four groups had two females that they determined to be reproductive (pregnant, lactating, or with perforate vaginas). In our study of 18 parental groups, three groups had two reproducing females but in two cases the second female did not breed until the founding female was over 1 year old. Restriction of breeding to founding females has been reported in laboratory populations of *M. ochrogaster* (Getz, 1978). Administration of estrogen and progesterone to our nonreproductive females induced perforate vaginas and estrus in these animals but did not result in pregnancy.

When we created small groups of two to three young females caged with an older, parous female, young females bred in only 25% of the groups. Alternatively, if no older female was present, 100% of the groups of young females produced litters. An established hierarchy for reproduction clearly existed in both the parental groups and the small groups with the older, parous female occupying the dominant position.

Most social groups monitored in the field by FitzGerald and Madison (1983) had more than one scrotal male as did those in the laboratory. However, that presence of testes in the scrotum did not constitute compelling evidence that male offspring were breeding. Two parental groups ceased reproduction when the founding father died. Control checks for fertility by pairing family members of parental groups resulted in no production of litters. Breeding appeared to be restricted to the founding parents with little or no participation in reproduction by other apparently mature, scrotal males.

Fifty percent of females past the chronological age for maturity had imperforate vaginas and appeared to be immature. However, most nonreproductive animals bred immediately when paired with unrelated mates. This fertility compares favorably with that noted previously for pine voles (Schadler, 1981; Schadler and Butterstein, 1979). Batzli et al. (1977) noted that in *M. ochrogaster* and *M. californicus* littermates reared together did not mature reproductively. These animals matured rapidly when removed from their littermates and paired with mature, unrelated animals of the opposite sex.

In the field, telemetry showed that breeding and establishment of new family groups took place readily when voles migrated from the parental group to live with unrelated animals of the opposite sex. Movement to a new location occurred only when all members of the receiving group were of the opposite sex or when the migrant found a new mate and established a family on a new or vacant territory.

Our data from freely reproducing parental groups added further support to Dewsbury's (1981) proposal that pine voles have a monogamous mating system. Of eight species of *Microtus*, Dewsbury (1981) rated *M. pinetorum* at the top of his scale for monogamy and the sympatric *M. pennsylvanicus* at the bottom. One correlate of monogamy not noted by Dewsbury (1981) that would further elevate the score of pine voles was male participation in rearing of young. We observed that males participated actively in retrieving and brooding infants, a finding also reported by Oliveras and Novak (1986). We also found avoidance of polygamous breeding in our familial groups but this may be attributed to avoidance of inbreeding. The fact that in small groups more than one female paired with a single strange male occasionally delivered a litter suggested polygyny may occur under opportune conditions. Pine voles, however, usually live in families, an arrangement that supports monogamy.

CONCLUSIONS

Pine voles in the laboratory and the field limited their own population size. Family groups normally had only one reproductive female (and probably one siring male as well). Exogenous hormonal stimulation induced estrus but not breeding in nonreproductive female members in a laboratory family group and thus had no effect on population growth. Chronologically mature but unreproductive animals possessed the physical capability for reproduction because both sexes bred readily under favorable social conditions. Social constraints dictated by communal living in family groups controlled population numbers.

ACKNOWLEDGMENTS

These studies could not have continued for 14 years without help from many people. I want to thank especially my colleague, George Butterstein, who joined with me in many of the studies that accompanied these experiments. Linda Schadler and Stanley Staveckis kept the log when I was out of town. Marijo Madonia has kept cages and enclosures clean and voles well fed. Many thanks in memorium to my Uncle, Frank Horsfall, Jr., for his generous help with the establishment of my pine vole work.

LITERATURE CITED

Batzli, G. O., L. L. Getz, and S. S. Hurley. 1977. Suppression of growth and reproduction of microtine rodents by social factors. Journal of Mammalogy, 58:583-591.

Benton, A. H. 1955. Observations on the life history of the northern pine mouse. Journal of Mammalogy, 36:52-62.

Colvin, M. A., and D. V. Colvin. 1970. Breeding and fecundity of six species of voles *(Microtus)*. Journal of Mammalogy, 51:417-419.

Dewsbury, D. A. 1981. An exercise in the prediction of monogamy in the field from laboratory data on 42 species of muroid rodents. The Biologist, 63:138-162.

FitzGerald, R. W., and D. M. Madison. 1983. Social organization of a free-ranging population of pine voles, *Microtus pinetorum*. Behavioral Ecological and Sociobiology, 13:183-187.

Forbes, J. E. 1972. The New York pine vole situation. Pp. 4-10, *in* Proceedings of the New York pine mouse symposium (J. F. Forbes, ed.). Bureau of Fish and Wildlife Special Reprint, 75 pp.

Getz, L. L. 1978. Speculation on social structure and population cycles of microtine rodents. The Biologist, 60:134-147.

Gourley, R. S., and M. E. Richmond. 1972. Vole populations in New York orchards. Pp. 61-71, *in* Proceedings of the New York pine mouse symposium (J. E. Forbes, ed.). Bureau of Fish and Wildlife Special Reprint, 75 pp.

Horsfall, F., Jr. 1953. Mouse control in Virginia orchards. Agricultural Experiment Station, Virginia Polytechnic Institute, Blacksburg, Virginia, Bulletin, 465:1-26.

Horsfall, F., Jr., R. E. Webb, and R. E. Beyers. 1973. How to successfully meet pine voles on their terms. Virginia Fruit, 61:3-15.

McGuire, B. A., and M. A. Novak. 1984. A comparison of maternal behaviour in the meadow vole *Microtus pennsylvanicus,* the pine vole *M. pinetorum* and the prairie vole *M. ochrogaster.* Animal Behaviour, 32:1132-1141.

Morrison, P., R. Dieterich, and D. Preston. 1976. Breeding and reproduction of fifteen wild rodents maintained as laboratory colonies. Laboratory Animal Science, 26:232-243.

Oliveras, D. M., and M. A. Novak. 1986. A comparison of parental behaviour in the meadow vole *Microtus pennsylvanicus,* the pine vole *M. pinetorum* and the prairie vole *M. ochrogaster.* Animal Behaviour, 34:519-526.

Paul, J. R. 1970. Observations on the ecology, population, and reproductive biology of the pine vole, *Microtus pinetorum,* in North Carolina. Reports of Investigations, Illinois State Museum, Springfield, Illinois, 20:1-28.

Schadler, M. H. 1981 Postimplantation abortion in pine voles *(Microtus pinetorum)* induced by strange males and pheromones of strange males. Biology of Reproduction, 25:295-297.

———. 1983. Male siblings inhibit reproductive activity in female pine voles, *Microtus pinetorum.* Biology of Reproduction, 28:1137-1139.

Schadler, M. H., and G. M. Butterstein. 1979. Reproduction in the pine vole, *Microtus pinetorum.* Journal of Mammalogy, 60:841-844.

———. 1987. Increase in serum levels of luteinizing hormone (LH) in pine voles, *Microtus pinetorum,* after induction of estrus and copulation. Journal of Mammalogy, 68:410-413.

Wolff, J. O. 1985. Behavior. Pp. 340-372, *in* Biology of New World *Microtus* (R. H. Tamarin, ed.). Special Publication, American Society of Mammalogists, 8:1-893.

A COMPARATIVE STUDY OF PHENOTYPIC CHANGES
IN *MICROTUS* SOCIAL ORGANIZATION

Jussi Viitala and Jyrki Pusenius

University of Jyväskylä, Department of Biology, Konnevesi Research Station, SF-44300 Konnevesi, Finland.

Summary.— Monogamy, polygyny, and promiscuity have been found in populations of *M. oeconomus* and *M. agrestis* in different environmental situations in northern Finland. Thus the mating systems seem to be more variable both between and within species in *Microtus* than in *Clethrionomys*. Spacing behavior in *Microtus* caused a temporary decline in population density in mid-summer, but in *Clethrionomys* a decline occurred only in the beginning of the breeding season. Habitat quality affected spacing behavior in similar ways in *Microtus* and *Clethrionomys* but did not affect differences in breeding limitation. Despite the differences in population regulation, both *Clethrionomys* and *Microtus* populations cycle synchronously in northern Fennoscandia.

INTRODUCTION

Previously we suggested (Viitala and Ylönen, 1985; Ylönen, this volume) that *Clethrionomys* social organization is an opportunistic strategy adapting the growth and size of the population to existing resources both in winter and in the breeding season. Viitala (1977) described the differences in social mechanisms between *Clethrionomys* and *Microtus*. He suggested that social mechanisms are part of the way in which voles cope with certain types of environments. A similar explanation for the differences in social behavior between *Microtus ochrogaster* and *M. pennsylvanicus* was suggested by Getz (1978). Viitala and Hoffmeyer (1985) suggested that species like *Clethrionomys* that live in stable, predictable environments and eat high quality but sparse food are characterized by philopatry and strict sociophysiological regulation of breeding (Bondrup-Nielsen, 1985; Bujalska, 1973; Kalela, 1957; Saitoh, 1981; Viitala 1977). Species living in ephemeral habitats that eat abundant lower quality food like many *Microtus* species exhibit a strong tendency to disperse and little or no social limitation of breeding (Myllymäki, 1971; Tast, 1966; Viitala, 1977). That is, *Clethrionomys* is more of a K-strategist and many *Microtus* species are r-strategists. Thus, changes in spacing behavior in females in these *Microtus* species may not have such drastic effects on limitation of breeding as in *Clethrionomys* (Ylönen et al., 1988). Because the variability in social behavior among North American *Microtus* species is extensive (Getz, 1978; Getz et al., 1981; Jannett, 1978, 1980; McGuire and Novak, 1984;

Tamarin, 1977a, 1977b; Viitala and Hoffmeyer, 1985; Wolff, 1980), in this paper we concentrate on North European species that are more typically r-strategists.

Herein we ask the following questions: Are there phenotypic changes in male and female social and spacing behavior in *Microtus?* If so, how similar are they with those of *Clethrionomys?* Do these behavioral mechanisms limit population growth? Is there a common behavioral mechanism associated with population decline in *Clethrionomys* and *Microtus?* Our examination of vole mating systems is based on investigations done at Kilpisjärvi, Finnish Lapland (Tast, 1966; Viitala, 1977), in the United States (Getz, 1978; Getz et al., 1981; Jannett, 1980; Madison, 1980; Ostfeld 1985), and in Norway (Ims, 1988). The examination of spacing behavior of female *Microtus*, which determines the density of breeding females and thus the growth of the population, is based mostly on studies done at Kilpisjärvi, Finnish Lapland by Tast (1966) and Viitala (1977) and in Konnevesi, Central Finland by Pusenius (1990). The Kilpisjärvi area belongs to the arctic-alpine birch forest zone of northern Fennoscandia and is characterized by patches of eutrophic meadow forests and fens that are inhabited by *Microtus,* among more ubiquitous oligotrophic and oligo - mesotrophic heath forests inhabited only by *Clethrionomys.* Konnevesi belongs to the mid-boreal coniferous forest zone with many types of forest and open habitats.

DIFFERENCES IN SOCIAL BEHAVIOR
BETWEEN *CLETHRIONOMYS* AND *MICROTUS*

Clethrionomys populations are characterized by philopatry, social stability, and a low rate of adult dispersal (Viitala, 1977). It long has been known that the territorial behavior of breeding *Clethrionomys* females restricts maturation of young females (Kalela, 1957). *M. agrestis* does not have such a mechanism (Viitala, 1977), but the density of mature females may be restricted by dispersal. This difference is exemplified by the degree of overlap of home ranges of mature female *C. rufocanus* and *M. agrestis* (Table 1; Viitala, 1980). There was little overlap of female home ranges in both species in early June. The overlap remained low and even decreased in *Clethrionomys* during the summer, but increased in *Microtus* due to the maturation of first litters in early July. Overlap decreased later when the young breeding females dispersed but remained still higher than in *Clethrionomys.* Viitala and Hoffmeyer (1985) suggested that *Microtus* species living in ephemeral habitats are characterized by low philopatry, only occasionally territorial behavior, and no social limitation of maturation of young females. It has been suggested that dominance and dispersal may limit the density of breeding populations (Taitt and Krebs, 1985).

Krebs et al. (1969, 1973) and Boonstra and Krebs (1977) found that enclosed *Microtus* populations reproduced until they destroyed the habitat and died out. Ylönen et al. (1988) repeated

Table 1.—Number of multiple captures in *Clethrionomys rufocanus* and *Microtus agrestis* in 1974 on a 6.7-ha study grid at Kilpisjärvi, Finnish Lapland. Multiple captures refers to the number of trap stations visited by two or more mature females; single captures refers to the number visited by only one mature female.

Date of Trapping	C. rufocanus[a]		M. agrestis[b]		χ^2
	Multiple Captures	Single Captures	Multiple Captures	Single Captures	
11-19 June	11	42	13	74	0.783
2-10 July	11	58	54	74	13.969***
21-31 July	1	42	18	92	5.565*

[a]Between-trapping period captures were significantly different, $\chi^2 = 7.115, P < 0.05$.
[b]Between-trapping period captures were significantly different, $\chi^2 = 28.175, P < 0.001$.
*$P < 0.05$
***$P < 0.001$.

this experiment with *C. glareolus*. They found in two consecutive years rapid reproduction early in the breeding season and high survival. Breeding stopped at least three weeks earlier inside the fence than outside. These findings are in agreement with the basic differences in social behavior between these two genera. However, all fenced *Microtus* populations do not show this "fence effect" (Gaines et al., 1979).

Boonstra and Hogg (1988) did not find mutual familiarity to have any effect on population statistics in *M. pennsylvanicus*. Ylönen et al. (1990) observed in an experiment with larger enclosures that populations of related and familiar *C. glareolus* individuals grew to twice the density of those composed of unfamiliar individuals. Frank (1954) noticed that unfamiliar mature females of *M. arvalis* were strictly territorial but that mature daughters of such a female stayed together with their mother and sisters on a common territory. The study of Pusenius (1990) indicated that similar clan formation may also take place in *M. agrestis*. The old females also seemingly try to improve their fitness by increasing their clan territory. Formation of female clans is best understood as a life history characteristic increasing fitness in productive environments.

Thus we conclude that social behavior is just one of the mechanisms that an individual vole can use to cope with a certain type of environment. There seem to be species-specific differences in social behavior, organization, and in the development of certain odor glands and their products used in social communication (Christiansen et al., 1978, Welsh et al., 1987). This genotypic basis does not exclude phenotypic plasticity, also observed in *Clethrionomys* (Ylönen, this volume), which aids animals to fit to changing physical and social environments. We feel that the evolution of these interspecific differences is best understood on the basis of individual selection on life history characteristics involving social behavior.

MICROTUS MATING SYSTEMS

In most live trapping studies we are forced to define the mating system on the basis of spacing behavior. In monogamy the home ranges of a breeding male and female greatly overlap and do not overlap with the home ranges of any other mature individuals. In polygyny males are territorial and overlap with the home ranges of several females. In promiscuity the home ranges of several males overlap extensively with those of many females.

Both pair bonds *(M. ochrogaster:* Getz et al., 1981; Thomas and Birney, 1979) and polygyny *(M. pennsylvanicus:* Madison 1980; *M. xanthognathus:* Wolff, 1980) have been found in different North American *Microtus* species. The usual mating system of *M. agrestis* in central Finland was polygyny with strictly territorial males (Myllymäki, 1971).

The mating systems of *Microtus oeconomus* and *M. agrestis* have been studied at Kilpisjärvi, Finnish Lapland, in different phases of a population cycle, throughout the breeding season, and in different habitats (Tast, 1966; Viitala, 1977, 1980). At high density promiscuous multi-male groups were found in both species in optimal habitats as the first summer-born females matured in highly overlapping home ranges. These aggregations of females became territorial and polygynous later in the summer. This change in the mating system was associated with a change in the habitat and home ranges of many females (Tast, 1966; Viitala, 1977). In Central Finland the females aggregated again in late summer but the males remained territorial (Fig. 1; Pusenius, 1990). At Kilpisjärvi some mature individuals of *M. oeconomus,* typically inhabitants of open grassy habitats, scattered into the moist grassy spots in eutrophic parts of the mountain birch forests during the highest density. Only monogamy was observed in this sparse population (Viitala, 1977, 1980). Thus the mating systems in *Microtus* seem to be more variable between and within species than in *Clethrionomys.*

Ostfeld (1985) and Ims (1987) suggested that spacing behavior in males depends on female dispersion in space and time. In Konnevesi estrous cycles of female *M. agrestis* became more synchronous toward the end of the breeding season (Pusenius, 1990). Aggregations of males were found in spring when females were densely aggregated and estrous cycles were not synchronous. When the breeding females aggregated again in late summer and estrous cycles became more synchronous, the males became territorial (Pusenius, 1990). *M. oeconomus* males overlapping the home range of one single female when the females were sparsely distributed in unfavorable habitats may be an attempt to optimize fitness in unfavorable circumstances.

In a study by Viitala (1977) many mature *M. agrestis* males disappeared from the study area and

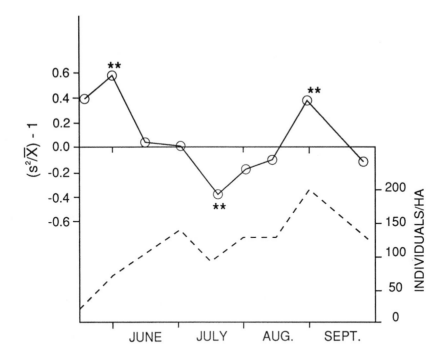

Fig. 1.—Distribution pattern of breeding *Microtus agrestis* females as determined with the index, $(s^2/\bar{X})$ - 1 (Southwood, 1978) in 1985 on a meadow study grid in Konnevesi, Central Finland. The asterisks denote deviations from random at $P < 0.01$. Positive deviations mean aggregations and negative ones mean territorial behavior. Broken line is the numbers of individuals known to be present (Pusenius, 1990).

new males invaded. Thus, male social organization seems to lack the stability found in *Clethrionomys*, in which the dominant males keep their position through the breeding season (Viitala 1977). *M. agrestis* males lack the well-developed preputial glands used to communicate social status (Christiansen et al., 1978; Hoffmeyer, 1983; Gustafsson et al., 1980). They had numerous wounds and scars, presumably gotten in territorial fights, not found among *Clethrionomys*.

In both genera the mature females outnumbered the mature males during high population density but not during low density. Thus there exists strong competition between males for females during peak densities (Ostfeld 1985; called "Männchenvernichtung"—male extermination; Stein, 1952). Even though male mating systems open many important possibilities in the study of evolutionary mechanisms (especially sexual selection), from the point of view of population dynamics, males are needed only for insemination and the many priming effects they have on females (Richmond and Stehn, 1976; Rogers and Beauchamp, 1976).

SPACING BEHAVIOR OF FEMALE *MICROTUS*

Home range sizes of female *Microtus agrestis* in optimal habitat in Northern Lapland in 1969 varied between 175 and $270/m^2$ (Viitala, 1977; Fig. 2). These were similar to the home range sizes in meadows in Central Finland and smaller than in transition habitat in more barren vegetation (Fig. 3). All areas were measured by the same method (Pusenius, 1990). At Kilpisjärvi there was greater overlap of the smaller home ranges of females in early summer than the larger ones in late summer (Fig. 2; Viitala, 1977). In Konnevesi, central Finland, there was a late summer peak in density not found at Kilpisjärvi. In both areas the oldest females remained mutually territorial through the breeding season. Thus territorial behavior of *M. agrestis* females is age dependent. The habitat quality and its seasonal dynamics seem to be important but they do not solely explain the dynamics of female spacing behavior.

Pusenius (1990) found a decline in population density (Fig. 1) in mid summer called a "mid-summer crisis" by Myllymäki (1977), who concluded that it was a consequence of food shortage. Pusenius (1990) did not find any evidence of a food shortage in his study population. The decline in

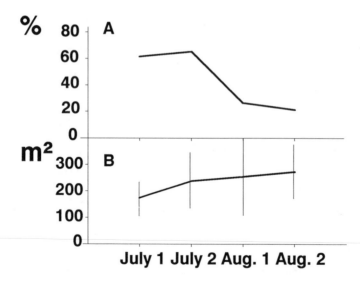

Fig. 2.—Percent of individual capture points that are in common with other individuals (A) and home range size (B), with standard deviations, of breeding *Microtus agrestis* females at Kilpisjärvi in 1969 (Viitala, 1977).

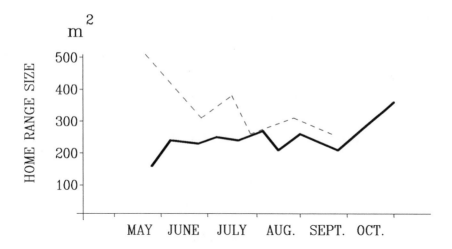

Fig. 3.—Changes in home range size in *Microtus agrestis* on a study grid in Konnevesi, Central Finland, in optimal meadow habitat (solid line) and in suboptimal forest habitat (broken line; Pusenius, 1990).

density coincided with an invasion of individuals from forest edges in early summer after the growth of herbs and grasses supplied sufficient cover and food. As a consequence unfamiliar individuals gathered together. The "mid-summer crisis" was characterized by increasing territoriality and decreasing juvenile survival and population density (Fig. 1). The young males of the second cohort were expelled most effectively. Later in the summer most of the breeding females were young of the year that lived together with their mothers and tolerated each other. At that time breeding females shifted to aggregative behavior, which resulted in a high density of breeding females and an increase in total population density. The short summer of Finnish Lapland was probably the reason why this autumn peak in density of females was not reached at Kilpisjärvi (Fig. 2).

The largest late-summer cohort was born during the "mid-summer crisis." Thus the aggressive behavior of females during and after parturition (Flanelly et al., 1986) could have affected spacing behavior. From the high survival of this mid-summer cohort we suggest that a food crisis did not exist.

In *Clethrionomys* territorial behavior of females prevented maturation of young females when there was no more space for new territories (Bondrup-Nielsen, 1987; Bujalska, 1973; Mihok, 1979; Saitoh 1981; Viitala, 1977). However, this prevention of maturation was more effective in cyclic than in noncyclic populations (Bondrup-Nielsen and Ims, 1986). This phenomenon did not occur in *Microtus*. Young females could get pregnant on the home range of their mother while overlapping with each other. Instead increasing territoriality may increase dispersal of breeding females (Pusenius, 1990; Viitala, 1977). Apparently the maturation of young females in *Microtus* was stopped by approaching winter and decreasing photoperiod at the end of summer. If there existed any social blocking of maturation in *Microtus*, its threshold density must be much higher than that in *Clethrionomys* and it may not be a consequence of territorial behavior but of female density (Pusenius, 1990). From the densities of several thousand individuals per hectare attained by some *Microtus* species (Frank, 1953; Lidicker, 1973, 1979) we suggest that a highly productive environment may block any social mechanisms that restrict breeding.

CONCLUSIONS

Based on the studies reviewed here we suggest that there does not exist any "microtine type" of social behavior and organization. The social systems of microtines are as variable as among any mammalian group. Behavioral traits have evolved under the pressure of environmental factors and most probably on the basis of individual selection. One of the most important factors may have been the quality and availability of food. In changing, unpredictable environments plasticity of behavior may also have been selected for.

From the point of view of mating systems and social organization the genus *Microtus* seems to be much more variable than *Clethrionomys*. There are also differences in their odor glands (Jannett, 1986) suggesting that these differences may have a genetic basis. Too little is known, however, about the odors, odor gland morphology, and how it is related to the habitat quality and way of life.

We have found sufficient data in two species of voles to demonstrate the existence of phenotypic changes in mating systems and female spacing behavior. In *Clethrionomys* changes in female spacing behavior may affect the maturation rate of young females. We have not found such an effect in *Microtus*. Increased territorial behavior of *Microtus* females resulted in increased dispersal and lowered population density. Despite the controversial results of Boonstra and Hogg (1988), perhaps lack of familiarity could temporarily affect spacing behavior and population statistics. Because of clan formation the effect may not last as long as in *Clethrionomys*, but it may cause just a temporary "mid-summer crisis." Phenotypic changes in spacing behavior occur both in male and female *Microtus*. They are, however, quite different from those of *Clethrionomys* and from those described by Madison and McShea (1987) for *M. pennsylvanicus*.

Population regulation and limitation among highly cyclic microtine populations may be a consequence of social behavior (Chitty, 1967; Krebs and Myers, 1974; Krebs et al., 1973). We have shown that sociophysiological blocking of maturation and breeding may set the upper limit to population growth in *Clethrionomys*. In *Microtus* density may be controlled by dispersal and food resources. There are temporary declines caused by changing from aggregations to territorial behavior. These occur in *Clethrionomys* in the beginning of the breeding season (Taitt and Krebs, 1985), but in *Microtus* as indicated here, they also occur later in the summer during the most successful breeding.

In northern Fennoscandia microtine populations belonging to both genera cycle in synchrony with characteristic summer declines (Hansson and Henttonen, 1988). We have not found evidence of any behavioral mechanism common to both genera that could cause the simultaneous declines from densities of tens or hundreds per ha to just few individuals per km^2. The synchrony of declines between *Clethrionomys* and *Microtus* may be evidence for a common extrinsic factor.

LITERATURE CITED

Bondrup-Nielsen, S. 1985. An evaluation of the effects of space use and habitat patterns on dispersal in small mammals. Annales Zoologici Fennici, 22:373-384.

———. 1987. Demography of *Clethrionomys gapperi* in different habitats. Canadian Journal of Zoology, 65:277-284.

Bondrup-Nielsen, S., and R. A. Ims. 1986. Comparison of maturation of female *Clethrionomys glareolus* from cyclic and non-cyclic populations. Canadian Journal of Zoology, 64:2099-2102.

Boonstra, R., and I. Hogg. 1988. Friends and strangers: a test of the Charnov-Finerty Hypothesis. Oecologia (Berlin), 77:95-100.

Boonstra, R., and C. Krebs. 1977. Fencing experiment on a high density population of *Microtus townsendii*. Canadian Journal of Zoology, 55:1166-1175.

Bujalska, G. 1973. The role of spacing behavior among females in the regulation of the reproduction in the bank vole. Journal of Reproduction and Fertility, Supplement, 19:461-472.

Chitty, D. 1967. The natural selection of self-regulatory behavior in animal populations. Proceedings of the Ecological Society of Australia, 2:51-78.

Christiansen, E., R. Wiger, and E. Eilertsen. 1978. Morphological variation in the preputial gland of wild bank vole. Holarctic Ecology, 1:321-325.

Flanelly, K. J., L. Flanelly, and R. Lore. 1986. Post partum aggression against intruding male conspecifics in Sprague-Dawley rats. Behavioral Processes, 13:279-286.

Frank, F. 1953. Zur Entstehung übernormaler Populationsdichten im Massenwechsel der Feldmaus, *Microtus arvalis* (Pallas). Zoologische Jahrbücher (Systematik), 81:611-624.

———. 1954. Beiträge zur Biologie der Feldmaus, *Microtus arvalis* (Pallas). Teil I: Gehege-versuche. Zoologische Jahrbücher (Systematik), 82:354-404.

Gaines, M. S., A. M. Vivas, and C. L. Baker. 1979. An experimental analysis of dispersal in fluctuating vole populations: demographic parameters. Ecology, 60:814-828.

Getz, L. L. 1978. Speculation on social structure and population cycles of microtine rodents. The Biologist, 60:134-147.

Getz L. L., C. S. Carter, and L. Gavish, 1981. The mating system of the prairie vole, *Microtus ochrogaster:* field and laboratory evidence for pair-bonding. Behavioral Ecology and Sociobiology, 8:189-194.

Gustafsson, T. O., C. B. Anderson, and P. Meurling. 1980. Effect of social rank on the growth of the preputial glands in male bank voles, *Clethrionomys glareolus.* Physiology of Behavior, 24:689-692.

Hansson, L., and H. Henttonen. 1988. Rodent dynamics as community process. Trends in Ecology and Evolution, 3:195-200.

Hoffmeyer, I. 1983. Interspecific behavioral niche separation in wood mice *(Apodemus flavicollis* and *A. sylvaticus)* and scent marking relative to social dominance in bank voles *(Clethrionomys glareolus).* Ph.D. dissertation, Department of Animal Ecology, University of Lund, Sweden, 116 pp.

Ims, R. A. 1987. Male spacing systems in microtine rodents. The American Naturalist, 130:475-484.

———. 1988. Spatial clumping of sexually receptive females induces space sharing among male voles. Nature, 335:541-543.

Jannett, F. J., Jr. 1978: The density-dependent formation of extended maternal families of the montane vole, *Microtus montanus.* Behavioral Ecology and Sociobiology, 3:245-263.

———. 1980. Social dynamics of the montane vole, *Microtus montanus,* as a paradigm. The Biologist, 62:3-19.

———. 1986. Morphometric patterns among microtine rodents, I. Sexual selection suggested by relative scent gland development in representative voles. Pp. 541-550, *in* Chemical signals in vertebrates, 4: ecology, evolution and comparative biology. Proceedings of the fourth international conference on chemical signals in vertebrates, Laramie, Wyoming (D. Duvall, D. Müller-Schwarze, and R. M. Silverstein, eds.). Plenum Press, New York, 742 pp.

Kalela, O. 1957. Regulation of the reproduction rate in subarctic populations of the vole *Clethrionomys rufocanus* (Sund.). Annales Academiae Scientiarum Fennicae (Series A, IV), 34:1-60.

Krebs, C. J., and J. H. Myers. 1974. Population cycles in small mammals. Advances in Ecological Research, 8:267-399.

Krebs, C. J., B. L. Keller, and R. H. Tamarin. 1969. *Microtus* population biology: demographic changes in fluctuating populations of *Microtus ochrogaster* and *M. pennsylvanicus* in southern Indiana. Ecology, 50:587-607.

Krebs, C. J., M. S. Gaines, B. L. Keller, J. H. Myers, and R. H. Tamarin. 1973. Population cycles in small rodents. Science, 179:35-41.

Lidicker, W. Z., Jr. 1973. Regulation of numbers in an island population of the California vole: a problem in community dynamics. Ecological Monogrographs, 43:271-302.

————. 1980. Analysis of two freely growing enclosed populations of the California vole. Journal of Mammalogy, 60:447-466.

Madison, D. M. 1980. Space use and social structure in meadow voles, *Microtus pennsylvanicus*. Behavioral Ecology and Sociobiology, 7:65-71.

Madison, D. M., and W. J. McShea. 1987. Seasonal changes in reproductive tolerance, spacing, and social organization in meadow voles: A microtine model. American Zoologist, 27:899-908.

McGuire, B., and M. A. Novak. 1984. A comparison of maternal behaviour in the meadow vole *(Microtus pennsylvanicus)*, prairie vole *(M. ochrogaster)*, and pine vole *(M. pinetorum)*. Animal Behaviour, 32:1132-1141.

Mihok, S. 1979. Behavioral structure and demography of subarctic *Clethrionomys gapperi* and *Peromyscus maniculatus*. Canadian Journal of Zoology, 57:1520-1535.

Myllymäki, A. 1971. Population ecology and its application to the control of field vole, *Microtus agrestis*. EPPO Publications, Series A, 58:27-48.

————. 1977. Demographic mechanisms in the fluctuating population of the field vole *Microtus agrestis*. Oikos, 29:468-493.

Ostfeld, R. S. 1985. Limiting resources and territoriality in microtine rodents. The American Naturalist, 126:1-15.

Pusenius, J. 1990. Peltomyyrän tilakäyttäytyminen ja maturoitumisen säätely. M.A. Thesis, Department of Biology, University of Jyväskylä, Finland, 52 pp.

Richmond, M., and R. Stehn. 1976. Olfaction and reproductive behavior in microtine rodents. Pp. 197-217, *in* Mammalian olfaction, reproductive processes and behavior (R. L. Doty, ed.). Academic Press, New York, 344 pp.

Rogers, J. G., Jr., and G. K. Beauchamp. 1976. Influence of stimuli from populations of *Peromyscus leucopus* on maturation of young. Pp. 318-330, *in* Mammalian olfaction, reproductive processes and behavior (R. L. Doty, ed.). Academic Press, New York, 344 pp.

Saitoh, T. 1981. Control of female maturation in high density population of the red backed vole, *Clethrionomys rufocanus bedfordiae*. Journal of Animal Ecology, 50:79-87.

Southwood, T. R. E. 1978. Ecological methods with particular reference to the study of insect populations. Chapman and Hall, London, 524 pp.

Stein, G. A. W. 1952. Über das Zahlenverhältnis der Geschlechter bai der Feldmaus *Microtus arvalis*. Zoologische Jahrbücher, Systematik, 81:1-26.

Taitt, M. J., and C. J. Krebs. 1985. Population dynamics and cycles. Pp. 567-620, *in* Biology of

New World *Microtus* (R. H. Tamarin, ed.). Special Publication, The American Society of Mammalogists, 8:1-893.

Tamarin, R. 1977a. Dispersal in island and mainland voles. Ecology, 58:1044-1054.

―――. 1977b. Demography of the beach vole *(Microtus breweri)* and the meadow vole *(Microtus pennsylvanicus)* in southeastern Massachusetts. Ecology, 58:1310-1321.

Tast, J. 1966. The root vole, *Microtus oeconomus* (Pallas), as an inhabitant of seasonally flooded land. Annales Zoologici Fennici, 3:127-171.

Thomas, J. A., and E. C. Birney. 1979. Parental care and mating system of the prairie vole, *Microtus ochrogaster.* Behavioral Ecology and Sociobiology, 5:171-186.

Viitala, J. 1977. Social organization in cyclic subarctic populations of the voles *Clethrionomys rufocanus* (Sund.) and *Microtus agrestis* (L.). Annales Zoologici Fennici, 14:53-93.

―――. 1980. Myyrien sosiologiasta Kilpisjärvellä (Sociology of *Microtus* and *Clethrionomys* in Kilpisjärvi). Luonnon Tutkija, 84:31-34.

Viitala, J., and I. Hoffmeyer. 1985. Social organization in *Clethrionomys* compared with *Microtus* and *Apodemus:* Social odours, chemistry and biological effects. Annales Zoologici Fennici, 22:359-371.

Viitala, J., and H. Ylönen. 1985. Variability of social overwintering strategies in *Clethrionomys.* Aquilo Serie Zoologica, 24:107-111.

Welsh, C. J., R. E. Moore, R. J. Bartelt, and L. L. Jackson. 1987. Novel, species-typical esters from preputial glands of sympatric voles, *Microtus montanus* and *M. pennsylvanicus.* Journal of Chemical Ecology, 14:143-158.

Wolff, J. O. 1980. Social organization of the taiga vole *(Microtus xanthognathus).* The Biologist, 62:34-45.

Ylönen, H., T. Kojola, and J. Viitala. 1988. Changing female spacing behavior and demography in an enclosed breeding population of *Clethrionomys glareolus.* Holarctic Ecology, 11:286-292.

Ylönen, H., T. Mappes, and J. Viitala. 1990. Different demography of friends and strangers: an experiment on the impact of kinship and familiarity in *Clethrionomys glareolus.* Oecologia (Berlin), 83:333-337.

SOCIAL STRUCTURE OF THE BEACH VOLE, *MICROTUS BREWERI*

Ken Zwicker

Biology Department, Boston University, Boston, MA 02215 U.S.A.

Present address: Whitehead Institute, 9 Cambridge Center, Cambridge, MA 02142 U.S.A.

Summary.—The beach vole *(Microtus breweri)* exhibits one of the most stable population densities of any microtine rodent. The social structure of the beach vole is similar to that of its mainland progenitor, the meadow vole *(Microtus pennsylvanicus),* with a few subtle, yet distinct, differences. The sex ratio of the beach vole is significantly biased toward males. The adult sex ratio of both beach vole and meadow vole populations exhibits dramatic fluctuations over several years, however the adult sex ratio of the beach vole never drops below a 1:1 (male:female) ratio. Unlike the daily ranges of meadow voles, there is no difference in the size or shape of daily ranges of adult male and female beach voles. Activity patterns of males and females are temporally distinct however. Several models of population regulation in voles are applied to *M. breweri.* The social structure, lack of a dispersal sink, and lack of heavy predation all may contribute to population stability.

NATURAL HISTORY

The beach vole *(Microtus breweri)* is endemic to Muskeget Island, Massachusetts, U.S.A. (Tamarin and Kunz, 1974). Muskeget is a 2.6-km^2 island located 32 km south of Cape Cod, Massachusetts, and 8 km west of Nantucket Island (41°21'N, 70°18'W). Muskeget was formed by the terminal moraine of the Laurentide ice sheet of the Pleistocene Epoch, which shaped much of the New England coastline. The meadow vole *(M. pennsylvanicus)* inhabits the larger, neighboring islands as well as the mainland. The islands have been isolated from the North American continent for ten to twelve thousand years, and from each other for three thousand years (Starrett, 1958; Wetherbee et al., 1972). It is during this isolation that the beach vole is believed to have diverged from the meadow vole (Starrett, 1958).

Muskeget Island has no fresh-water table. The vegetation of Muskeget consists primarily of beach grass *(Ammophila breviligulata)* interspersed with poison ivy *(Rhus radicans).* There are also patches of beach rose *(Rosa rugosa),* juniper *(Juniperus virginiana),* and bayberry *(Myrica pennsylvanicus).* The only terrestrial mammal of Muskeget other than the beach vole is the white-footed mouse *(Peromyscus leucopus),* which has not diverged significantly from its mainland ancestors (Wetherbee et al., 1972).

All historical reports of the beach vole describe the population as being abundant or excessively abundant (Allen, 1869; Baird, 1857; Miller, 1896). The population was extirpated by 1890, however, due to the accidental release of cats on Muskeget a few years earlier. In 1893, the beach vole population was reestablished by the release of 26 individuals (sex ratio unknown) from a subpopulation which had been isolated from the main island on a grassy sand spit of Muskeget (South Point). The sand spit, connected to the larger land mass of Muskeget Island during a United States Coast Survey in 1887, was isolated from the main island just before, or during the extirpation of the beach voles from the main island. By 1895, the Muskeget mainland population was flourishing, whereas the South Point colony had gone extinct and the point completely washed away (Miller, 1896).

Current traits of the beach vole are probably products of both island adaptation and genetic drift. Although the majority of evolutionary changes associated with speciation are believed to have occurred during the three thousand year separation of Muskeget Island from Nantucket Island, the species has also experienced at least two genetic bottlenecks. The magnitude of the founder effects due to the initial isolation of the population on Muskeget Island can only be speculated. The reintroduction of *M. breweri* onto Muskeget from a transitory sand spit was relatively well documented however. The extent of this genetic drift is exemplified by the high proportion (44%) of individuals on South Point with a white blaze located on their foreheads, which was not previously reported in the species. Of the founding individuals reintroduced to the Muskeget mainland, 38% had a blaze (currently the proportion fluctuates around 20%: Tamarin et al., 1987).

LIFE HISTORY

Microtus breweri is K-selected relative to other microtine rodents (Tamarin, 1978). On average, beach voles are larger, reach sexual maturity later, have a lower pregnancy rate, significantly smaller litter size, and a slightly longer life span than meadow voles (Tamarin, 1977a, 1977b, 1977c, 1978). The beach vole does not exhibit the periodic multi-annual fluctuations in population density (population cycles) common to many *Microtus* species. In fact, beach vole population density is one of the most stable of any microtine rodent (Ostfeld, 1988), with levels comparable to high population densities of cycling meadow vole populations (Fig. 1; Tamarin, 1977b; Tamarin et al., 1987).

Although the sex ratio (determined by trapping) of meadow voles does not differ significantly from 1:1 (male:female), the sex ratio of beach voles is significantly biased toward males (Tamarin, 1977b). Sex ratios of adult beach vole are skewed even more toward males. Monthly sex ratios of adults in cyclic populations of meadow voles appear to fluctuate dramatically from being male biased to female biased over the course of a three to four year cycle. Monthly sex ratios of adult beach voles undergo fluctuations as well, but never have dropped below a 1:1 sex ratio (Fig. 1).

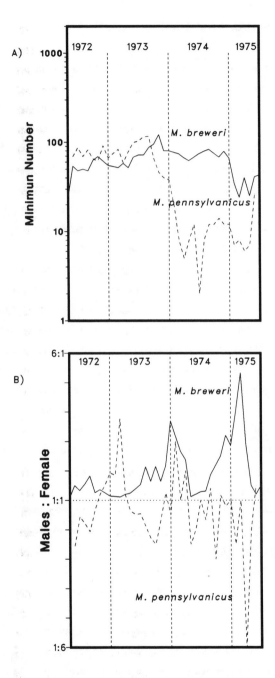

Fig. 1.—Monthly censusing of populations of beach and meadow voles in Massachusetts. A) Minimum numbers known alive per 0.8-ha trapping grid (from Tamarin, 1977b). B) The adult sex ratio (males:female) of the same populations from the same time interval.

SPATIAL AND TEMPORAL ORGANIZATION

The social structure of the beach vole during the breeding season is similar to that of the meadow vole. Beach voles appear to have a promiscuous mating system. Females maintain exclusive daily ranges, whereas male ranges overlap the ranges of both females and other males (Zwicker, 1989). Females also exhibit dramatic shifts in location, and reduction in size of their home ranges at the time of parturition and during early lactation, similar to female meadow voles (Zwicker, 1990). Levels of intrusion and home range overlap are comparable between the species. Dispersal into suboptimal habitat has been observed with indications that it is socially mediated. Finally, the spatial organization of beach voles appears to break down during the nonbreeding season (home range overlap among females increases, while male overlap decreases); however there is no evidence that beach voles form huddling groups (Zwicker, 1989, 1990).

Unlike meadow voles, the sizes and shapes of daily ranges of beach voles do not differ between the sexes (Zwicker, 1989). Home range areas of male and female beach voles are comparable to those of male meadow voles, but they are two to three times larger than the home ranges of female meadow voles (Zwicker, 1989). Madison (1980) has reported that female meadow vole ranges are over-dispersed, and that males possibly are forced to feed in the areas between female ranges. In contrast, ranges of female beach voles are contiguous, and male ranges overlap female ranges extensively (Zwicker, 1989). Despite the overlap of male and female ranges and the fact that adult males outnumber adult females, there is still an equal probability that the neighbor closest to a given female beach vole will be either male or female. Unlike the males, females are closest to each other during specific periods of the day (Zwicker, 1990). Because of the male-biased sex ratio and the ranging habits of males through the habitat, this apparent equality in proximity of either sex to females may be due to repulsion of males by females.

Patterns of activity reveal temporal partitioning between male and female beach voles. Both male and female beach voles exhibit ultradian activity rhythms of four and twelve hours during the breeding season. These rhythms are depressed during the nonbreeding season. The activity rhythms are more pronounced in males than in females, and overall locomotor activity is greater in males. For males, the period of greatest activity occurs at dawn, whereas for females, highest activity occurs at dusk. Furthermore, the 4-hour rhythm is the strongest component of male activity, while the 12-hour rhythm is strongest in females (Zwicker, 1990). Use of core areas within a home range, and exploratory forays of individual beach voles, were also separated in time between the sexes. These sex-specific temporal patterns of activity have not been reported for other microtine rodents.

These aspects of the social system of beach voles indicate that, although much of the social structure is similar to that reported for meadow vole populations, there are key differences. The "packaging" of home ranges into the habitat may be more efficient in the beach vole than the meadow vole, with males and females utilizing the same food resources (Zwicker, 1989). The sharing of resources could be accomplished through the temporal partitioning exhibited by beach voles rather than separation in space, and might also explain the larger female ranges.

The ultimate cause for the differences in social structure between beach and meadow voles may be the lack of an adequate dispersal sink for the beach vole population (Tamarin, 1978). The potential disperser, therefore, is under greater pressure to remain in the population. Any individual that is able to remain in the population (perhaps by temporally shifting its activity patterns to partition available resources) will increase its chances to survive and to reproduce relative to those individuals forced to disperse into poor habitat. This scenario would also account for the male-biased sex ratio, since the social structure of the beach vole would more easily permit males to remain in the population, with their overlapping ranges, than females, requiring large, exclusive ranges. High population densities may be maintained by temporal partitioning of resources between males and females, which allows more males to remain in the breeding population. The temporal partitioning of resources between the sexes, and the male-biased adult sex ratio, may contribute to greater social stability of the beach vole population at high density, and prevent extreme fluctuations in adult sex ratios (Fig. 1). These behavioral characteristics of the beach vole may stabilize its population dynamics, and their absence in other microtine rodents may result in population crashes.

THE APPLICATION OF DENSITY REGULATING MECHANISMS

The social and ecological constraints on the beach vole provide a unique perspective from which to examine a variety of population regulation models proposed for microtine rodents. Below I will review briefly some models of population regulation in fluctuating populations of voles and evaluate them in light of the natural history and population stability of the beach vole.

Food resource hypotheses.—It has been hypothesized that the quantity, quality, and secondary compounds in food fluctuate on a multiannual basis that may contribute to microtine cycles (Taitt and Krebs, 1985). Time lags in the feedback between voles and their food supply are thought to destabilize vole populations. Beach grass, the primary source of food for beach voles (Rothstein and Tamarin, 1977), is abundant and quickly renewable. There has been no evidence during the past 19 years that the beach vole population depletes this food supply. Food supplement studies on other microtine rodents have indicated that the addition of food increases vole population densities but does not prevent their eventual crash (Cole and Batzli, 1978; Desy and Thompson, 1983; Krebs and Delong, 1965; Taitt and Krebs, 1981). The food supply of beach voles does not appear to cause any dramatic declines in population density. It is possible that the stability of the beach vole population is related to its stable food supply.

Predation hypotheses.—Hansson (1971, 1987) suggested that generalized predators act to prevent cycling in populations of field voles *(Microtus agrestis),* whereas specialized predators may facilitate cycles. The beach vole is unusual among naturally occurring *Microtus* populations in that it experiences extremely low predation pressure. Beach voles have no mammalian, reptilian, or amphibian predators. Marsh hawks *(Circus cyaneus)* and gulls *(Larus* sp.) are potential avian predators but their rates of vole predation are thought to be low (Tamarin, 1978). Hansson (1987) suggested that populations of folivorous rodents on small islands without predators would maintain high densities for "an extended period of time," but would be susceptible to acute adverse factors (weather, disease). Tamarin et al. (1987) suggested that low spring density of beach voles may be directly due to the severity of preceding winter storms, which result in flooding.

The current consensus seems to be that predation pressures do not prevent or initiate declines in population density, but affect the amplitude of the crash and prolong the low density phase (Pearson, 1971, 1985). The lack of strong predation pressure on Muskeget Island may contribute to the stability of beach vole density. Unfortunately, the lack of a reliable and accurate measure of predation on natural populations has yet to substantiate its role in vole population processes.

Behavioral hypotheses.—All of the proposed behavioral mechanisms for population regulation stem from the notion that increased population density leads to increased levels of interaction among individuals. The various behavioral hypotheses then diverge into either phenotypic or genotypic mechanisms.

Christian (1950) was the first to propose a behavioral mechanism for population cycles in mammals. His "stress hypothesis" is based on the assumption that social interactions are fundamentally stressful to an individual, and as interactions increase with increasing density, so, in turn, do levels of stress. Christian linked stressful stimuli with increased pituitary - adrenocortical activity and a corresponding decrease in pituitary-gonadal activity, leading to a drop in individual reproductive capability (Christian, 1975).

To and Tamarin (1977) found a significant correlation between the weight of adrenal glands and population density in the beach vole, but not in a meadow vole population. The results indicated that stress levels vary directly with population density, and are greater in the noncyclic beach vole population, but do not seem related to population cycles of a meadow vole population. These findings are in direct opposition to predictions made by the stress hypothesis.

Chitty (1967) proposed the first genetically based mechanism of vole population regulation, postulating that aggressiveness was genetically determined (i.e., heritable). As population density increased, aggressive individuals would have an advantage in acquiring and maintaining the resources necessary for survival. The population crash would occur because less aggressive individuals would be driven out of the population leaving a population numerically dominated by aggressive individuals that are less successful in mating and rearing young. The Chitty hypothesis is a polymorphism model (involving aggressive behavior) with natural selection acting in the 3- to 5-year interval between population crashes.

To test the Chitty hypothesis, at least two facets of the model must be examined: 1) The degree of heritability of aggressive behavior, and 2) whether levels of aggressiveness in a population fluctuate with population densities (less aggressive individuals making up the majority of dispersers). In examining these assumptions, it is important not to take a narrow view of the concept of aggressive behavior. In the Chitty hypothesis, aggressive behavior is generally described as any genetic trait that predisposes an individual to successfully acquire and maintain the resources necessary to survive in an increasing population. If the Chitty hypothesis is correct, then the population dynamics of the beach vole would have to be explained in one of two ways; either the heritability of aggressive behavior is too low, or selection against nonaggressive genotypes in high density populations is too weak.

There are numerous problems associated with measuring aggressiveness and determining heritability in natural populations (Boonstra and Boag, 1987), and no general consensus has emerged on what is a sufficient level of heritability of aggressiveness for natural selection to act. True heritability (in the broad sense) is measured as that proportion of the variance of a phenotype that is attributable to genetic factors. The genetic variance of the beach vole population may be extremely low, given that the population is descended from as few as 26 founding individuals (Miller, 1896). Therefore, even if there is a strong genetic component to aggressive behavior, the heritability of aggressive behavior in the beach vole may be low due to its low genetic variability in relation to its overall phenotypic variability.

According to the Chitty hypothesis, selective pressures result in the removal of the nonaggressive genotypes from the gene pool at high densities either through dispersal or increased mortality, which are difficult to distinguish in the field. The lack of a true dispersal sink, coupled with the extremely low predation pressure on the beach vole population, may effectively prevent the removal of nonaggressive individuals from the breeding population, thus preventing selection pressure on the nonaggressive genotypes. Therefore, one or both of the exceptions to the Chitty mechanism of population regulation could apply to the beach vole population. To test the Chitty hypothesis thoroughly, levels of aggressiveness, and the heritability of aggressive behavior must be compared between beach vole and meadow vole populations.

Smith et al. (1975) proposed a different model of population regulation involving genetically based aggressive behavior. According to Smith et al. (1975), outbreeding increases with increasing density, which, in turn, increases the level of heterozygosity of the population. Smith et al. (1975, 1978) proposed that heterozygous individuals are predisposed to disperse from a high density population, and because of their relative vigor, are better able to survive in suboptimal habitat as well as surviving the act of dispersing itself. Behaviorally, Smith et al. (1975) predicted that dispersing (heterozygous) individuals will be more aggressive than the population average, whereas Chitty (1967) predicted that dispersers will be less aggressive than the population average.

Little is known of the genetic variability of *M. breweri*. Kohn and Tamarin (1978) found that one of 15 blood allozyme systems tested was polymorphic, and that system (transferrin) showed low levels of polymorphism relative to *M. pennsylvanicus* populations. Keith and Tamarin (1981) later reported *M. breweri* to be polymorphic for esterase as well. Since the founder population of the beach vole was small and the population since has remained isolated, low levels of heterozygosity might explain the lack of population cycles in the beach vole population, based on the outbreeding model.

Heterozygosity has been associated with aggressive behavior among male *Peromyscus* (Garten, 1976), although the correlations were among populations, not individuals. Information from the beach vole population is inconclusive regarding the outbreeding hypothesis.

The third genetically based model of population regulation was proposed by Charnov and Finerty (1980). Working within the theoretical framework of kin selection (Hamilton, 1964), Charnov and Finerty (1980) proposed that as population density increases, the degree of relatedness among neighbors decreases, and individuals would behave more aggressively toward nonrelatives than relatives. The model does not specify the exact mechanism of the decline but it is linked intricately to levels of dispersal.

The Charnov and Finerty (1980) model is difficult to assess because of its genetic basis. Critics of the model may state that the stability of the beach vole population at high density disproves the relatedness model. The social system of the beach vole is similar to that of the meadow vole, and their population density is equivalent to peak densities reported for meadow voles; therefore, if low levels of relatedness among neighbors precipitate a decline in meadow vole population density, they should cause the beach vole population density to decline as well. Supporters of the model would argue that the beach vole population represents a case in which aggressiveness toward nonrelatives may have been lost (or more precisely, tolerance toward relatives fixed) in the founding population. Overall levels of aggression in the beach vole are expected to be lower because, in essence, overall levels of relatedness are higher.

The Watson and Moss (1970) criteria of socially limited animal populations have been supported by numerous tests on a variety of *Microtus* species (Tamarin, 1983, 1985; Taitt and Krebs, 1985), with no evidence to the contrary. The social structure and population dynamics of *M. breweri*, in comparison to cyclic populations of *M. pennsylvanicus,* as well as the lack of support for any extrinsic mechanism, indicate some behavioral component to the mechanism of population regulation in voles. Clearly, the role of aggressive behavior and its genetic basis need further study. The impact of predation on population processes in small mammals also requires further quantitative study. Genetic mechanisms of population regulation are intuitively pleasing to evolutionary ecologists and population geneticists, but technology is only now becoming available to properly test the models of Chitty (1967), Smith et al. (1975), and Charnov and Finerty (1980). With these tests will come a better understanding of microtine population dynamics, and a possible solution to the enigma of vole cycles.

ACKNOWLEDGMENTS

I thank Don Little for allowing me access to Muskeget Island. Marita Sheridan helped in all aspects of the field work. My research was supported by Van Alan Clarke, Jr. and the Island Foundation and grants to R. Tamarin at Boston University from the National Science Foundation (DEB81-03483) and the National Institutes of Health (HD18620).

LITERATURE CITED

Allen, J. A. 1869. Mammalia of Massachusetts. Bulletin of the Museum of Comparative Zoology, 1:143-252.

Baird, S. F. 1857. Mammals, *in* Reports of explorations and surveys from the Mississippi river to the Pacific ocean, 8:xxi-xlviii + 1-757.

Boonstra, R., and P. T. Boag. 1987. A test of the Chitty hypothesis: Inheritance of life-history traits in meadow voles *Microtus pennsylvanicus.* Evolution, 41:929-947.

Charnov, E. L., and J. P. Finerty. 1980. Vole population cycles; a case for kin selection? Oecologia (Berlin), 45:1-2.

Chitty, D. 1967. The natural selection of self regulatory behavior in animal populations. Proceedings of the Ecological Society of Australia, 2:51-78.

Christian, J. J. 1950. The adeno-pituitary system and population cycles in mammals. Journal of Mammalogy, 31:247-259.

———. 1975. Hormonal control of population growth. Pp. 205-274, *in* Hormonal correlates of behavior (B. E. Eleftheriou and R. L. Sprott, eds.). Plenum Press, 1:1-439.

Cole, F. R., and G. O. Batzli. 1978. Influence of supplemental feeding on a vole population. Journal of Mammalogy, 59:809-819.

Desy, E. A., and C. F. Thompson. 1983. Effects of supplemental food on a *Microtus pennsylvanicus* population in central Illinois. Journal of Animal Ecology, 52:127-140.

Garten, C. T., Jr. 1976. Relationships between aggressive behavior and heterozygosity in the old field mouse, *Peromyscus polionotus*. Evolution, 30:59-72.

Hamilton, W. D. 1964. The genetical evolution of social behavior. Journal of Theoretical Biology, 7:1-16.

Hansson, L. 1971. Small rodent food, feeding and population dynamics. Oikos, 22:183-198.

———. 1987. An interpretation of rodent dynamics as due to trophic interactions. Oikos, 50:308-318.

Keith, T. P., and R. H. Tamarin. 1981. Genetic and demographic differences between dispersers and residents in cycling and noncycling vole populations. Journal of Mammalogy, 62:713-725.

Kohn, P. H., and R. H. Tamarin. 1978. Selection at electrophoretic loci for reproductive parameters in island and mainland voles. Evolution, 32:15-28.

Krebs, C. J., and K. DeLong. 1965. A *Microtus* population with supplemental food. Journal of Mammalogy, 46:566-573.

Madison, D. 1980. Space use and social structure in meadow voles, *Microtus pennsylvanicus*. Behavioral Ecology and Sociobiology, 7:65-71.

Miller, G. S., Jr. 1896. The beach mouse of Muskeget Island. Proceedings of the Boston Society of Natural History, 27:75-87.

Ostfeld, R. S. 1988. Fluctuations and constancy in populations of small rodents. The American Naturalist, 131:445-452.

Pearson, O. P. 1971. Additional measurements on the impact of carnivores on California voles *(Microtus californicus)*. Journal of Mammalogy, 52:41-49.

———. 1985. Predation. Pp. 535-566, *in* Biology of New World *Microtus*. Special Publication, The American Society of Mammalogists, 8:1-893.

Rothstein, B. E., and R. H. Tamarin. 1977. Feeding behavior of the insular beach vole, *Microtus breweri*. Journal of Mammalogy, 58:84-85.

Smith, M. H., C. T. Garten, Jr., and P. R. Ramsey. 1975. Genetic heterozygosity and population dynamics in small mammals. Pp. 85-102, *in* Isozymes IV: Genetics and Evolution (C. L. Markert, ed.). Academic Press, New York, 965 pp.

Smith, M. H., M. N. Manlove, and J. Joule. 1978. Spatial and temporal dynamics of the genetic organization of small mammal populations. Pp. 99-113, *in* Populations of Small Mammals Under Natural Conditions (D. P. Snyder, ed.). Pymatuning Laboratory of Ecology Special Publication, 5:1-237.

Starrett, A. 1958. Insular variation in mice of the *Microtus pennsylvanicus* group in southeastern Massachusetts. Ph.D. dissertation, University of Michigan, Ann Arbor, 137 pp.

Taitt, M. J., and C. J. Krebs. 1981. The effect of extra food on small rodent populations: II Voles

(Microtus townsendii). Journal of Animal Ecology, 50:125-137.

———. 1985. Population dynamics and cycles. Pp. 567-620, *in* Biology of New World *Microtus.* (R. H. Tamarin, ed.). Special Publication, The American Society of Mammalogists, 8:1-893.

Tamarin, R. H. 1977a. Dispersal in island and mainland voles. Ecology, 58:1044-1054.

———. 1977b. Demography of the beach vole *(Microtus breweri)* and the meadow vole *(Microtus pennsylvanicus)* in southeastern Massachusetts. Ecology, 58:1310-1321.

———. 1977c. Reproduction in the island beach vole, *Microtus breweri,* and the mainland meadow vole, *Microtus pennsylvanicus* in southeastern Massachusetts. Journal of Mammalogy, 58:536-548.

———. 1978. Dispersal, population regulation, and k-selection in field mice. The American Naturalist, 112:545-555.

———. 1983. Animal population regulation through behavioral interactions. Pp. 698-720, *in* Advances in the study of mammalian behavior (J. F. Eisenberg and D. G. Kleiman, eds.). Special Publication, The American Society of Mammalogists, 7:1-753.

———. 1985. Intrinsic mechanisms of population regulation in microtine rodents. Acta Zoologica Fennica, 173:19-21.

Tamarin, R. H., and T. H. Kunz. 1974. *Microtus breweri.* Mammalian Species, 45:1-3.

Tamarin, R. H., G. H. Adler, M. Sheridan, and K. Zwicker. 1987. Similarity of spring population densities of the island beach vole *(Microtus breweri),* 1972-1986. Canadian Journal of Zoology, 65:2039-2041.

To, L. P., and R. H. Tamarin. 1977. The relation of population density and adrenal gland weight in cycling and noncycling voles *(Microtus).* Ecology, 58:928-934.

Watson, A., and Moss, R. 1970. Dominance, spacing behavior and aggression in relation to population limitation in vertebrates. Pp. 167-218, *in* Animal populations in relation to their food resources (A. Watson, ed.). Blackwell Scientific Publications, 477 pp.

Wetherbee, D. K., R. P. Coppinger, and R. E. Walsh. 1972. Time Lapse Ecology, Muskeget Island, Nantucket, Massachusetts. MSS Educational Publishing Co. Inc., New York, 173 pp.

Zwicker, K. 1989. Home range and spatial organization of the beach vole, *Microtus breweri.* Behavorial Ecology and Sociobiology, 25:161-170.

———. 1990. A telemetric study of space use and social structure of the insular beach vole, *Microtus breweri.* Ph.D. Dissertation, Boston University, 195 pp.

SOCIAL SYSTEM OF THE BANK VOLE, CLETHRIONOMYS GLAREOLUS

Gabriela Bujalska

Institute of Ecology, PAS, 05-092 Dziekanów Leśny, Poland

Summary.—A survey of the literature and original data were used to describe the social system of the bank vole. Up to seven mature, territorial females and up to six mature males with overlapping home ranges, constitute a breeding colony. Young of the year usually remain within the area occupied by the breeding colony with females at the periphery of their mother's home range. Immature males and females replace mature individuals that die. Mature males employ one of two alternative breeding tactics: higher reproductive effort related to a large home range and short life-span, or lower reproductive effort related to a small home range size (limited access to mature females) and long life-span. This social system seems to exclude the possibility of density-dependent regulation of population size (only the breeding potential is regulated). Models of population dynamics based on "local" interrelations between closest neighbors, nontransferable to more distant individuals, are suggested.

LIFE-CYCLE AND BEHAVIOR

Bank voles inhabit primeval forests in Europe: boreal coniferous forests in the north, broad-leaved oak and beech forests in the south, and mixed forests of Central Europe. They prefer dense mixed forests with abundant herb and undergrowth layers (Pucek, 1983; Raczyński, 1983). Their polyphagy is associated with ecological plasticity and wide geographical distribution (Gębczyńska, 1983; Hansson, 1985). However, because of their cryptic nature, bank voles are rarely seen under natural conditions. The only exceptions are the studies of Mironov (1977) and Petrov and Mironov (1972).

The estrous cycle lasts for 8 (Larina and Golikova, 1960) or 5 days (on the average; Bujalska, 1983). The fertile period (proestrus and estrus) lasts on the average 52.4 h. A female may mate with several males (Kalela, 1957; A. Mironov, pers. comm.), or it may choose a single male from those whose home ranges overlap with hers (Viitala and Hoffmeyer, 1985). The latter description is consistent with a study by Kawata (1985) who found no multiple paternity in *Clethrionomys rufocanus*, a behaviorally similar species. Pregnancy lasts 17-18 days (Popov, 1960), or 22 ± 2 days (Bujalska and Ryszkowski, 1966).

The litter consists usually of 4-5 young (Zejda, 1966), born blind and naked. Their eyes open at

10-12 days at which time they begin to eat solid food (Bashenina, 1981) that is carried to the nest by the mother (Mironov, 1977).

Young females can attain sexual maturity at 1 month (Buchalczyk, 1970) or earlier (Bujalska et al., 1968). Males can attain sexual maturity at 2 months (Buchalczyk, 1970). However, the actual age of maturation depends on the number of mature individuals in the surrounding habitat (see below).

Bank voles move along a path system. The home ranges of males are marked by urine and secretions of the preputial gland. Urinary marking appears to maintain a dominance hierarchy among males (Viitala and Hoffmeyer, 1985). The signal system among females has not been evaluated as yet, however, one is expected to exist.

SOCIAL STRUCTURE

Home ranges of immature individuals are smaller than those of sexually mature ones. Average home ranges of immature females (737 m^2) and immature males (832 m^2) are the smallest, whereas those of mature females are slightly larger (897 m^2) and those of mature males (1,753 m^2) are the largest (Bujalska and Grüm, 1989). For mature males home range size decreases with increasing population density (Bujalska and Grüm, 1989). Home range size in all bank voles seems to vary in relation to food conditions (Bondrup-Nielsen and Karlsson, 1985; Bujalska, 1975a; Mazurkiewicz, 1983; Nikitina and Merkova, 1963).

The spatial distribution of immature bank voles is usually random or clumped (Bujalska and Grüm, 1989). Mature females are distributed either evenly (especially at low population density) or randomly, whereas mature males exhibit either a highly clumped (mostly at low population density) or random pattern (Bujalska and Grüm, 1989; Fig. 1). The degree of home range overlap seems to be high in immature bank voles and among mature males, but is low among mature females. Mature females need an exclusive space for breeding and defend these territories against intruders (Bujalska, 1985b; Kalela, 1957; Viitala, 1977). Therefore females will not mature unless they occupy an exclusive territory (Bujalska, 1970; Koshkina, 1965; Naumov, 1948; Saitoh, 1981; Tanaka, 1953). Intrusion onto the breeding territory by other mature females may inhibit reproduction by the territory holder. In females suppressed by intruders a phenomenon of anestrus in the breeding season, resembling winter anestrus, is observed, and such females can regain reproductive condition when the intruders depart (Bujalska, 1970, 1985b).

Newly weaned females seem to establish home ranges between those of reproductive females (Mironov and Bieltiukova, 1976; Bujalska, 1985b). When a breeding female dies, an adjacent immature female may occupy her place and attain maturity. Such a "sit and wait" strategy (Bujalska, 1988) does not seem to be the only way to find a free breeding territory. Mazurkiewicz and Rajska (1975) found that juvenile bank voles dispersed from their nests to establish breeding ranges on average (±*SE*) 62.7 ± 5.4 m (males) or 48.6 ± 4.7 m (females) away.

Home ranges of mature males encompass home ranges of a few mature females (Bujalska and Grüm, 1989). Mature males form "clans" (Brown, 1966; Kalela, 1957) of mutually tolerant males (Kalela, 1957) with overlapping home ranges. However, the members of different clans are mutually intolerant (Bujalska and Grüm, 1989; Wiger, 1982). Immature males seem to behave in a manner similar to the sit and wait strategy of immature females. Bujalska and Grüm (1989) postulated that maturation of males requires the presence of reproductive females within their range. A number of mature females and the overlapping clan of males constitute a "breeding colony" (Kalela, 1957).

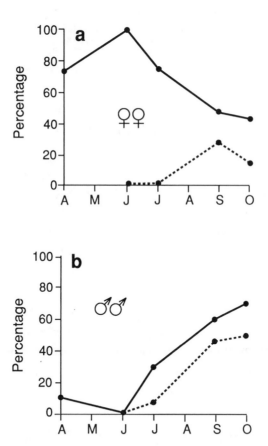

Fig. 1.—Seasonal changes in patterns of spatial distribution, as shown by percentage of uniform distributions among all of the distributions (one value for each trapping series) in the population of Crabapple Island in 1975-1988. Solid lines denotes mature, and dashed lines immature, individuals. Months are abbreviated on the abscissa. The sample size is 14 throughout except: June, immature females, *n* = 5; October, immature females, *n* = 13; June, immature males, *n* = 10.

The social structure changes in winter (Bujalska, 1973; Bujalska and Grüm, 1989; Petrov et al., 1978; Viitala,1977). After the end of the breeding season mature females (being in anestrus) as well as immature ones are distributed at random. In winter, voles aggregate and share nests, which lowers the energetic cost of thermoregulation (Gębczyński, 1975; Karlsson and Ås, 1987). However, when winter breeding occurs the aggregations are not stable; females move to home ranges in the aggregation or in its close vicinity, and home ranges of males expand (Kalela, 1957; Ylönen and Viitala, 1985). Winter home ranges vary from 307 to 492 m^2 in males and from 260 to 475 m^2 in females (Petrov et al., 1978), and are smaller than reported for the breeding season.

A consequence of a social system consisting of breeding colonies is that social relations occur only between closest neighbors. Thus, the effects of interactions within a breeding colony cannot be extrapolated to other breeding colonies, nor can interactions between two neighboring individuals be considered representative of more distant animals (Bujalska and Grüm, 1989). Therefore, the population can be seen as a system of relatively independent, self-sustained breeding colonies.

SOME IMPLICATIONS OF THE SOCIAL SYSTEM IN THE BANK VOLE

The social system in the bank vole limits the numbers of reproductive individuals (Bondrup-Nielsen and Ims, 1986; Bujalska, 1970; 1985a; 1985b; Bujalska and Grüm, 1989; Kalela, 1957; Koshkina, 1965; Saitoh, 1981). On Crabapple Island (4 ha), the number of mature females varies from 30 to 90 (June-October), and that of mature males from 25 to 70, whereas the total population size changes from 100 to over 500 individuals (Fig. 2). Hence, there can be as many as 200 females and 220 males that are capable of replacing mature individuals upon their deaths (Bujalska, 1988).

At the beginning of the breeding season (mid April) the population on Crabapple Island consists of several to 130 overwintered voles (Fig. 2), all able to reproduce. As the breeding season progresses the social structure becomes more complex; progeny of overwintered, and later the current year, voles enter the population (Fig. 2). Newly matured voles either join established breeding colonies or form new ones. New breeding colonies are smaller—up to four females and three males (Bujalska and Grüm, 1989)—and as a result the pattern of spatial distribution of mature males slowly changes from clumped to random. At places of high density of females, mature females lose their ability to reproduce, and immature females cannot find vacant areas in which to establish breeding territories (Bujalska, 1985b). As a consequence, the number of females able to reproduce decreases with increasing density and the pattern of spatial distribution of mature females slowly shifts from uniform to random (Bujalska and Grüm, 1989).

Voles born in the spring are capable of reproduction in the year of their birth whereas those born in the autumn usually are not (Schwarz et al., 1963). However, the experimental removal of most females belonging to the spring generation resulted in substantial reproduction by females of the autumn generation (Bujalska, 1973). Thus, reproduction by the autumn generation appears to be suppressed by the spring generation.

Other differences between spring and autumn generations, such as a more rapid gain in body weight by individuals in the spring generation, can be explained by the fact that mature individuals gain weight more quickly than immatures of the same age (Bujalska, 1988; Bujalska and Gliwicz, 1972). In addition, the lower survival rates of members of the spring generation appear to be due to higher mortality rates experienced by mature, as opposed to immature, bank voles (Bujalska, 1975b; 1985a; Bujalska and Grüm, 1989). Dispersal rates in unconfined populations are probably associated with searching for a place in which it is possible to attain maturity and breed, because dispersers are mostly immature individuals (Bondrup-Nielsen and Karlsson, 1985).

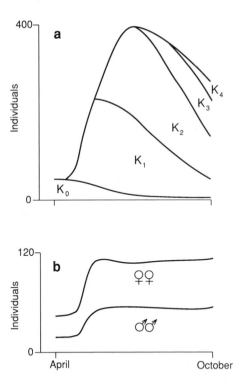

Fig. 2.—Generalized pattern of seasonal changes in some aspects of population structure of bank voles inhabiting Crabapple Island. (A) Age structure (individuals of each cohort differ in their age by 6 weeks). $K_1 + K_2$ are the spring generation, and $K_3 + K_4$ are the autumn generation. (B) Abundance of mature fraction of bank voles.

Breeding colonies established at the beginning of the breeding season consist only of overwintered individuals and tend to occupy the most favorable sites. Those established later in the breeding season may be mostly composed of the current-year animals forced to settle in unoccupied places (Bondrup-Nielsen, 1985). Hence, the breeding colonies may differ in their age composition and colony size, as well as in quality of surrounding habitat.

Clan territoriality in mature males and limited home range overlap in mature females contribute to relative isolation of breeding colonies; the members of a colony may encounter only the individuals from the neighboring colonies. Thus, dominance hierarchies within colonies may not extend between them (Shilov, 1976; Viitala, 1977). The dominant bank voles are, supposedly, the holders of large home ranges (Andrzejewski et al., 1967; Korn, 1986; Viitala, 1977).

Dominant individuals achieve higher fitness than subordinates. Longevity of mature bank voles may be used as an indirect index of their reproductive success (the longer a mature individual lives the higher can be the number of its progeny). Studies on *Microtus pennsylvanicus* (Ostfeld et al., 1988) provided evidence that successful females had smaller home ranges than did unsuccessful ones. In addition, Sheridan and Tamarin (1988) showed interrelations between breeding success of females of that species and their survival, body weight, and spatial mobility. Therefore, interrelations between home range size and breeding success as well as other population correlates in the bank vole should be expected.

To examine this expectation, I analyzed correlates of home range size, survival rate, body weight and behavior of bank voles. The data from the population on Crabapple Island sampled in 1975-1988 were used. Each year I conducted five trapping series each lasting 7 days (14 trap inspections), starting in mid April and continued at 6-week intervals. Live traps forming a grid (15 m between rows and columns) were distributed over the entire island and were inspected twice daily. The animals were marked individually, and released after processing. The details of the sampling procedure can be found in Bujalska (1985a). For all the individuals caught at least five times in a trapping series the following data were taken: reproductive condition of females (stage of estrous cycle or pregnancy—assessed from vaginal smears taken from females with perforate vaginas) and of males (position of testes); body weight; number of trap sites visited; the maximum distance (range) between visited trap sites; frequency of visits to traps (the inverse of the mean interval between the consecutive captures of the individual); and whether a given individual survived to the next trapping series.

For all sex and age categories there was a significant positive correlation between the mean values of the maximum range and the number of different trap sites visited (Table 1). Hence, the maximum range is a good index of the size of home range estimated by the method of Wierzbowska (1972) Maximum range and frequency of visits to trap sites are not significantly correlated in any of the age or sex categories of bank voles. Maximum range and body weight are correlated significantly only for

Table 1.—Correlation coefficients between the estimates of the mean value of maximal range in a trapping series and of the mean number of different trap sites visited by individuals bank voles in five consecutive captures in the same series on Crabapple Island, Poland.

Category	Trapping series (n)	Correlation coefficient	P
Immature females	16	0.68	<0.01
Immature males	25	0.80	<0.001
Mature females	46	0.81	<0.001
Mature males	46	0.83	<0.001

mature males ($r = +0.335$, $n = 46$, $P < 0.05$). Mature males that survived from one trapping series to the next had significantly shorter maximum ranges (estimated in the first of the series) than those that died (Table 2).

Mating strategies of males should be influenced by timing of estrus in mature females (Eisenberg, 1981; Kawata, 1985; McShea, 1989). In 80% of the trapping series analyzed (40 of 50), the onset of estrus among individual females was indistinguishable from a uniform distribution. When females enter

Table 2.—Mean values of maximal range (m) for individual bank voles on Crabapple Island, Poland, that survived the 6-week intervals between consecutive trapping series and those that did not.

Category	Survived			Died			Wilcoxon test P
	n	$\bar{X}$	95% confidence limits	n	$\bar{X}$	95% confidence limits	
Immature females	584	26.8	25.1–28.4	103	26.1	22.6–29.6	>0.05
Immature males	894	28.8	27.2–30.5	186	29.8	26.2–33.4	>0.05
Mature females	1,249	31.7	30.4–33.1	412	30.5	28.7–32.2	<0.05
Mature males	873	53.8	51.1–55.9	374	64.1	60.2–67.9	<0.0005

estrus asynchronously, males with larger home ranges may have access to more receptive females than males with smaller home ranges. However, a large home range may result in a lower probability of surviving. Therefore, males with large and small home ranges may attain similar breeding success. Whether variation of the home range size is genetically controlled or depends mostly on social factors, is a question open for further discussion. According to Bujalska and Grüm (1989), home range size of mature males decreases over the course of the breeding season because of clan territoriality.

Mature females with larger home ranges seem to survive better than those having smaller home ranges (Table 2). However, it is doubtful that their breeding success is higher, because they are more likely to overlap with daughters that remain on the territory and suppress their mother's breeding capacity.

Apart from the influence of the social system on reproduction, there is a strong impact of it on survival. Immature bank voles survive on the average better than mature ones in the breeding season (Table 3). During the breeding season the survival of mature females seems to depend essentially on the intensity of their mutual encounters (Bujalska and Grüm, 1989), and that of mature males on both the intensity of encounters between males of different clans and on the size of their home ranges (Bujalska and Grüm, 1989). As a consequence, survival of bank voles does not seem to depend on their age: bank voles aged 4 months survived equally well as those aged 8 months, 89.2% and 86.7% per 6 weeks, respectively. Nor does survival seem to depend on their previous participation in reproduction (Petrusewicz et al., 1971). Winter survival of immature and mature females is not different, but it is higher in mature than immature males, the reverse of the situation in the breeding season (Table 3).

Table 3.—Percent of bank voles surviving 6-week periods between trapping series in 1975-1988, Crabapple Island, Poland. Probabilities of the one-tailed, signed-rank, Wilcoxon matched-pairs test are shown.

Period and sex	Mature	Immature	P
Breeding season:			
Females	66.8	72.0	<0.02
Males	60.8	71.2	<0.02
Winter:			
Females	67.1	72.0	>0.05
Males	74.2	68.7	<0.02

CONCLUSIONS

The basic social unit in the bank vole is the breeding colony, which consists of a group of a few mature females with partly overlapping home ranges and separate breeding territories, and a group of mutually tolerant mature males whose home ranges overlap those of the females. This unit has developed mechanisms of limitation of reproduction. A population can be regarded as a system of breeding colonies. Since the social system of bank voles contradicts many of the basic assumptions of the logistic equation, new, formal approaches to evaluate population dynamics of the bank vole are badly needed (Stenseth, 1985).

The social system of bank voles seems to allow breeding success by both dominant and subordinate males (higher mortality rates of dominants than of subordinates) as well as by more- and less-productive females (females that reproduce more rapidly can loose their ability to reproduce due to suppression by their daughters).

ACKNOWLEDGMENTS

I wish to thank K. Banach, D. Mieszkowska, and H. Plewka, for their help in data sampling. My husband, Leszek Grüm, helped me in data analysis and discussed the results. R. H. Tamarin suggested the topic of this paper to me, and R. S. Ostfeld contributed much, with his critical remarks, to its present shape. Also S. Bondrup-Nielsen, L. Hansson, and two anonymous reviewers helped me much with their criticism. In 1988, when I was preparing data analysis for this paper, W. Grodzinski died. I would like to commemorate his influence on me with this paper.

LITERATURE CITED

Andrzejewski, R., K. Petrusewicz, and J. Waszkiewicz-Gliwicz. 1967. The trappability of *Clethrionomys glareolus* (Schreber, 1780) and other ecological parameters obtained by the CMR capture method. Ekologia Polska A, 15:709-725.

Bashenina, N. V. 1981. Ontogenez. Pp. 211-226, *in* Evropejskaja ryžaja polevka (N. V. Bashenina, ed.). Nauka, Moskva, 351 pp.

Bondrup-Nielsen, S. 1985. An evaluation of the effects of space use and habitat patterns on dispersal in small mammals. Annales Zoologici Fennici, 22:373-383.

Bondrup-Nielsen, S., and R. A. Ims. 1986. Reproduction and spacing behavior of females in a peak density population of *Clethrionomys glareolus*. Holarctic Ecology, 9:109-112.

Bondrup-Nielsen, S., and F. Karlsson. 1985. Movements and spatial patterns in populations of

Clethrionomys species: a review. Annales Zoologici Fennici, 22:385-392.

Brown, L. E. 1966. Home range and movement of small mammals. Symposia of the Zoological Society of London, 18:111-142.

Buchalczyk, A. 1970. Reproduction, mortality and longevity of the bank vole under laboratory conditions. Acta Theriologica, 15:153-176.

Bujalska, G. 1970. Reproduction stabilizing elements in an island population of *Clethrionomys glareolus* (Schreber, 1780). Acta Theriologica, 15:381-413.

––––. 1973. The role of spacing behaviour among females in the regulation of the reproduction in the bank vole. Journal of Reproduction and Fertility, Supplement, 19:463-472.

––––. 1975a. The effect of supplementary food on some parameters in an island population of *Clethrionomys glareolus* (Schreber, 1780). Bulletin de l'Academie Polonaise des Sciences, Serie des Sciences Biologiques, 23:23-28.

––––. 1975b. Reproduction and mortality of bank voles and the changes in the size of an island population. Acta Theriologica, 20:41-56.

––––. 1983. Reproduction. Pp. 148-161, *in* Ecology of the bank vole (K. Petrusewicz, ed.). Acta Theriologica, 28 (Supplement 1):1-242.

––––. 1985a. Fluctuations in an island bank vole population in the light of the study on its organization. Acta Theriologica, 30:3-49.

––––. 1985b. Regulation of female maturation in *Clethrionomys* species, with special reference to an island population of *C. glareolus.* Annales Zoologici Fennici, 22:331-342.

––––. 1988. Life history consequences of territoriality in the bank vole. Pp. 75-90, *in* Evolution of life histories: theories and patterns from mammals (M. S. Boyce, ed.). Yale University Press, New Haven, 373 pp.

Bujalska, G., and J. Gliwicz. 1972. Growth and reproduction of female bank voles under field conditions. Acta Theriologica, 17:33-40.

Bujalska, G., and L. Grüm. 1989. Social organization of the bank vole *(Clethrionomys glareolus,* Schreber 1780) and its demographic consequences: a model. Oecologia (Berlin), 80:70-81.

Bujalska, G., and L. Ryszkowski. 1966. Estimation of the reproduction of the bank vole under field conditions. Acta Theriologica, 11:351-361.

Bujalska, G., R. Andrzejewski, and K. Petrusewicz. 1968. Productivity investigation of an island population of *Clethrionomys glareolus* (Schreber, 1780). II. Natality. Acta Theriologica, 13:415-425.

Eisenberg, J. F. 1981. The mammalian radiations. University of Chicago Press, Illinois, 610 pp.

Gębczyńska, Z. 1983. Feeding habits. Pp. 40-48, *in* Ecology of the bank vole (K. Petrusewicz, ed.). Acta Theriologica, 28 (Supplement 1):1-242.

Gębczyński, M. 1975. Heat economy and the energy cost of growth in the bank vole during the first month of postnatal life. Acta Theriologica, 20:379-434.

Hansson, L. 1985. Geographic differences in bank voles *Clethrionomys glareolus* in relation to ecogeographical rules and possible demographic and nutritive strategies. Annales Zoologici Fennici, 22:319-328.

Kalela, O. 1957. Regulation of reproduction rate in subarctic populations of the vole *Clethrionomys rufocanus* (Sund.). Annales Academiae Scienciarum Fennicae, Serie A IV Biologica, 34:1-60.

Karlsson, A. F., and S. Ås. 1987. The use of winter home ranges in a low density *Clethrionomys glareolus* population. Oikos, 50:213-217.

Kawata, M. 1985. Mating system and reproductive success in a spring population of the red-backed vole, *Clethrionomys rufocanus bedfordiae*. Oikos, 45:181-190.

Korn, H. 1986. Changes in home range size during growth and maturation of the wood mouse *(Apodemus sylvaticus)* and the bank vole *(Clethrionomys glareolus)*. Oecologia (Berlin), 68:623-628.

Koshkina, T. V. 1965. Plotnost' populacii i eyo znachenye v regulacii chislennosti krasnoy polevky. Bulletin Moskovskogo Obshchestva Ispytateley Prirody, 70:3-65.

Larina, N. J., and T. V. Golikova. 1960. Izuchenye polovogo cikla samok lesnykh myshevidnykh gryzunov v prirode. Fauna i Ekologia Gryzunov, 6:96-110.

Mazurkiewicz, M. 1983. Spatial organization of the population. Pp. 117-127, *in* Ecology of the bank vole (K. Petrusewicz, ed.). Acta Theriologica, 28 (Supplement 1):1-242.

Mazurkiewicz, M., and E. Rajska. 1975. Dispersion of young bank voles from their place of birth. Acta Theriologica, 20:71-81.

McShea, W. J. 1989. Reproductive synchrony and home range size in a territorial microtine. Oikos, 56:182-186.

Mironov, A. D. 1977. Viesennye zapasanie korma ryzhey polevki. Vestnik Leningradskogo Universiteta, 9:19-23.

Mironov, A. D., and O. P. Bieltiukova. 1976. Stanovlenye territorialnykh otnosheniy i kormovogo povedenya u mlodykh osobiey ryzhey polevki. Pp. 255-257, *in* Gruppovoe povedenye zhivotnykh. Doklady II Vsesoyuznoy Konferencii po povedenyu zhivotnykh. Nauka, Moskva, 451 pp.

Naumov, N. P. 1948. Očerki sravnitelnoj ekologii myševidnych gryzunov. AN SSSR, Moskva, 202 pp.

Nikitina, N. A., and M. A. Merkova. 1963. Ispolzovanie territorii myšami i polevkami po dannym mečenija. Bulletin Moskovskogo Obshchestva Ispytateley Prirody, Otdel Biologiceskij, 48:15-21.

Ostfeld, R. S., S. R. Pugh, J. O. Seamon, and R. H. Tamarin. 1988. Space use and reproductive success in a population of meadow voles. Journal of Animal Ecology, 57:385-394.

Petrov, O. V., and A. D. Mironov. 1972. Peredvizhenye ryzhey polevki v predelakh individualnogo uchastka. Ekologija, 1:101-103.

Petrov, O. V., Le Vou-Khoy, and A. D. Mirinov. 1978. O zimney podvizhnosti ryzhey polevki v lesostepnykh dubravakh. Bulletin Moskovskogo Obshchestva Ispytateley Prirody, Otdel Biologiceskij, 83:36-44.

Petrusewicz, K., G. Bujalska, R. Andrzejewski, and J. Gliwicz. 1971. Productivity processes in an island population of *Clethrionomys glareolus*. Annales Zoologici Fennici, 8:127-132.

Popov, V. A. 1960. Mlekopitayushchye Volzhsko-Kamskogo Kraya. AN SSSR, Kazanski Filyal, 1:1-467.

Pucek, M. 1983. Habitat preference. Pp. 31-40, *in* Ecology of the bank vole (K. Petrusewicz, ed.). Acta Theriologica, 28 (Supplement 1):1-242.

Raczyński, J. 1983. Taxonomic position, geographical range and the ecology of distribution. Pp. 3-10, *in* Ecology of the bank vole (K. Petrusewicz, ed.). Acta Theriologica, 28 (Supplement 1):1-242.

Saitoh, T. 1981. Control of female maturation in high density populations of the red-backed vole, *Clethrionomys rufocanus bedfordiae*. Journal of Animal Ecology, 50:79-87.

Schwarz, S. S., A. V. Pokrovski, V. G. Istschenko, V. G. Olenjev, N. A. Ovtchinnikova, and O. A. Pjastolova. 1963. Biological peculiarities of seasonal generations of rodents, with special reference to the problem of senescence in mammals. Acta Theriologica, 8:11-43.

Sheridan, M., and R. H. Tamarin. 1988. Space use, longevity, and reproductive success in meadow voles. Behavioral Ecology and Sociobiology, 22:85-90.

Shilov, J. A. 1976. Ekologo-fizyologicheskie osnovy populacyonnykh otnosheni u zhivotnykh. Moskovskogo Universiteta, Moskva, 261 pp.

Stenseth, N. C. 1985. Models of bank vole and wood mouse populations. Pp. 339-376, *in* The ecology of woodland rodents, bank voles and wood mice (J. R. Flowerdew, J. Gurnell, and J. W. H. Gipps, eds.). Zoological Society Symposia London, 55:1-418.

Tanaka, R. 1953. Home ranges and territories in a *Clethrionomys* population on a peat-bog grassland in Hokkaido. Bulletin, Kochi Woman's College, 2:10-120.

Viitala, J. 1977. Social organization in cyclic subarctic populations of the voles *Clethrionomys rufocanus* (Sund.) and *Microtus agrestis* (L.). Annales Zoologici Fennici, 14:53-93

Viitala, J., and I. Hoffmeyer. 1985. Social organization in *Clethrionomys* compared with *Microtus* and *Apodemus*. Social odours, chemistry and biological effects. Annales Zoologici Fennici, 22:359-371.

Wierzbowska, T. 1972. Statistical estimation of home range size of small rodents. Ekologia Polska, Series A, 20:781-831.

Wiger, R. 1982. Roles of self regulatory mechanisms in cyclic populations of *Clethrionomys*, with special reference to *C. glareolus:* a hypothesis. Oikos, 38:60-71.

Ylönen, H., and J. Viitala. 1985. Social organization of an enclosed winter population of the bank vole *Clethrionomys glareolus*. Annales Zoologici Fennici, 22:353-358.

Zejda, J. 1966. Litter size in Clethrionomys glareolus (Schreber, 1780). Zoologické Listy, 15:193-206.

Social Systems and
Population Cycles in Voles
Advances in Life Sciences
© Birkhäuser Verlag Basel

HABITAT-DEPENDENT REPRODUCTIVE SUCCESS
IN BANK VOLES

J. Gliwicz

Agricultural University of Warsaw, Department of Wildlife Management, Warsaw, Poland.

Summary.—Reproductive performance of *Clethrionomys glareolus* in optimal and suboptimal habitats was investigated. Female reproductive success was estimated for one breeding season based on numbers of pregnancies. Reproductive opportunity in males was estimated based on inter- and intrasexual spatial patterns of males at the time of conception of pregnancies of females. Reproductive success of overwintered voles of both sexes was higher than that of young of the year. Reproductive success of young of the year was equal in optimal and suboptimal habitats. Thus, since winter mortality is high and chances to mature in the year of birth in densely populated optimal habitat are low, successful emigration to suboptimal habitats is a viable alternative for young *C. glareolus*.

INTRODUCTION

In small rodents reproduction is related to home range acquisition by mature males and females (Bujalska, 1973; Gipps, 1985a). When available space becomes limiting at higher population densities, individuals inferior in competition for space (mostly young of the year) are either reproductively suppressed or forced to disperse. Different strategies may be favored by natural selection in individual male and female voles who can: stay in the high-density population waiting for a home-range vacancy; postpone breeding in the year of birth, save energy to survive the winter, and acquire a breeding home range in a low-density spring population; or disperse, settle in less populated, usually suboptimal habitat, and start breeding without delay. These strategy options lend understanding of dispersal (Lidicker, 1975; Stenseth, 1983), of forces driving population cycles (Krebs and Myers, 1974), and of breeding strategies in small mammals (Fleming, 1979; Łomnicki, 1978; Stenseth et al., 1985).

One way to address these issues is to compare the reproductive success of old and young adults in optimal and suboptimal habitats. The secretive life of small rodents makes this evaluation very difficult under natural conditions, especially in the case of males. Although an electrophoresis technique has been successfully applied to determine the paternity in rodents (Ostfeld et al., 1988; Sheridan and Tamarin, 1988; Sikorski, 1990), and new DNA methods have been recently developed (Burke, 1989), most data on small rodents are gathered by livetrapping, which can only give indirect estimations of reproductive success.

In the bank vole *(Clethrionomys glareolus)*, mature females hold exclusive breeding territories (Bondrup-Nielsen, 1985; Bujalska, 1970), and males have individual home ranges that overlap one to several territories of females (Gipps, 1985b; Wolton and Flowerdew, 1985). It is assumed that male microtine rodents mate with those females whose territories are located within their home ranges (Gaulin and FitzGerald, 1988; Sikorski, 1990; Wolff, 1985). Such spatial organization allows us to estimate the reproductive success (or rather "the reproductive opportunity") of an individual male, based on an analysis of spatial relationships among males and between males and females, if the reproductive success of the female is known.

Reproductive success of females and reproductive opportunity of males were estimated in this study by analyzing spatial behavior in three different types of habitats: high quality insular habitat, from which voles could not disperse; high quality forest habitat (donor), from which many young voles emigrated during the breeding season; and small, suboptimal patches of woods, which provided recipient habitat for young dispersers (Gliwicz, 1989).

The method used here for estimating the breeding success of individual voles is not precise, and the absolute values given here should be treated with caution. Yet, this is the first attempt to examine reproductive performance of individuals across different habitats. It can be done effectively using this technique as long as relative values are comparable.

MATERIAL AND METHODS

Study areas.—This study was conducted in northeastern Poland near Suwalki (54°10'N, 22°55'E) from April 1984 to October 1986 (Gliwicz, 1989). All three study areas lie within 3 km of each other. Turtul Island (0.5 ha), is situated on a small lake. It is covered with forest habitat and is highly suitable for bank voles during the entire year. Population density in this habitat is the highest of the three areas studied (mean of 46 bank voles/ha). The second area, the "forest" plot (0.7 ha), is located within a large alder *(Alnus* sp.) forest. Its habitat is rich and offers high quality living conditions for bank voles regardless of season. Density in this habitat averaged 33 bank voles/ha. The third area (0.7 ha) was situated in a much poorer habitat. It consisted of two small patches of woods surrounded by pasture, and offered good living conditions to bank vole immigrants only in the middle of the breeding season. Density in this habitat averaged 20 bank voles/ha.

The two most relevant differences between the three habitats were: the degree of openness of each area to dispersal—the two mainland sites were open to dispersal whereas the island was not—and the preferences shown by overwintered voles settling for the new breeding season. In spring the forest habitat was densely populated whereas the patches of woods were nearly empty. Later in the season, the patches became more densely populated by young immigrants from other habitats (including the forest habitat). Due to the above characteristics the studied areas were treated as: optimal insular habitat (Turtul Island), optimal donor habitat (the forest plot), and suboptimal recipient habitat (the patches of woods).

Field methods.—All data were collected by livetrapping in 15 by 15 m grids. Trapping was conducted four times each year (three in 1985) between late April and the beginning of October. Six- to ten-day trapping sessions were separated by 6-7 weeks. Males with scrotal testes and females with perforated vaginae were considered mature. Vaginal smears were taken from all mature females at each capture to identify stages of estrus and early pregnancy (Bujalska, 1970). Additionally, all signs of pregnancy, parturition, lactation, and presence of vaginal plugs were recorded. High probability of capture of mature females (Gliwicz, in press), synchrony of pregnancies of overwintered females in the first months of the breeding season (Sikorski, 1990), recognition of early pregnancies by vaginal smears, and long lasting signs of lactation assured that all pregnancies of resident females were detected.

Determination of reproductive success.—Reproductive success of female voles was measured as the number of pregnancies per season. For males reproductive opportunity was estimated according to a male's access to receptive females based on inter- and intrasexual spatial patterns at the time before pregnancies by females. Home range size and location of mature males and females were assessed by the exclusive boundary strip method (Stickel, 1954). This assessment was made for each trapping period separately. Overlap of the home ranges of males and females assessed for two consecutive trapping sessions were compared. The shifts in home ranges between two consecutive sessions were usually very small. Because of the spatial stability it was possible to identify the males whose home ranges overlapped the territory of each mature female between trapping sessions.

When estimating the reproductive opportunity of males, I assumed that if the territory of a female was visited by several males at the estimated time of her conception, each of them sired an equal proportion of the litter. Although this assumption may be biologically questionable, it seems to be mathematically justified, as it defines a male's opportunity to become a father according to the location of its home range relative to the location of female territories and the home ranges of other males. Reproductive opportunity of males was estimated as the sum of pregnancies of a female (i) whose territories were overlapped by the home range of the male in a period before her pregnancy (F_i), divided by the number of home ranges of males (N_i) overlapping the territory of that female: $\Sigma(F_i/N_i)$.

RESULTS

Female reproductive success.—The maximum number of pregnancies per female was four in both optimal habitats for overwintered females that survived to the end of the breeding season (Fig. 1). Reproductive success of females was significantly higher in both optimal habitats than in the suboptimal habitat (Table 1). Reproductive success also differed significantly between overwintered females and young of the year in both optimal habitats, and between overwintered females in suboptimal and optimal habitats (Table 1). These differences resulted from significantly shorter times of residency of less successful females (Gliwicz, 1989), not from a lower frequency of pregnancies.

As I found in an earlier study (Gliwicz, 1989), different dispersal behavior and maturation rates in each habitat resulted in a significantly different age composition of mature females. Young mature females in insular habitat were on average significantly older than those in the patches of woods or in the forest habitat. Despite the differences in the age composition of the young females, their reproductive success in all habitats was similar (Table 1).

Although individual reproductive success was estimated for only one breeding season, it is a good approximation of lifetime reproductive success at least for females inhabiting optimal habitats. Only two females reproduced during two breeding seasons, both of which increased their reproductive success by one pregnancy (from two to three). The vast majority (86%) of overwintered females were born late in the previous breeding season and were immature until the spring of the next season. For overwintered, dispersing females settling in the suboptimal habitat the reproductive history before dispersal was unknown.

Table 1.—Reproductive success (number of pregnancies) of female bank voles in three habitats in northeastern Poland, 1984-1986.

Habitat	All			Overwintered			Young of the year		
	n	$\bar{X}$	SD	n	$\bar{X}$	SD	n	$\bar{X}$	SD
Island	13	2.2[a]	1.3	8	2.7[ce]	1.2	5	1.2[c]	0.8
Forest	11	2.2[b]	0.9	6	2.8[df]	0.8	5	1.4[d]	0.6
Patches of woods	20	1.4[ab]	0.6	6	1.5[ef]	0.6	14	1.4	0.7

[a-f]Means with the same superscript letter are significantly different at $P = 0.05$ as determined by Student's t-test.

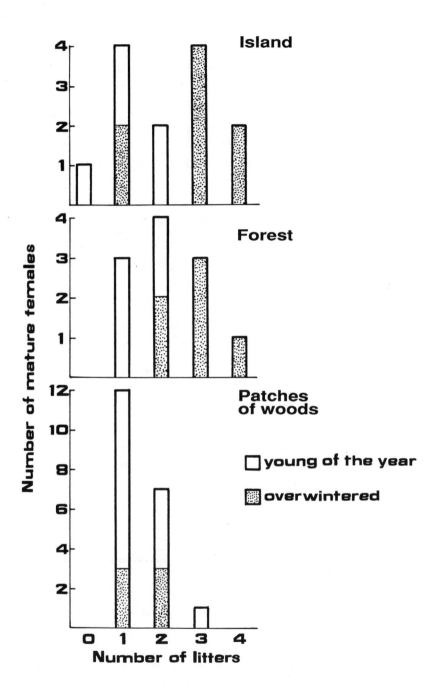

Fig. 1.—Variation in female reproductive success: frequency of pregnancies of overwintered and young bank voles in the three habitats in northeastern Poland, 1984-1986.

Reproductive opportunity of males.—The reproductive opportunity of males ranged from zero to nine litters per breeding season. The highest variance in reproductive opportunity was found on the island and the lowest in the suboptimal habitat (Table 2, Fig. 2). The mean reproductive opportunity differed between habitats and between overwintered and young males, but because of large variation within habitats these differences were not always significant (Table 2). Average reproductive opportunity of males was greatest in the forest and least in the patches of woods (Table 2). The significant difference between these two habitats was due primarily to shorter residency time of males in the suboptimal habitat.

For all males pooled together the reproductive opportunity was correlated with body weight ($r = 0.48$, $P < 0.01$), but the slopes of the regressions were different in the three habitats. The slope of the regression line was greatest in the two optimal habitats and lowest in the suboptimal habitat (Fig. 3). In the latter habitat reproductive opportunity of males was not correlated significantly with body weight (the slope was not significantly different from zero).

For males the reproductive opportunity estimated for one breeding season was equivalent to. lifetime reproductive opportunity; no male was sexually active in two consecutive breeding seasons. However, little is known about the reproductive opportunity of overwintered males before immigrating into the suboptimal habitat.

The average reproductive success of females and reproductive opportunity of males inhabiting the same habitat were similar. However,the variance in the reproductive opportunity of males was greater than the variance in the reproductive success of females in the two optimal habitats ($F = 4.64$, $0.05 > P > 0.02$, and $F = 7.11$, $P < 0.02$, respectively), whereas in the suboptimal habitat the variance in the reproductive opportunity of males was not significantly different than the variance in the reproductive success of females ($F = 2.25$, $0.1 > P > 0.05$).

Table 2.—Reproductive opportunity (average number of litters potentially sired) of male bank voles in three habitats in northeastern Poland, 1984-1986.

Habitat	All			Overwintered			Young of the year		
	n	$\bar{X}$	SD	n	$\bar{X}$	SD	n	$\bar{X}$	SD
Island	12	2.3	2.8	4	5.2[bc]	2.6	8	0.9[c]	1.4
Forest	8	3.0[a]	2.4	5	3.8[d]	1.9	3	1.7	2.9
Patches of woods	17	1.7[a]	0.9	7	2.1[bd]	0.6	10	1.4	0.8

[a-d]Means with the same superscript letter are significantly different at $P = 0.05$ as determined by Student's *t*-test.

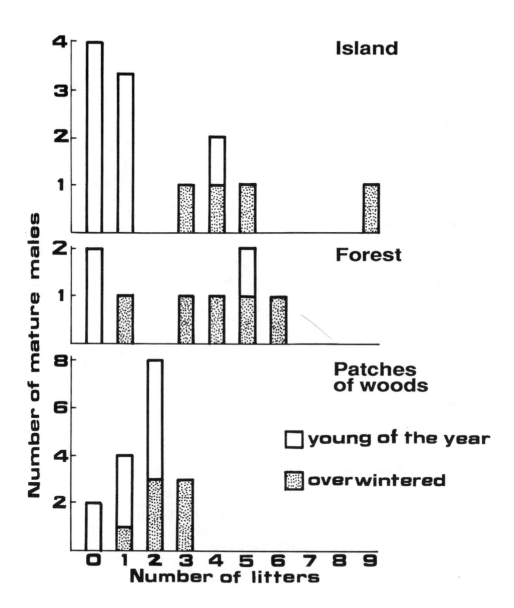

Fig. 2.—Variation in the reproductive opportunity of males: frequency of litters potentially sired by overwintered and young male bank voles in the three habitats in northeastern Poland, 1984-1986, based on their access to females.

176

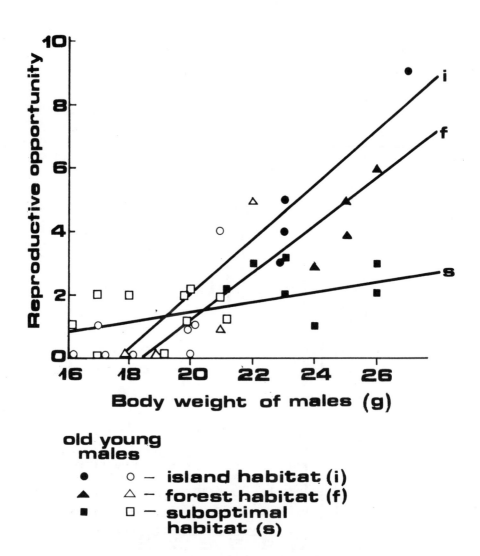

Fig. 3.—Regressions of the reproductive opportunity (Y) on body mass (X) of male bank voles, northeastern Poland, 1984-1986. Island: Y = -13.6 + 0.8X; forest: Y = -12.9 + 0.7X; suboptimal habitat: Y = -1.6 + 0.2X. The slopes of the regressions for the island and forest habitats differ significantly from that of the suboptimal habitat $(F = 4.81$ and 4.56, respectively, $P < 0.05$ for both).

DISCUSSION

Since reproductive success of overwintered males and females seems to be much greater than that of mature young of the year, and since only a few individuals manage to reproduce in two consecutive seasons, the best strategy for bank voles is to try to survive the winter and settle in optimal habitats for the breeding season. For males it is important to survive the winter in a good physical condition because in these habitats male reproductive performance is correlated with body weight.

However, winter survival is low: only 20% of individuals present in the optimal habitat in October managed to survive until April (Gliwicz, 1989). Thus for the majority of voles reproduction in the year of birth is the only chance for leaving any offspring. In optimal habitats crowded with overwintered voles maturation of young is suppressed in comparison with maturation rate in low-density suboptimal habitats. Moreover, the reproductive success of young adults seems to be equal in optimal and suboptimal habitats. Thus, dispersal from natal optimal habitats and settlement in suboptimal ones seems to be a viable option for young of the year. This conclusion may be changed if there are high interhabitat differences in offspring mortality.

The method used here to estimate the individual reproductive performance of males is based on the assumption that there is a relationship between male access to females and characteristics of the male's home range (Gaulin and FitzGerald, 1988; Wolff, 1985). If this assumption is correct, the reproductive opportunity of males estimated here should be closely related to their reproductive success, measured in number of litters sired (although not necessarily in number of offspring alive at maturity—see below). However, Ostfeld et al., (1988) and Sheridan and Tamarin (1988) found no relationship between reproductive success of males (assessed as offspring surviving to trappable age) and either home range size or inter- and intrasexual overlap for *Microtus pennsylvanicus*.

I believe that in the case of rodents the relationship between spatial characteristics of home ranges of males and their breeding success strongly depends on the method used to measure reproductive success. The same is true for the relative value of variances in the reproductive success of males and females. In this study, the variation in reproductive opportunity of males supported the theory of Trivers (1985) that in polygynous species with low paternal investment the variance in the reproductive success of males should be greater than that of females. This hypothesis was corroborated by Clutton-Brock et al. (1982) for the red deer *(Cervus elaphus)* and recently by Sikorski (1990) for the bank vole. It was refuted, however, by results of Sheridan and Tamarin (1988) for the meadow vole. It seems that in the case of animals with large litters (like voles but unlike deer), and great among-litter variation in survival of young to maturation, the relationship between the variances in the reproductive success of males and females is difficult to predict. Greater "primary" variance in reproductive success of males, measured in number of litters sired (or number of copulations) combines randomly with the great variance in litter survival, and produces an "ultimate" variance in reproductive success in males that may happen to be lower than reproductive success in females.

In addition, in the vole species considered here, fathers (unlike mothers) have no influence on survival of young from birth to maturity. Therefore, individual male characteristics, like home range size or body size (Ostfeld et al., 1988; Sheridan and Tamarin, 1988), which can affect male access to receptive females, cannot be assumed to correlate with "ultimate" reproductive success in males, measured in the number of mature offspring recruited, because of the large variance in litter survival independent of the above characteristics.

ACKNOWLEDGMENTS

I am grateful to two anonymous reviewers for helpful comments on the manuscript. The study was supported by a grant from CPBP 04.10.07.

LITERATURE CITED

Bondrup-Nielsen, S. 1985. An evaluation of the effects of space use and habitat patterns on dispersal in small mammals. Annales Zoologici Fennici, 22:373-384.

Bujalska, G. 1970. Reproduction stabilizing elements in an island population of *Clethrionomys glareolus* (Schreber, 1780). Acta Theriologica, 15:381-412.

———. 1973. The role of spacing behaviour among females in the regulation of reproduction in bank voles. Journal of Reproduction and Fertility, 19:465-474.

Burke, T. 1989. DNA fingerprinting and other methods for the study of mating success. Trends in Ecology and Evolution, 4:139-144.

Clutton-Brock, T. H., F. E. Guinness, and S. D. Albon 1982. Red deer: behaviour and ecology of two sexes. University of Chicago Press, 378 pp.

Fleming, T. H. 1979. Life-history strategies. Pp. 1-61, *in* Ecology of small mammals (D. M. Stoddart, ed.). Chapman and Hall, London, 280 pp.

Gaulin S. J. C., and R. W. FitzGerald. 1988. Home-range size as a predictor of mating systems in *Microtus*. Journal of Mammalogy, 69:311-319.

Gipps, J. H. W. 1985a. Spacing behaviour and male reproductive ecology in voles of the genus *Clethrionomys*. Annales Zoologici Fennici, 22:343-351.

———. 1985b. The behaviour of bank voles. Symposia of the Zoological Society of London, 55:61-87.

Gliwicz, J. 1989. Individuals and populations of the bank vole in optimal, suboptimal and insular habitats. Journal of Animal Ecology, 58:237-247.

————. In press. Dispersal in rodents: do females benefit from dispersal of their kin? Journal of Animal Ecology.

Krebs, C. J., and J. H. Myers, 1974. Population cycles in small mammals. Advances in Ecological Research, 8:267-399.

Lidicker, W. Z., Jr. 1975. The role of dispersal in the demography of small mammals. Pp. 103-128, in Small mammals: their productivity and population dynamics (F. B. Golley, K. Petrusewicz, and L. Ryszkowski, eds.). Cambridge University Press, London, 451 pp.

Łomnicki, A. 1978. Individual differences between animals and the natural regulation in their numbers. Journal of Animal Ecology, 47:461-475.

Ostfeld, R. S., S. R. Pugh, J. O. Seamon, and R. H. Tamarin. 1988. Space use and reproductive success in a population of meadow voles. Journal of Animal Ecology, 57:385-394.

Sheridan, M., and R. H. Tamarin. 1988. Space use, longevity and reproductive success in meadow voles. Behavioral Ecology and Sociobiology, 22:85-90.

Sikorski, M. 1990. Mating system and reproductive success in the natural population of the bank vole [in Polish]. Ph.D. dissertation, Jagiellonian University, Cracow, 61 pp.

Stenseth, N. C. 1983. Causes and consequences of dispersal in small mammals. Pp. 63-101, in The ecology of animal movements (I. Swingland and P. Greenwood, eds.). Oxford University Press, 311 pp.

Stenseth, N. C., T. O. Gustafsson, L. Hansson, and K. I. Ugland. 1985. On the evolution of reproductive rates in microtine rodents. Ecology, 66:1795-1808.

Stickel, L. F., 1954. A comparison of certain methods of measuring home ranges of small mammals. Journal of Mammalogy, 35:1-15.

Trivers, R., 1985. Social evolution. The Benjamin/ Cummings Company, Menlo Park, California, 462 pp.

Wolff, J. O., 1985. Behavior. Pp. 340-372, in Biology of New World Microtus (R. H. Tamarin, ed.). Special Publications, The American Society of Mammalogists, 8:1-893.

Wolton R., and J. R. Flowerdew. 1985. Spatial distribution and movements of wood mice, yellow-necked mice and bank voles. Symposia of the Zoological Society of London, 55:249-275.

SPATIAL AND TEMPORAL ORGANIZATION OF POPULATIONS
OF THE BANK VOLE, *CLETHRIONOMYS GLAREOLUS*

A. D. Mironov

Biological Faculty, Leningrad State University, Leningrad, U.S.S.R.

Summary.—I used visual observational methods to determine the aboveground activity of bank voles *(Clethrionomys glareolus)* in three locations in the European part of the U.S.S.R. One hardwood- and two coniferous-forest sites were studied. Bank voles usually have one nighttime and four to seven daytime activity periods. There are differences in duration of activity and distance traveled depending on sex, age, and physiological condition of the voles. Females average 69 minutes and males 51 minutes per active phase. There was no significant seasonal variation in duration of activity. The home ranges of bank voles are made up of refuges, feeding places, and travel routes. Sizes of home ranges vary seasonally and with reproductive condition of females during the breeding season.

INTRODUCTION

The European bank vole *(Clethrionomys glareolus)* is one of the most abundant and best studied species of small mammals (Bashenina, 1981; Gashev, 1978; Mazurkiewicz, 1969; Petrusewicz, 1983; Stenseth, 1985). For this reason the bank vole can be considered a suitable model for investigating various questions of territorial behavior. The objective of this study is to describe the use of home range by bank voles.

METHODS

Study areas.—Investigations were carried out in three localities in the range of the bank vole in the European part of the U.S.S.R. The first area was in an oak *(Quercus)* forest in the forest steppe zone (49°N, 36°E), the second in a coniferous forest in the subzone of southern taiga (59°N, 36°E), and the third in a coniferous forest in the subzone of northern taiga (65°N, 36°E).

Our principle study site was in a typical oak forest where *Quercus robur, Tilia cordata,* and *Fraxinus excelsior* predominate. The understory consists of *Acer platanoides, Fraxinus excelsior, Padus avium,* and *Euonymus verrucosa.* The herb layer consists of 20-25 species, the most abundant of which are *Aegopodium podagraria, Carex pilosa, Stellaris nemorum,* and *Poa* sp. Oak forests may be considered optimal habitats for bank voles. A rich food base, a variety of protective shelters, and favorable climate promote high density and intensive reproduction of voles.

The second study site was in a coniferous forest typical of the southern taiga. *Picea abies, Betula pubescens,* and *Pinus sylvestris* form the canopy layer. The understory consists of *Picea abies, Betula pubescens, Alnus incana, Sorbus aucuparia, Populus tremula,* and *Frangula alnus.* Large areas are covered by *Vaccinium myrtillus* interspersed with *Vaccinium vitis-idaea.* The herb layer is very sparse and consists mainly of *Agrostis canina, Majanthemum bifolium,* and *Pyrola* sp. In open mossy places, vegetation is more varied. The high water table is conducive to formation of bogs in low spots. A notable feature of the forest is an abundance of fallen tree trunks concealed under a cover of moss.

The third study site is in a coniferous forest typical of islands in the White Sea. The main tree species are *Picea abies* and *Betula pubescens,* whose shoots are surrounded by characteristic hummocks. The dominant species in the herb layer are *Vaccinium myrtillus, Ledum palustre, Carex* sp., and *Empetrum nigrum.*

Behavioral observations.—The main method I used for studying details of the ecology of bank voles was direct visual observation of marked individuals. Similar studies are rare (Gipps, 1981; Kawata, 1987; Mironov, 1979, 1984; Ylönen and Viitala, 1985) mainly because of the large amount of labor required, the small amount of comparative data, and the complexity of the statistical analysis of territorial-behavior data. However, the chance to look into the intimate life of the bank vole in its natural environment makes this technique worthwhile.

The work was carried out from year to year on permanent plots varying in size from 3 to 9 ha. The abundance of rodents on experimental plots as well as the distribution of voles and the general level of density of territorial groups was determined by the capture-mark-recapture technique. Sherman traps baited with either seeds of *Helianthus annuus* or bread were used to capture animals. On the central part of the plot (1 ha), traps were placed at 10-m intervals; on the rest of the plot, at 20-m intervals. We marked animals by toe clipping. Most of our observations were made in spring, but in some years investigations were made in fall and winter. In the oak forest, observations were made from 1970 to 1988 with minor interruptions; in the southern taiga from 1978 to 1981; and in the northern taiga in 1981 and 1982. Altogether, 4,325 voles were captured.

Preliminary visual observations were made in part of the forest with a large area of minimal understory or in early spring before new growth began. Later, we learned to follow movements of voles even in thick grass. We marked animals with a system of symbols produced by shearing patches of hair on both sides of the body. This enabled us to mark up to 200 individuals and distinguish with confidence individual voles at a distance of 20 m in daylight. We observed from a 2-m portable ladder through 8X binoculars. We made >3,000 hours of observations in the oak forest, >500 hours in the southern taiga, and 50 hours in the northern taiga. The daily average was 8 to 10 hours. Times were recorded to the nearest minute. Movements of voles, and location of trails, shelters, and feeding areas were mapped at a scale of 1:100.

Definition of home range.—The idea of a home range, introduced in works by Burt (1943, 1949), Hayne (1949), and Naumov (1948), was developed with a temporal component in later works by Bondrup-Nielsen (1985), Grüm (1988), Khlyap (1983), Myllymäki (1977), and Nikitina (1979). We use the following definition: "Home range is a space, the resources of which (food, shelter, and mates) are used during a definite, biologically significant, interval of time." Temporal intervals may consist of anything from a few hours to a few months. Therefore, it is correct to speak of daily, seasonal, or phasal home range. Application of the temporal component is necessary for defining the stability-of-use of a home range and for solving problems of competitive relationships.

RESULTS AND DISCUSSION

Temporal organization of populations of bank voles.—I studied the circadian activity rhythm of bank voles in natural conditions by observing the times when an animal left, and returned to, a permanent nesting burrow (Flowerdew, 1973; Mironov, 1979, 1984). That interval of time I called the active phase, and time spent in the burrow the resting phase.

Bank voles have a polyphasic activity rhythm with 5-8 periods of activity in the course of a 24-h day (Khlyap et al., 1979; Saint-Girons, 1960, 1961) with day-time activity predominant; the animals have only one active phase during the night. The average length of the active phase is 1-1.5 hours and that of the resting phase is 1.5-2 hours (Table 1). The activity rhythm of adult females, especially during lactation, is most stable. The activity rhythm of adult males is determined frequently by the activity of females, especially during estrus. At that time, a male persistently follows a female, and when she enters a burrow the male remains on the surface near the exit hole and waits for her to emerge. The activity rhythm of juveniles is variable and depends on the size and composition of the

Table 1.—Rhythm of activity (in minutes) of bank voles during phases of activity in European U.S.S.R.

Individuals (n)		Active phase			Resting phase			Both phases		
		n	Range	$\bar{X}$	n	Range	$\bar{X}$	n	Range	$\bar{X}$
Females	24	202	1-226	69	166	11-250	103	136	22-321	170
Males	45	45	1-149	51	35	10-216	66	32	30-245	98

group. At 15-19 days of development young voles are active on the surface only after the beginning of the mother's active period, and with her return, they go back into the burrow. The group activity rhythm is preserved among littermates up to 20-28 days of development.

Great variation in the duration of activity of adult voles (males, 1-149 minutes; females, 1-226 minutes) impedes comparative analysis of activity by sex, age, and population group (Table 1). It would be possible to attribute the differences to external conditions, physiological state, or age. However, we had a unique opportunity to observe individual variability in activity rhythm. Two adult females with litters of almost the same age lived in burrows located within 2 m of each other. Their home ranges had a 70% overlap. We concluded that they lived under nearly identical ecological conditions. Nevertheless, their activity rhythms differed (Table 2). Differences were noted in the timing of the first emergence to the surface following their resting phase. One female emerged at 0420 h on June 6, and at 0407 h on June 9 whereas the other female emerged at 0545 h and 0610 h on the same two days. Subsequent phases of activity gradually came closer together and even coincided.

A large proportion of the time budget of the voles is devoted to feeding behavior (>50% of the active phases). Different components of the population have different peculiarities in their feeding behavior. Females have two peaks of feeding in the course of each active phase; one at the beginning and one at the end. Adult males begin to feed actively just before completion of the active phase. Young animals are occupied in searching for and consuming food for almost the entire active period. Voles spend a significant part of their time visiting different kinds of shelters and burrows in their home range.

During our observations in the field, we did not detect significant seasonal variation in duration of the active phase. Only the frequency and proportion of different kinds of activity varied. For example, we noted that with completion of the breeding season and the onset of cold weather in autumn, up to 70% of the active phase was spent in different kinds of refuges. (The comparable figure for summer was only 8-10%.) The time of absence from the main nest burrow—the length of the active phase—and time spent in burrows after returning—the resting phase—did not differ seasonally.

Table 2.—Rhythm of activity (in minutes) of two female bank voles during phases of activity in European U.S.S.R.

	Active phase			Resting phase			Both phases		
	n	Range	$\bar{X}$	n	Range	$\bar{X}$	n	Range	$\bar{X}$
First female	20	28-185	110	13	89-230	142	13	159-349	252
Second female	19	13-143	78	16	99-229	157	16	126-366	235

We do not have data for other geographical regions.

We can demonstrate only a few peculiarities of the activity rhythms in southern and northern taiga because of limited sample size (e.g., $n = 8$ for adult females). Here, the active phase averages 90-110 minutes and the resting phase, 150 minutes; the period of activity is longer than in the oak forest.

Structure of the home range and its use.—Based on analysis of vole movements and intensity of use of different parts of the territory, we established that the home range of bank voles is made up of a set of jointly used refuges, feeding places, and a system of travel routes (Fig. 1a). At the center of activity is a nest burrow and its immediate surroundings. The voles use holes, depressions, fallen logs, thickets of herbaceous cover, and so forth as refuges and cover. The nest burrow, in which the vole sleeps, has special significance. The vole usually covers its entrance hole with dry leaves both before leaving for an excursion and after returning. This behavior probably provides additional thermal insulation or serves to camouflage the nest burrow.

In the nest burrow adult females bear and suckle their litters. At the termination of lactation, the female expels her young, or more often, she herself abandons the burrow and takes up residence in another burrow in the same home range (Mironov and Beltjukova, 1977). Sometimes a female disperses >20-25 m to a new home range. The moment when lactation ends and the female changes her nest burrow is critical for the stability of the boundaries of a home range. During the breeding season, adult males make irregular use of burrows, but they are never found in a burrow with young.

Voles seek and use food in four or five feeding places in the home range, which are spread out from 4-40 m apart (Mironov, 1979). The feeding places are found in the vicinity of refuges and burrows or as small "patches" in clumps of grasses. Here, the voles search out, gather, and eat food. The uneven distribution of refuges results in a mosaic use of food resources. Feeding places are usually small in area and occupy about 10% of a home range. Feeding places are more strictly localized for females than for males.

The formation of trails is determined by the distribution of burrows and cover. During movement in the home range the animals orient themselves by means of well known shelters (burrows, trees, stumps); each shelter on the route becomes the starting place for the next segment of movement. The way in which trails are constructed is similar in the different forest types (taiga or oak forest). They differ only in more frequent use of subterranean trails in taiga where a large amount of forest litter and a high density of shrubs *(Vaccinium myrtillus* and *V. vitis-idaea)* make rapid surface movement more difficult.

During 10-15 years we observed that animals of different generations followed the same routes. In the zone of contact between two or three home ranges bank voles use trails in common. The principal features of routes are preserved in winter. The system of runways has a more complex structure in the

186

snow cover because the voles use different layers in the snow. According to the amount of fresh snowfall, the rodents construct new passages that frequently lie above older ones (Petrov et al., 1978). Thus, the structure of the home range of bank voles is a mosaic of feeding places, nesting burrows, and temporary burrows that are connected by a network of travel routes (Fig. 1a).

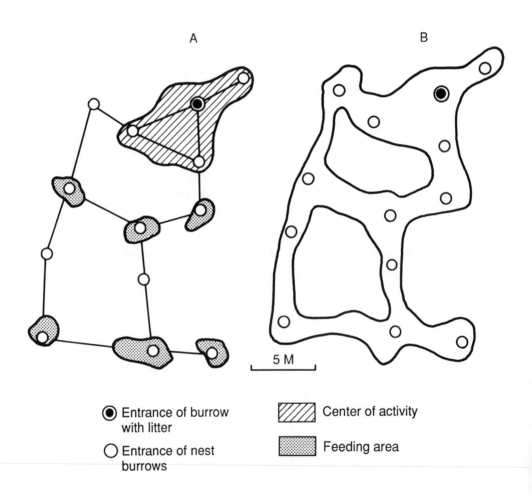

A   B

● Entrance of burrow
  with litter

○ Entrance of nest
  burrows

▨ Center of activity

▦ Feeding area

5 M

Fig. 1.—Spatial structure of bank vole home range. A. Component parts; B. Area actually used.

Size of home range.—In this study based on visual observation, we considered the boundary of a home range to be a line passing along the external margin of feeding places, burrows, and travel routes (Fig. 1b). There is no problem of calculating the size of the home ranges (Andrzejewski and Babinska-Werka, 1986; Calhoun and Casby, 1958; Grüm, 1988; Hayne, 1949; Mazurkiewicz, 1969, 1971; Wierzbowska, 1983). Difficulty arises in determination of the temporal aspect of the stability of the borders. On this question, opinion is not unanimous: different authors have used intervals ranging from "during the whole life" to "the time during which the voles used the indispensable minimum of resources." Analysis of our data indicates that the minimum time segment for characterizing use of territory is the "phase of activity" (Mironov, 1979, 1984). Because of difficulty in clearly distinguishing the phase of activity by application of other methods of field study, the 24-h day could be used for analysis (Nikitina et al., 1977). According to our data, bank voles cover a distance of 100-150 m (range, 10-350 m) during one active phase. The amount of territory used fluctuates and depends on sex, age, and physiological condition. Even among females, the size of the "phasal" home range varies widely from 10 to 500 m^2. For example, one female visited areas of 8-468 m^2 in different activity phases. In April, in 80% of cases, the size of territory used was no greater than 100 m^2 (mean = 35 m^2). In the absence of a litter (May) the area visited by a female in each phase of activity increased (mean = 47 m^2). The area used by an animal in the course of a 24-h day is made up of the nonoverlapping parts of each "phasal area" and a basic nucleus (Fig. 2).

According to our data from the oak forest, the size of the home range of males is small at the beginning of the breeding season (up to 80-100 m^2 in April), which may be explained by the prolonged lactation of the females. In June, the males were more mobile as they searched for estrus females. Their area enlarged up to 3,000 m^2. The range of females varied in size from 33-647 m^2 in April-May, and from 50-1,323 m^2 in June-July. The mean value in April was 147 m^2, and in June it was 387 m^2. In southern and northern taiga males use an area of up to 7,200 m^2 in the breeding season, and females average 900 m^2 (range: 120-1,500 m^2).

CONCLUSIONS

It is believed generally that with range extension to the south there is a regular decrease in the size of area used by an animal (Brown, 1966; Maza et al., 1973; Nikitina and Merkova, 1963). For example, Nikitina (1980) noted that in northern parts of the range of the bank vole the home range area of males was about 3,000 m^2 and that of females was about 2,200 m^2. Geographical differences in home range size, in the opinion of certain authors (Andrzejewski and Mazurkiewicz, 1976; Bujalska and Janion, 1981; Korn, 1986) are caused by the abundance and quality of food. Indeed, if data from a relatively large time interval (more than 1 month) are used for comparison, as was done in the

188

majority of works of this kind, the area of the home range, summed over time, really is larger in northern regions than in southern parts of the range. But that, it seems to me, is related to differences in population density and the quality of refuges in the habitats. Detailed visual observations of territorial behavior of marked individuals showed that "phasal" area, as well as its sum, the "daily" area, used by adult females is practically the same in different forest types (oak and taiga). Of course, food resources are an important ecological factor. Seasonal fluctuations in abundance and quality of food may be considered analogous to geographical differences. Indeed, the size of the territory used decreases sharply in autumn. At that time, reproduction ceases and climatic conditions are significantly changed, both of which have a definite influence on the mobility of rodents, so that it is simplistic to speak of the action of single factors. Distribution and quantity of food determine the way in which a home range is used, rather than the size of the home range. Several authors (Andrzejewski and Babinska-Werka, 1986; Karlsson, 1988; Kutenkov, 1979; Mazurkiewicz, 1981, 1983; Okulova et al., 1971) showed that home range size decreases with an increase in population density. According to our data from southern and northern taiga, population density in June - August reached 10 - 15 individuals/ha, and in the oak forest in the same period it reached 100/ha.

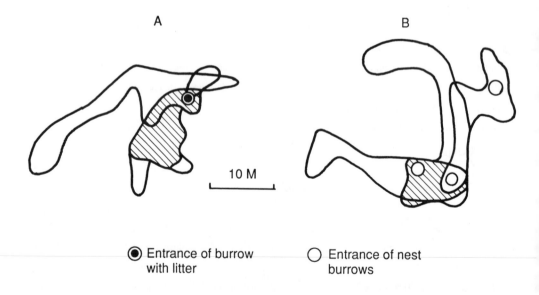

Fig. 2.—Daily home ranges of one female bank vole. A. During lactation (18 April 1974); B. During pregnancy (9 May 1974). Enclosed areas represent different activity phases.

Social behavior can regulate the use of individual home ranges (Bujalska, 1973, 1985; Gipps, 1985; Mironov, 1979; Viitala and Hoffmeyer, 1985). Contacts between individuals at the borders of home ranges and in areas of overlap are reduced by "isolating" forms of behavior, which is expressed by irregular visits to parts of the home range (spatial isolation) and asynchronous use of the territory (temporal isolation). Territorial integrity of home ranges of females is maintained by direct contacts with active defense of the resources of the territory. Adult female bank voles determine the basic social organization of the population (Bujalska, 1973, 1985; Mironov, 1984) at a time when males are a mobile element and immatures constitute a reserve. Investigation of the mechanism of regulation of spatial and temporal relations is possible only as a result of very detailed study of the ecology of individuals—"personal ecology"—by means of direct methods. In this article we wished to demonstrate the feasibility of observing visually individually marked bank voles.

ACKNOWLEDGMENTS

I am very grateful to Dr. William Fuller and Dr. Gabriela Bujalska for valuable help and advice in the preparation of this manuscript. [A very special thanks to Bill Fuller for translating and transcribing the original manuscript from the Russian.—Editors.]

LITERATURE CITED

Andrzejewski, R., and J. Babinska-Werka. 1986. Bank vole populations: are their densities really high and individual home range small? Acta Theriologica, 31:409-422.

Andrzejewski, R., and M. Mazurkiewicz. 1976. Abundance of food supply and size of the bank vole's home range. Acta Theriologica, 21:237-253.

Bashenina, N. V., ed. 1981. Evropejskaja ryžaja polevka. Nauka, Moskva, 351 pp.

Bondrup-Nielsen, S. 1985. An evaluation of the effects of space use and habitat patterns on dispersal in small mammals. Annales Zoologici Fennici, 22:373-383.

Brown, L. E. 1966. Home range and movements of small mammals. Symposia of the Zoological Society of London, 18:111-142.

Bujalska, G. 1973. The role of spacing behaviour among females in the regulation of the reproduction in the bank vole. Journal of Reproduction and Fertility, Supplement, 19:463-472.

———. 1985. Regulation of female maturation in *Clethrionomys* species, with special reference to an island population of *C. glareolus*. Annales Zoologici Fennici, 22:331-342.

Bujalska, G., and S. M. Janion. 1981. Bank vole response to an increase of environmental capacity. Bulletin, Academie Polonaise des Sciences, Serie des Sciences Biologiques, 29:129-133.

Burt, W. H. 1943. Territoriality and home range concepts as applied to mammals. Journal of Mammalogy, 24:346-352.

———. 1949. Territoriality. Journal of Mammalogy, 30:25-27.

Calhoun, J. B. , and J. U. Casby. 1958. Calculation of home range and density of small mammals. United States Public Health Monograph, 55:1-24.

Flowerdew, J. R. 1973. A new method for recording the activity of small mammals in the field. Journal of Zoology, London, 171:449-455.

Gashev, N. S. 1978. Dynamics of population of small rodents with special reference to controlled groups of the common redbacked vole. Ekologiya, 6:55-60.

Gipps, J. H. W. 1981. Behavior of bank voles, Clethrionomys glareolus, in the field. Journal of Mammalogy, 62:382-384.

———. 1985. Spacing behaviour and male reproductive ecology in voles of the genus Clethrionomys. Annales Zoologici Fennici, 22:343-351.

Grüm, L. 1988. On the home range concept and principles of comparability of its aspect estimates. Wiadomości Ekologiczne, 34:61-72.

Hayne, D. W. 1949. Calculation of size of home range. Journal of Mammalogy, 30:1-18.

Karlsson, A. F. 1988. Social organization of a low density spring population of the bank vole, Clethrionomys glareolus. Oikos, 52:19-26.

Kawata, M. 1987. The effect of kinship on spacing among female red-backed voles, Clethrionomys rufocanus bedfordiae. Oecologia (Berlin), 72:115-122.

Khlyap, L. A. 1983. Peculiarities of structure of home ranges and their use by shrews and forest voles. Fauna and Ecology of Rodents, Moskva, 15:162-203.

Khlyap, L. A., et al. 1979. Diurnal activity of the common red-backed vole, Clethrionomys glareolus. Zoologicheskii Zhurnal, 58:97-104.

Korn, H. 1986. Changes in home range size during growth and maturation of the wood mouse (Apodemus sylvaticus) and the bank vole (Clethrionomys glareolus). Oecologia (Berlin), 68:623-628.

Kutenkov, A. P. 1979. Utilization of territory by Clethrionomys glareolus under low population density. Zoologicheskii Zhurnal, 58:234-240.

Maza, B. G., N. R. French, and A. P. Aschwanden. 1973. Home range dynamics in a population of heteromyid rodents. Journal of Mammalogy, 54:405-425.

Mazurkiewicz, M. 1969. Elliptical modification of the home range pattern. Bulletin, Academie Polonaise des Sciences, Serie des Sciences Biologiques, 17:427-431.

———. 1971. Shape, size and distribution of home ranges of Clethrionomys glareolus (Schreber, 1780). Acta Theriologica, 16:23-60.

———. 1981. Spatial organization of a bank vole population in years of small or large numbers.

Acta Theriologica, 26:31-45.

————. 1983. Spatial organization of the population. Pp. 117-127, *in* Ecology of the bank vole (K. Petrusewicz, ed.). Acta Theriologica, 28 (Supplement 1):1-242.

Mironov, A. D. 1979. Spatial behavior of the bank vole. Avtoreferat Dissertation, Leningrad State University, 14 pp.

————. 1984. The use of territory by the bank vole. Animal in ecosystem. Syctyvkar, [1984]:131-141.

Mironov, A. D., and O. P. Beltjukova. 1977. Stanovlenyr territorialnykh otnosheniy i kormovogo povedenya u mlodykh osobiey ryzhey polevki. Pp. 255-257, *in* Gruppovoe povedenye zhivotnykh. Doklady II Vsesoyuznoy Konferencii po povedenyu zhivotnykh. Nauka, Moskva.

Myllymäki, A. 1977. Intraspecific competition and home range dynamics in the field vole, *Microtus agrestis.* Oikos, 29:553-569.

Naumov, N. P. 1948. Očerki sravnitelnoj ekologii myševidnych gryzunov. AN SSSR, Moskva, 202 pp.

Nikitina, N. A. 1979. On the concept of individual range in small mammals. Zoologicheskii Zhurnal, 58:1055-1058.

————. 1980. The Bank Vole. Pp. 189-219, *in* Itogi mechenikila mlekopitakilushchikh (V. V. Kucheruk, ed.). Nauka, Moskva, 289 pp.

Nikitina, N. A., and M. A. Merkova. 1963. Ispolzovanie territorii myšami i polevkami po dannym mečenija. Bulletin Moskovskogo Obshchestva Ispytateley Prirody, Otdel Biologiceskij, 48:15-21.

Nikitina, N. A., et al. 1977. Daily range extent and probable structural characteristics of individual ranges of some rodent species. Zoologicheskii Zhurnal, 56:1860-1869.

Okulova, N. M., V. A. Aristova, and T. V. Koshkina. 1971. Effect of population density upon the size of home range of small rodents in the West Siberian taiga. Zoologicheskii Zhurnal, 50:908-915.

Petrov, O. V., Le Vou-Khoy, and A. D. Mirinov. 1978. O zimney podvizhnosti ryzhey polevki v lesostepnykh dubravakh. Bulletin Moskovskogo Obshchestva Ispytateley Prirody, Otdel Biologiceskij, 83:36-44.

Petrusewicz, K. (ed.). 1983. Ecology of the bank vole. Acta Theriologica, 28 (Supplement 1):1-242.

Saint-Girons, M. C. 1960. Le rhythme nysthéméral d'activité du campagnol roux, *Clethrionomys glareolus* (Schreber, 1780). I. Les males. Mammalia, 24:516-532.

————. 1961. Le rhythme nysthéméral d'activité du campagnol roux, *Clethrionomys glareolus* (Schreber, 1780). II. Les females. Mammalia, 25:342-357.

Stenseth, N. C., ed. 1985. *Clethrionomys* biology: population dynamics, dispersal, reproduction and social structure. Annales Zoologici Fennici, 22:205-395.

Viitala, J., and J. Hoffmeyer. 1985. Social organization in *Clethrionomys* compared with *Microtus* and *Apodemus:* Social odours, chemistry, and biological effects. Annales Zoologici Fennici, 22:359-371.

Wierzbowska, T. 1983. Sample size in the problem of statistical estimation of home range size in small rodents. Polish Ecological Studies, 9:507-563.

Ylönen, H., and J. Viitala. 1985. Social organization of an enclosed winter population of the bank vole, *Clethrionomys glareolus*. Annales Zoologici Fennici, 22:353-358.

MATING SYSTEM AND REPRODUCTIVE SUCCESS IN A FREE-LIVING POPULATION OF THE BANK VOLE, *CLETHRIONOMYS GLAREOLUS*

Michał D. Sikorski and Anna M. Wójcik

Mammal Research Institute, Polish Academy of Sciences, 17-230 Białowieża, Poland

Summary.—The mating system in a free-living population of the bank vole *(Clethrionomys glareolus)* was examined by mark-recapture and electrophoretic techniques. All overwintered animals from a spring population were sexually active. The home ranges of females were mutually exclusive; they adjoined or overlapped, on average, with 12.5 males. The home ranges of males were larger and overlapped extensively. Mean litter size was 5.8 pups. The mean interval between litters was 19.2 days with a high synchrony in parturition. On the basis of genotypic analysis the paternity of 13 litters was determined. Multiple paternity was not observed. Three males out of ten had offspring simultaneously with two females each. Reproductively successful males were not distinguishable from all available males by age, mass, or body size. However, in the groups of males competing for one female, the successful males were recognizable from competitors by being older and having smaller home ranges.

INTRODUCTION

The mating system of some animals such as birds and large mammals can be observed directly in the field. However, rodents are secretive and often nocturnal; direct observation of them in the field is difficult if not impossible. Mating systems of various rodent species have been described on the basis of patterns of dispersion of individuals in different age and sex categories (Jannett, 1980; Lidicker, 1980; Myllymäki, 1977). Gliwicz (1988), on the basis of detailed examination of the mutual relationship of home ranges between adult males and females, described the mating system in the bank vole *(Clethrionomys glareolus)* as promiscuous. However, patterns of space use of individual voles give only indirect information concerning mating systems. Particularly lacking in such studies is paternity determination, for which electrophoretic techniques and DNA fingerprinting have been used recently (Burke, 1989). Electrophoretic techniques have revealed a monogamous mating system in *Peromyscus polionotus*, harem-polygyny in *Cynomys ludovicianus,* and multiple paternity in *Peromyscus maniculatus* (Birdsall and Nash, 1973; Foltz, 1981; Foltz and Hoogland, 1981). A promiscuous mating system was demonstrated in a population of *Clethrionomys rufocanus* using biochemical markers (Kawata, 1985).

In the present study, we determined paternity, analyzed the mating system, and gave characteristics of reproductively successful males in a natural population of bank voles using methods adapted

194

from Kawata (1985).

MATERIALS AND METHODS

The study was carried out in the Białowieża National Park in an oak-hornbeam *(Querco-Carpinetum)* forest more than 170 years old. Trapping was conducted from 17 April to 21 May 1987. Over an area of 5.8 ha, 288 live traps (wooden boxes with metal valves) were distributed in a grid at 20- by 20-m intervals with two traps at each station. Traps were inspected daily in the morning. To reduce the time spent by voles in traps and to shorten the interruption of free movement in the field the traps were closed after the morning inspection and opened in the evening.

During the first 20-day period, the catch-mark-release method was used. During each inspection, animals caught for the first time were marked uniquely by toe clipping. Each time a vole was captured, its identity, trap station, body weight, sex, and reproductive condition were recorded. More advanced pregnancies were detected by palpation. Vaginal smears were taken for each female with a perforate vaginal opening. We could not distinguish the stages of estrus, but the smears were helpful in determining the time of copulation according to the presence of sperm.

After a 1-day break, all voles captured during the following five days were brought to the laboratory. The length of the capture-mark-release period was set to approximate the gestation period in this species (18-20 days: Buchalczyk, 1970). In this way parturition in the laboratory would have to be a result of copulations during the trapping period. We conducted an additional 5-day trapping period that started one week after the end of the removal period.

All trapped males were killed within 2-7 days after trapping and their sexual activity was checked during autopsy. The presence of sperm in the cauda epididymis was used as an indicator of sexual maturity (Jameson, 1950). Females were housed singly in breeding cages and were inspected daily until parturition. Females and laboratory-born offspring were killed four to six weeks after parturition. Blood, kidneys, and livers were collected from all voles for electrophoresis. After the skulls had been cleaned, the first lower molar of adults was removed and the root length measured to determine age (Gustafsson et al., 1982).

The home range of each vole was estimated by the inclusive-boundary-strip method (Blair, 1940) to select individuals for paternity determination. Home ranges determined by this method are larger than home ranges estimated by other cartographic boundary strip methods. We chose this method to include the maximum number of ranges of males that adjoined and overlapped the home ranges of a given female, and to reduce mistakes of excluding potential fathers from the paternity analysis.

Electrophoretic analysis was conducted according to standard methods on a starch gel (Selander et al., 1971). The following four polymorphic loci were detected: plasma esterase *(Es-7,* three alleles), hemolysate esterase *(Es-1,* two alleles), malic enzyme *(Me,* two alleles), and leucine aminopeptidase *(Lap,* three alleles).

To analyze the spatial and temporal distributions of individuals and the temporal distribution of parturitions in the laboratory, the ratio of the variance to the mean $(s^2/\overline{X})$ was calculated. For spatial distribution, the number of individuals of each sex captured at each trap station was determined, and for temporal distribution the number of parturitions per day was analyzed. The $s^2/\overline{X}$ ratio is an index of randomness of distribution $(s^2/\overline{X} < 1$: uniform; $s^2/\overline{X} = 1$: random; $s^2/\overline{X} > 1$: clumped; Southwood, 1966).

Multiple paternity was assessed using the criteria described by Hoogland and Foltz (1982): the occurrence in a litter of more than two different paternal alleles for loci having more than two alleles *(Es-7* and *Lap* had three alleles each), and the occurrence in a litter of genotypes different from that of any single male adjoining or overlapping the mother. Thirty-five litters were examined according to the first criterion. It was possible to apply the second criterion to ten litters in which the genotypes of the mothers, all the offspring, and all the potential fathers were known.

Paternity was determined using criteria according to Kawata (1985). Among the males whose home ranges adjoined or overlapped the home range of the female in question, only those which could have sired all its offspring were considered to be possible fathers. Then, if more than one male was a possible father, the log likelihood of paternity was compared according to Foltz and Hoogland (1981). Finally, in some cases, not all potential sires of a litter could be analyzed electrophoretically. Sometimes marked males whose ranges overlapped those of females could not be removed, and occasionally unmarked males may have overlapped with females, especially at the periphery of the grid. The probability that electrophoretically uncharacterized males outside the grid could have a genotype consistent with all the offspring of females trapped at the edge of the grid was estimated. The number of unknown males was established on the basis of the maximum number of adjoining or overlapping males per female. The maximum number of such males per female was 20 $(\overline{X} \pm SD = 12.5 \pm 3.97, n = 31)$. The hypothesis that unremoved, marked males or unknown males could have genotypes consistent with all the offspring was tested on the basis of the equation of Kawata (1985:185).

RESULTS

Population characteristics.—During the first trapping period 117 voles were trapped. Of these, four animals (two male, two female) died in the traps during the trapping. At the end of this period, there were 67 marked males and 46 marked females in the study area. Of these, 57 males and 41 females were removed to the laboratory (85.1% and 89.1% of surviving voles, respectively). Of these, one female died before parturition, one female died when the young were already independent, three litters were lost (offspring were either still-born or died during the first day after birth), and one female did not give birth. To determine paternity there were 35 females, 181 laboratory-born offspring by these females, and 57 males. During the additional 5-day trapping series, 14 bank voles were caught: nine overwintered individuals (seven males, two females) and five young. None of these individuals was previously marked. All overwintered individuals were caught in the traps located in two peripheral rows of traps.

The population density of bank voles in the study area was 20.3 animals/ha. Males constituted 59% of the sample of voles from trapping. In the sample of laboratory-born offspring 48.4% were males. In both instances the difference from a 1:1 sex ratio was not significant (chi-square test).

The field study was begun in the spring when the vole population consisted only of animals born in the previous year. The mean age for all voles at the time they were taken to the laboratory was 10.5 months. The mean age of males was approximately 20 days greater than that of females. The age span indicated that the overwintered population consisted of animals born during the entire reproductive season of the previous year. However, about 70% of the animals were born between May and August.

Range size and spatial structure.—The mean size of home ranges and the mean maximum distance between all captures in males were significantly greater than those in females. In order to exclude the individuals with ranges only partly incorporated into the study area, the females that were captured only on the peripheral line of traps and males captured only on the two peripheral lines were excluded from calculating mean ranges and distances. Different criteria for exclusion of males and females were justified by the significantly larger ranges and distances covered by males.

Home ranges of females, as determined by minimum area, did not overlap except for one instance, which indicated territoriality during the reproductive period. Home ranges of males overlapped intrasexually, and each of them overlapped an average of 3.64 ($\pm$2.14, $n = 67$) female ranges. No more than two individual females ($\bar{X} = 0.83 \pm 0.71$) were captured at any given trap station, but up to seven males ($\bar{X} = 1.99 \pm 1.76$) co-occurred at individual trap stations. The $s^2/\bar{X}$ values were 1.75 for males, and 0.61 for females. In both instances the difference from one was significant (Student's t-test, $P < 0.001$), and indicated the clumped distribution of males and uniform distribution of females. For each female the trap station where it was captured most often was determined. The mean number of males captured at these trap stations was 2.75 ($\pm 1.78, n = 48$) and was significantly greater than the mean in the remaining stations (1.61 $\pm$ 1.62, $n = 96$; $t = 3.816$, $P < 0.01$).

Reproductive cycle.—From the beginning of trapping advanced pregnancies were noted. During the initial livetrapping period, all females gave birth to their first litters of the year. Of the 41 females taken into the laboratory only one did not give birth.

For 13 females in which the date of parturition in the field was determined with an accuracy of ±1 day, the mean interval between successive parturitions was 19.2 days (±1.21). This interval corresponds to the gestation period (Buchalczyk, 1970), indicating that the next estrus occurs immediately after parturition.

Parturition in the laboratory occurred from 20 May to 7 June. Thirty-one of 39 females (79.5%) gave birth between 25 May and 7 June. The $s^2/\overline{X}$ ratio was 2.06, which was significantly greater than unity (Student's t-test, $P < 0.001$), indicating that parturitions were synchronous.

Determination of paternity.—The paternity of 13 of 35 litters was determined. In six cases, only one male was genetically compatible with all offspring. In three cases, the log likelihood method was used to select one of several potential fathers. The paternity of three litters was determined after rejecting the hypothesis that unremoved or unknown males could have genotypes consistent with the offspring. The paternity of one male was recognized on the basis of the following facts: on 14 May the adult pair was captured together; a copulatory plug was found in the female; and after 19 days (2 June) offspring were born. The genotype of this male was consistent with those of the litter, and therefore it was accepted as the father although several other males adjoined or overlapped the range of the female. Three males out of ten each sired the litters of two different females.

Reproductive success and male characteristics.—The mean litter size was 5.8 (±1.6, range 1-9, $n = 39$). The mean number of offspring per successful male was 8.3 (±3.5, range 5-14, $n = 10$). No significant correlation was observed between the number of offspring and either age or body mass for both males and females, and between the number of offspring and body length for males only.

In all 13 cases in which paternity could be determined, successful males had home ranges overlapping (not adjoining) the ranges of the females. In six instances the male's range encompassed the entire range of the female; in four cases the sire overlapped 50% of the female's home range, and in three cases less than 50% of the female's home range. In four cases, the father had a lesser degree of overlap with the female than did other males. In the remaining pairs the father was the male whose range overlapped the female range to the greatest extent.

Successful males were compared to all available males with respect to the following traits: age, body mass and length, condylobasal length of skull, and size of home range. The distributions of measurements of all traits and the mean values for the first four traits in both groups of males did not differ (Kolmogorov-Smirnov test, Student's t-test: Fig. 1). Successful males had significantly smaller home ranges than did unsuccessful males ($t = 2.147$, $P < 0.05$).

The traits listed above were also compared within the groups of several males whose home ranges adjoined or overlapped with that of a single female. In all groups of competitors, successful males had home ranges smaller than the average for the group (Fig. 2). With one exception, only the oldest males had reproductive success (Fig. 2); however, the difference in mean age of successful and unsuccessful males was not significant. Successful males could not be distinguished from their competitors by body mass, body length, or condylobasal length.

DISCUSSION

The assumptions on which the methods of determining paternity are based were formulated by Kawata (1985). In his first method (1) the following assumptions were made: (a) all copulations resulting in offspring born in the laboratory involved a male trapped in a home range that either overlapped or adjoined the female's home range; (b) multiple paternity did not occur; (c) each genetic polymorphism was controlled by codominant alleles at a single locus. Kawata's second method (2) required an additional condition: (d) the loci are governed by the Mendelian laws of segregation and independent assortment (also assumed by Foltz and Hoogland, 1981). In his third method (3), in addition to assumptions (b) and (c) it was assumed that: (e) the spatial distribution of alleles in males was random.

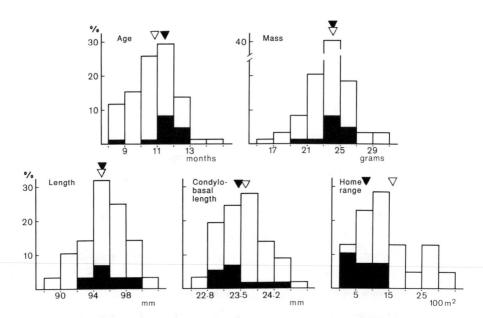

Fig. 1.—Frequency distributions of age, body mass, body length, condylobasal length, and home range in available males (open bars) and 10 successful males (solid bars). Mean values are indicated for available males (open triangles) and successful males (solid triangles).

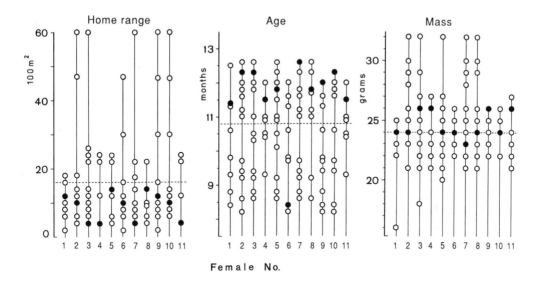

Fig. 2.—Values of home range area, age, and body mass within a group of males whose home ranges adjoined or overlapped that of a female. The points on vertical lines above the identification numbers of females show the data for males adjoining and overlapping with the female. Open circles—unsuccessful males; solid circles—successful males. The horizontal broken lines are the means for all males.

Assumption (a) is difficult to verify because it requires the exact estimation of number of potential fathers for each litter. Such estimation, however, may be inaccurate because the trapping method is not well suited for mapping of home ranges, and the number of males visiting the female's home range may increase when the female is in estrus (Madison, 1980a, b).

Some individual voles that occupy a grid of live traps may not be caught (Boonstra and Krebs, 1978; Tanaka, 1981). This factor might have affected the precision of our estimation of numbers of males. The percentage of trap-shy individuals in different populations has been estimated at 10 to 25% (Krebs, 1966; Krebs et al., 1969). Additional trapping series that we conducted led us to estimate that in our study the trap-shy males were fewer than 10% of all individuals and were mostly located on the edge of the trapping grid. In the case of females whose ranges were located along the edges of trapping grid, method (3) of paternity determination includes the probability that trap-shy males were present. We think that these facts corroborate assumption (a) in our study.

Assumption (b), which is a condition for the paternity determination to be correct, precludes the possibility that multiple paternity occurs. Multiple paternity has not been recorded in microtine rodents so far, but in promiscuous populations it may occur. Although we cannot reject the hypothesis that multiple paternity may occasionally occur in bank voles, we think it was not common in our study population. The results of studies on protein polymorphism in the bank vole do not give reasons for doubting assumptions c-e (Fedyk and Gębczyński, 1980; Hall and Semeonoff, 1985; Wójcik and Fedyk, 1984).

A social structure in which mature females have exclusive home ranges and the home ranges of mature males overlap is known for several vole species such as *M. oeconomus* (Tast, 1966), *M. pennsylvanicus* (Madison, 1980a) and all species of *Clethrionomys* (Bondrup-Nielsen and Karlsson, 1985; Bujalska, 1985). The uniform spatial distribution of sexually receptive females, which are considered to be a key resource for breeding males (Williams, 1966), causes a nonterritorial spacing system of males (Ostfeld, 1985). Nonterritoriality reflects male strategies for obtaining access to the maximum number of matings by searching for potential mates rather than defending a home range. Such a strategy should be advantageous in the case of asynchronous female reproduction and most likely results in promiscuous mating (Ims, 1987). However, we found nonterritoriality of males and synchronous breeding of females incompatible with the model by Ims (1987). It seems that this incompatibility is caused by the way reproductive synchrony is analyzed. Temporally clumped parturitions led us to conclude that breeding was synchronous. However, even more significant than the timing of parturitions is the length of the period in which breeding females are receptive to males. Most females (about 80%) were vulnerable to impregnation for about 10 days per estrous cycle, a period long enough that a single male could search for and mate with more than one female. That this time was sufficient to search for additional females is supported by three instances that we observed in which a male sired offspring with two females within an average interval of 7 days. In spite of the lack of direct evidence that a single female mated with different males during the breeding season, we think that it is highly probable that the mating system of our population was promiscuous.

Successful males did not differ in age, body mass, body length, and condylobasal length from all available males. All males that bred successfully had small home ranges not exceeding the mean for the population. Perhaps subordinate males are forced to move over large areas because they are chased by dominant males away from the vicinity of receptive females. This situation can change when old males die and their places are taken by the young of that year.

Our data should be considered preliminary because our conclusions regarding mating system are based on only a portion of one breeding season, and we do not present data on lifetime reproductive success in comparing successful and unsuccessful males.

LITERATURE CITED

Birdsall, D. A., and D. Nash. 1973. Occurrence of successful multiple insemination of females in natural populations of deer mice *(Peromyscus maniculatus)*. Evolution, 27:106-110.

Blair, W. F. 1940. Home ranges and populations of the meadow vole in southern Michigan. Journal of Wildlife Management, 4:149-161.

Bondrup-Nielsen, S., and F. Karlsson. 1985. Movements and spatial patterns in populations of *Clethrionomys* species: A review. Annales Zoologici Fennici, 22:385-392.

Boonstra, R., and C. J. Krebs. 1978. Pitfall trapping of *Microtus townsendii*. Journal of Mammalogy, 59:136-148.

Buchalczyk, A. 1970. Reproduction, mortality and longevity of the bank vole under laboratory conditions. Acta Theriologica, 15:153-176.

Bujalska, G. 1985. Regulation of female maturation in *Clethrionomys* species, with special reference to an island population of *C. glareolus*. Annales Zoologici Fennici, 22:331-342.

Burke, T. 1989. DNA fingerprinting and other methods for the study of mating success. Trends in Ecology and Evolution, 4:139-144.

Fedyk, A., and M. Gębczyński. 1980. Genetic changes in seasonal generation of the bank vole. Acta Theriologica, 25:475-485.

Foltz, D. W. 1981. Genetic evidence for long-term monogamy in a small rodent, *Peromyscus polionotus*. The American Naturalist, 117:665-675.

Foltz, D. W., and J. L. Hoogland. 1981. Analysis of the mating system in the black-tailed prairie dog *(Cynomys ludovicianus)* by likelihood of paternity. Journal of Mammalogy, 62:706-712.

Gliwicz, J. 1988. The private life of mice. Wiadomości Ekologiczne, 34:187-202. [In Polish with English summary.]

Gustafsson, T. G., C. B. Andersson, and L. M. Westlin. 1982. Determining the age of bank voles—a laboratory study. Acta Theriologica, 27:275-282.

Hall, S. J. G., and R. Semeonoff. 1985. Plasma esterase polymorphism in the bank vole, *Clethrionomys glareolus* in Britain. Journal of Zoology (London), 207:213-222.

Hoogland, J. L., and D. W. Foltz. 1982. Variance in male and female reproductive success in a harem-polygynous mammal, the black-tailed prairie dog (Sciuridae: *Cynomys ludovicianus)*. Behavioral Ecology and Sociobiology, 11:155-163.

Ims, R. A. 1987. Male spacing systems in microtine rodents. The American Naturalist, 130:475-484.

Jameson, E. W. 1950. Determining fecundity in small mammals. Journal of Mammalogy, 31:433-436.

Jannett, F. J., Jr. 1980. Social dynamics of the montane vole, *Microtus montanus,* as a paradigm. Biologist, 62:3-19.

Kawata, M. 1985. Mating system and reproductive success in a spring population of the red-backed vole, *Clethrionomys rufocanus bedfordiae.* Oikos, 45:181-190.

Krebs, C. J. 1966. Demographic changes in fluctuating populations of *Microtus californicus.* Ecological Monographs, 36:239-273.

Krebs, C. J., B. L. Keller, and R. H. Tamarin. 1969. *Microtus* population biology: demographic changes in fluctuating populations of *M. ochrogaster* and *M. pennsylvanicus* in southern Indiana. Ecology, 50:587-607.

Lidicker, W. Z., Jr. 1980. The social biology of the California vole, *Microtus californicus.* Biologist, 62:46-55.

Madison, D. M. 1980a. Space use and social structure in the meadow vole, *Microtus pennsylvanicus.* Behavioral Ecology and Sociobiology, 7:65-71.

———. 1980b. An integrated view of the social biology of *Microtus pennsylvanicus.* Biologist 62:20-33.

Myllymäki, A. 1977. Interspecific competition and home range dynamics in the field vole, *Microtus agrestis.* Oikos, 29:553-569.

Ostfeld, R. S. 1985. Limiting resources and territoriality in microtine rodents. The American Naturalist, 126:1-15.

Selander, R. K., M. H. Smith, S. Y. Yang, W. E. Johnson, and J. B. Gentry. 1971. Biochemical polymorphism and systematics in the genus *Peromyscus.* I. Variation in the old-field mouse *(Peromyscus polionotus).* Studies in Genetics, University of Texas, 6:49-90.

Southwood, T. R. E. 1966. Ecological methods with particular reference to the study of insect populations. Methuen, London, 391 pp.

Tanaka, R. 1981. Controversial problems in advanced research on estimating population densities in small rodents. Researches on Population Ecology, Supplement, 2:1-67.

Tast, O. 1966. The root vole, *Microtus oeconomus* Pallas, as an inhabitant of seasonally flooded land. Annales Zoologici Fennici, 3:127-171.

Williams, G. C. 1966. Natural selection, the cost of reproduction and refinement of Lack's principle. The American Naturalist, 100:687-690.

Wójcik, A. M., and S. Fedyk. 1984. Breeding parameters in the bank vole of different esterase phenotypes. Acta Theriologica, 29:305-316.

PHENOTYPIC FLEXIBILITY IN THE SOCIAL ORGANIZATION
OF *CLETHRIONOMYS*

Hannu Ylönen

University of Jyväskylä, Konnevesi Research Station, SF 44300 Konnevesi, and

Department of Biology, Yliopistonkatu 9, SF-40100 Jyväskylä, Finland

Summary.—I review the flexibility of social organization and spacing behavior in *Clethrionomys*. This review is based on a 6-year comparative study and several experimental studies on cyclic populations of the bank vole, *C. glareolus*, in Central Finland. The social organization of *Clethrionomys* populations shows great flexibility during both the breeding and nonbreeding season, and is dependent on habitat patchiness, food availability, predation, kinship, philopatry, and familiarity between individuals. The first three factors are most important in destabilizing a population, whereas the last three stabilize a population without exhausting its resources. Female territoriality can weaken in a productive environment perhaps due to increasing kinship between reproductive females during the breeding season. During the winter, food availability seems to determine the social structure of the population, which consists of either large or small aggregations of both sexes. Winter territoriality may be influenced by relatively homogenous habitat with low productivity. Forest-dwelling species of *Clethrionomys* seem to adopt behavioral tactics different from those of most *Microtus* that live in a productive, but unstable habitat. Despite these behavioral differences, both genera cycle synchronously in northern Fennoscandia. This leads to the conclusion that we have to seek explanations for microtine cycles not based on the behavior of individual voles.

INTRODUCTION

Clethrionomys inhabits forested areas of the Holarctic region (Niethammer and Krapp, 1982; Stenseth, 1985a). In a relatively predictable habitat, the genus has evolved a fairly stable social system based on the territoriality of breeding females, first described by Kalela (1957) for *C. rufocanus* and by Bujalska (1970) for *C. glareolus*. North American and Eurasian species exhibit the same kind of social system (Bondrup-Nielsen and Karlsson, 1985).

The social system of the main rodent competitors of *Clethrionomys*, *Microtus* species (Boyce and Boyce, 1988; Grant, 1969; Henttonen and Hansson, 1984; Henttonen et al., 1977; Myllymäki, 1977; Ostfeld, 1985; Ostfeld et al., 1985; Viitala, 1977; Wolff, 1980) is much more variable than in *Clethrionomys*. All European *Microtus* species *(M. agrestis, M. oeconomus, M. arvalis)* and at least *M.*

pennsylvanicus of North America are considered "non-regulators" (Viitala and Hoffmeyer, 1985), characterized by low social stability, lack of social regulation of maturity, and high rates of adult dispersal (Boyce and Boyce, 1988; Getz, 1978; Viitala, 1977). The social organization of some other New World *Microtus—M. ochrogaster, M. montanus, M. xanthognathus—*is more like *Clethrionomys,* in that social stability and regulation of maturity are more pronounced (Getz, 1978; Viitala and Hoffmeyer, 1985; Wolff, 1980).

Because the social system of *Clethrionomys* is similar throughout Holarctic region whereas population dynamics vary considerably, they have been used to study the role of social behavior in population regulation (Stenseth, 1985b). This social stability also makes them suitable for studies of phenotypically determined changes in social behavior (Ims, 1987; Ylönen and Viitala, 1987; Ylönen et al., 1988). If the social system is determined mainly by the environment, then by introducing voles into a new environment, or by manipulating different environmental factors, it should be possible to induce different behavioral patterns, and study their population consequences.

At the Konnevesi Research Station of the University of Jyväskylä, we have followed the social organization of an enclosed bank vole population over one cycle of density, 1982-1987 (Ylönen and Viitala, 1985; Ylönen et al., 1988). In addition, we have conducted several experiments on the effects of food, familiarity between individuals, and predation on the social behavior of the bank vole (Ylönen, 1989; Ylönen and Viitala, in press; Ylönen et al., 1990), and have introduced northern grey-sided voles into a new environment 900 km south of their origin (Ylönen and Viitala, 1987). Herein we describe the characteristic features of the social organization and spacing behavior of *C. glareolus* populations under different environmental conditions throughout a cycle. The paper is based on observations on an enclosed bank vole population from 1982 to 1987. Additional experiments were designed to explain the patterns observed.

PATTERNS IN THE SOCIAL ORGANIZATION OF *CLETHRIONOMYS*

The pattern of social organization of *Clethrionomys* during the breeding season can be divided into strict or weak territoriality among females, the latter indicated by greater overlap among their home ranges. Female territoriality has been reported for *C. rufocanus* and *C. rutilus* in Finnish Lappland (Kalela, 1957; Viitala, 1977, 1988), for *C. rufocanus* on islands in Central Finland (Ylönen and Viitala, 1987), for *C. glareolus* on islands (Bujalska, 1970), and for *C. gapperi* in North America (Mihok, 1979; Bondrup-Nielsen, 1984). Exceptions to this pattern occur with supplemental feeding *(C. rufocanus:* Ims, 1987, 1989) or with enclosed populations *(C. glareolus:* Ylönen et al., 1988). Ylönen et al. (1988) concluded that increasing overlap of breeding females was due to the food resources of the old field habitat and not to the fencing of the area.

During winter, small rodents either maintain a territorial system or aggregate in groups, depending on environmental factors (West and Dublin, 1984). In almost all studies of *Clethrionomys*, only winter aggregations have been observed *(C. rutilus:* West, 1977; *C. gapperi:* Criddle, 1932; *C. glareolus* and *C. rufocanus:* Ylönen and Viitala, 1985, 1987). The only observations of possible winter territoriality were made on *C. rutilus* and *C. rufocanus* in Finnish Lappland in which Viitala (1984) interpreted the site tenacity of voles in late autumn and the following spring as an indication of territoriality throughout winter. Perhaps in a relatively even habitat with low productivity, territorial behavior could evolve as a means of protecting sufficient food resources over winter.

STUDY SITE AND RESULTS

A population of *C. glareolus* in a 0.8-ha enclosure at the Konnevesi Research Station was livetrapped for 1 week every month between 1982 and 1987 (Ylönen and Viitala, 1985; Ylönen et al., 1988). Since 1987 we have used four 0.5 ha enclosures for experimental studies with the bank vole (Ylönen and Viitala, in press; Ylönen et al., 1990).

The enclosed bank vole population showed cyclic fluctuations in density similar to those in populations of *Clethrionomys* and *Microtus* outside the fence (Ylönen, in press; Ylönen et al., 1988). After the crash in spring of 1983 only one male remained in the enclosure, and we introduced new animals (five females, five males) into it in May.

During the summer 1983 the number of breeding females remained at the same level as the number of introduced females (Table 1). Only one young female born in the enclosure matured during the breeding season. The size of the home ranges was the largest ever observed during the 6-year study and home-range overlap was minimal.

After the autumn decline 10 voles remained to form the overwintering population. They stayed in two overwintering groups in bushy areas. The individual home ranges decreased in size and their overlap increased (Table 1). Survivorship in the population was very good and breeding began early— young voles of trappable age first occurred in February under the 80-cm snow cover (Ylönen and Viitala, 1985). Early breeding and good survival of voles caused a rapid growth of the populations and dispersal from the overwintering patches. The daughters born during winter and spring stayed near their mothers, the mean distance between the home range centers being only 30 m. Due to plentiful food in the old field and surrounding alder *(Alnus incana)* and spruce *(Picea abies)* patches—both of the tree species had an exceptionally good seed crop that year—nearly all of the females born in winter, spring, and early summer matured. The number of breeding females reached its peak of 22 (27/ha) at the end of June, and breeding stopped in the beginning of August (Ylönen et al., 1988). The overlap of home ranges was the same as for winter aggregations. The highest population density

Table 1.—Characteristic features of the social system of a bank vole population within a 0.8-ha enclosure, June 1983-February 1987, central Finland.

Period	Mature females (n)	Mature males (n)	Juveniles (n)	Average home range of females m²	SD	Average overlap[a] (%)
Increase year						
June 1983	6	5	13	630	170	2
December 1983	6	4		450	40	33
Peak year						
June–July 1984	22	12	50	480	160	37
After-peak Winter						
January 1986	10	9		390	180	40
Crash breeding season						
January 1986	5	5	7	390	130	0
After-crash winter						
February 1987	4	4		330	130	55

[a]Home-range overlap is percent of traps used by at least two reproductive females of the total number of traps used.

was observed in the portion of the enclosure that consisted of an abandoned field. Field voles *(M. agrestis)* were excluded from the enclosure but occurred at high densities outside the fence.

Due to the abundant food, survivorship was high during autumn, and density of the overwintering population was high (Ylönen et al., 1988). A relatively early start of breeding caused the second peak with a high maximum number (15/ha) of breeding females in the enclosure. Breeding stopped early again.

During the next winter the number of overwintering voles was still relatively high (24 voles/ha, Table 1), as was the home range overlap among females. Breeding in the overwintering population started early but the survival of the young was very low. Five females bred in June, but altogether only seven young reached trappable age. The summer decline resulted in extinction in October. The old females in the population, which survived until September, remained in breeding condition.

In October we introduced four female and four male voles into the enclosure. They were captured in the surrounding areas from populations of the same, low density, phase of the cycle as that inside the enclosure. Thus, we created an overwintering population with much higher density than the surrounding populations. Three females formed an aggregation in the abandoned field site, showing a high overlap of home ranges. The survival of the population until spring was 100%.

DISCUSSION

In the summer of 1983, with a moderate density of breeding female bank voles, the mean size of the home ranges of females was larger than at any other time of the cycle (Table 1). Predators were scarce (Ylönen, in press) and the maximum density was influenced by the quality of the habitat and an abundance of preferred food items such as spruce and alder seeds (Kaikusalo, 1972; Hansson, 1985). The survival rates during the winter 1983-1984 were high (Ylönen and Viitala, 1985) as is typical for populations at moderate density during the snowy period (Kaikusalo, 1972; Karlsson, 1988).

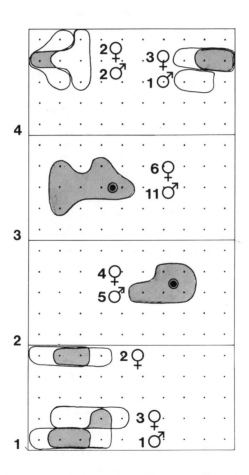

Fig. 1.—Spatial distribution of the mid-winter (January 1988) bank vole populations in two experimental sets of 0.5-ha enclosures in central Finland: with a patchy food distribution (enclosures 2 and 3) and with even food distribution (enclosures 1 and 4). Shading represents overlap of individuals; trapping points are separated by 10 m.

High survival and breeding during winter caused a rapid increase in population density, which was promoted by the familiarity between the voles after overwintering together (Ferkin, 1988a; Ylönen and Viitala, in press; Fig. 1). Ylönen et al. (1990) showed the significant positive effect of familiarity on the growth rate of *Clethrionomys* populations. Depending on habitat quality, young females stay as near to their mother as possible, with a high degree of overlap of home ranges with each other and their mother (Ims, 1989). Mutual familiarity has been shown to have a positive influence on the survival of young *Microtus* as well (Boonstra, 1984; Ferkin 1988b). During the breeding season of the peak year, the segment of the population in an old field had the highest density among the different habitats (Ylönen et al., 1988), probably because field voles, *M. agrestis,* were excluded by the fence. During peak years, bank voles reached densities of up to 150/ha, higher than the density of *Clethrionomys* in forested habitats. However, we did not observe a fence effect as Krebs et al. (1969) and Boonstra and Krebs (1977) documented in studies with enclosed *Microtus* populations. The home range size of breeding females decreased and the breeding stopped significantly earlier in the year of high density than during the years of low or moderate density (Ylönen et al., 1988). There is evidence that reproduction is socially suppressed in *Clethrionomys* populations at high density (Bujalska, 1970, 1973; Gipps, 1985; Saitoh, 1981).

During autumn of the peak year predation pressure—especially the occurrence of small mustelids (Ylönen, in press)—had already increased. In the winter of high density, voles remained in the optimal habitat with overlapping territories, rather than dispersing more evenly over suboptimal habitat. Supplemental food in the forest area caused it to be preferred over the abandoned field normally preferred. In this experiment I tried to induce the voles to move from the normally optimal, open wintering habitat with especially thick snow cover, to forest, where snow cover was thin or lacking. Eight of ten winter home ranges of females occurred, and about 75% of the total captures during the winter were made, on this previously suboptimal habitat. The results indicated that food availability was the most important factor in determining habitat choice of voles that winter (Ylönen and Viitala, in press). Due to supplemental feeding, the survival rate of the peak winter population was high (Ylönen et al., 1988), but the spring decline started the crash, which was completed by the summer extinction. Without supplemental feeding the high density in the optimal habitat could have caused an overexploitation of food resources resulting in an earlier decline than that observed in the enclosure. However, the crash in the enclosure was synchronous with that of the population outside the fence in spite of extra food (Hansson, 1987). Thus the cause of the decline should be sought in the combined effect of nutritional conditions, diseases or parasites spreading in the dense population under the snow cover, possible stress reactions in the voles, and in predation (Hansson and Henttonen, 1988; Lidicker, 1988).

CONCLUSIONS

A long-term study of the social organization of *C. glareolus* showed that strict female territoriality, often assumed to be a species- or genus-specific characteristic, is subject to considerable flexibility. This flexibility seems to be dependent on such environmental factors as, habitat patchiness, food availability, and perhaps predation, and also on intraspecific factors such as kinship and familiarity between individuals.

One major extrinsic factor affecting the behavior of individual voles must be the cyclicity of microtine species in some parts of the Holarctic region. However, since such behaviorally different genera as *Clethrionomys, Microtus,* and *Sorex* (shrews), cycle synchronously in northern Fennoscandia, we must seek an explanation for population cycles from hypotheses other than those based mainly on spacing behavior (Hansson and Henttonen, 1988; Lidicker, 1988). An individual vole reacts to the environmental conditions in which it lives. Intra- and inter-specific competition, predation pressure, food supply, parasites, and diseases form the main features of that environment.

ACKNOWLEDGMENTS

I would like to thank Bill McShea, Rick Ostfeld and one unknown referee for constructive criticism on the manuscript.

LITERATURE CITED

Bondrup-Nielsen, S. 1984. The role of habitat heterogeneity and female spacing behaviour in density regulation of *Clethrionomys gapperi.* Unpublished Ph.D. dissertation. University of Alberta, Edmonton, 134 pp.

Bondrup-Nielsen, S., and F. Karlsson. 1985. An evaluation of the effects of space use and habitat patterns on dispersal in small mammals. Annales Zoologici Fennici, 22:385-392.

Boonstra, R. 1984. Aggressive behaviour of adult meadow voles *(Microtus pennsylvanicus)* towards young. Oecologia (Berlin), 62:126-131.

Boonstra, R., and C. J. Krebs. 1977: A fencing experiment on a high-density population of *Microtus townsendii.* Canadian Journal of Zoology, 55:1166-1175.

Boyce, C. C. K., and J. L. Boyce. 1988. Population biology of *Microtus arvalis.* III. Regulation of numbers and breeding dispersion of females. Journal of Animal Ecology, 57:737-754.

Bujalska, G. 1970. Reproduction stabilizing elements in an island population of *Clethrionomys glareolus* (Schreber, 1780). Acta Theriologica, 15:381-412.

————. 1973. The role of spacing behaviour among females in the regulation of reproduction in the bank vole. Journal of Reproduction and Fertility, 19:461-472.

Criddle, S. 1932. The red-backed voles *(Clethrionomys gapperi loringi* Bailey) in southern Manitoba. Canadian Field Naturalist, 46:178-181.

Ferkin, M. H. 1988a. Seasonal differences in social behaviour among adult and juvenile meadow voles, *Microtus pennsylvanicus.* Ethology, 79:116-125.

————. 1988b. The effect of familiarity on social interactions in meadow voles, *Microtus pennsylvanicus:* a laboratory and field study. Animal Behaviour, 36:1816-1822.

Getz, L. L. 1978. Speculation on social structure and population cycles of microtine rodents. The Biologist, 60:134-147.

Gipps, J. H. W. 1985. Spacing behaviour and male reproductive ecology in voles of the genus *Clethrionomys.* Annales Zoologici Fennici, 22:343-351.

Grant, P. R. 1969. Experimental studies of competitive interactions in a two-species system. I. *Microtus* and *Clethrionomys* species in enclosures. Canadian Journal of Zoology, 47:1059-1082.

Hansson, L. 1985. *Clethrionomys* food: Generic, specific and regional characteristics. Annales Zoologici Fennici, 22:315-318.

————. 1987. An interpretation of rodent dynamics as due to trophic interactions. Oikos, 50:308-318.

Hansson, L., and H. Henttonen. 1988. Rodent dynamics as a community process. Trends in Ecology and Evolution, 3:195-200.

Henttonen, H., and L. Hansson 1984. Interspecific relations between small rodents in European boreal and subarctic environments. Acta Zoologica Fennica, 172:61-65.

Henttonen, H., A. Kaikusalo, J. Tast, and J. Viitala 1977. Interspecific competition between small rodents in subarctic and boreal ecosystem. Oikos, 29:581-590.

Ims, R. A. 1987. Responses in spatial organization and behaviour to manipulations of the food resource in the vole *Clethrionomys rufocanus.* Journal of Animal Ecology, 56:585-596.

————. 1989. Kinship and origin effects of dispersal and space sharing in *Clethrionomys rufocanus.* Ecology, 70:607-616.

Kaikusalo, A. 1972. Population turnover and wintering of the bank vole, *Clethrionomys glareolus* (Schreb.), in southern and central Finland. Annales Zoologici Fennici, 9:219-224.

Kalela, O. 1957. Regulation of the reproduction rate in subarctic populations of the vole *Clethrionomys rufocanus* (Sund.). Annales Academiae Scientiarum Fennicae, (A IV) 34:1-60.

Karlsson, A. F. 1988. Interindividual proximity and the probability of winter survival in the bank vole, *Clethrionomys glareolus.* Canadian Journal of Zoology, 66:1841-1845.

Krebs, C. J., B. L. Keller, and R. H. Tamarin 1969. *Microtus* population biology: Demographic changes in fluctuating population of *M. ochrogaster* and *M. pennsylvanicus* in southern Indiana. Ecology, 50:587-607.

Lidicker, W. Z., Jr. 1988. Solving the enigma of microtine "cycles." Journal of Mammalogy, 69:225-235.

Mihok, S. 1979. Behavioural structure and demography of subarctic *Clethrionomys gapperi* and *Peromyscus maniculatus*. Canadian Journal of Zoology, 57:1520-1535.

Myllymäki, A. 1977. Demographic mechanisms in the fluctuating populations of the field vole *Microtus agrestis*. Oikos, 29:553-569.

Niethammer, J., and F. Krapp (eds.) 1982. Handbuch der Säugetiere Europas. Band 2/I, Nagetiere II. Akademischer Verlagsgesellschaft, Wiesbaden, Federal Republic of Germany, 649 pp.

Ostfeld, R. S. 1985. Experimental analysis of aggression and spacing behavior in California voles. Canadian Journal of Zoology, 63:2277-2282.

Ostfeld, R. S., W. Z. Lidicker, Jr., and E. J. Heske 1985. The relationship between habitat heterogeneity, space use, and demography in a population of California voles. Oikos, 45:433-442.

Saitoh, T. 1981. Control of female maturation in high-density populations of the red-backed vole, *Clethrionomys rufocanus bedfordiae*. Journal of Animal Ecology, 50:79-87.

Stenseth, N. C. 1985a. Geographic distribution of *Clethrionomys* species. Annales Zoologici Fennici, 22:215-219.

―――. 1985b. The Konnevisi symposium on *Clethrionomys* biology. Conclusions: A speculative account. Annales Zoologici Fennici 22:393-395.

Viitala, J. 1977. Social organization in cyclic subarctic populations of the voles *Clethrionomys rufocanus* (Sund.) and *Microtus agrestis* (L.). Annales Zoologici Fennici, 14:53-93.

―――. 1984. Stability of overwintering populations of *Clethrionomys* and *Microtus* at Kilpisjärvi, Finnish Lappland. Special Publications of the Carnegie Museum of Natural History, 10:109-112.

―――. 1988. Social organization of *Clethrionomys rutilus* (Pall.) at Kilpisjärvi, Finnish Lappland. Annales Zoologici Fennici, 24:267-273.

Viitala, J., and I. Hoffmeyer 1985. Social organization in *Clethrionomys* compared with *Microtus* and *Apodemus:* Social odours, chemistry and biological effects. Annales Zoologici Fennici, 22:359-371.

West, S. D. 1977. Mid-winter aggregation in the northern red-backed vole, *Clethrionomys rutilus*. Canadian Journal of Zoology, 55:1404-1409.

West, S. D., and H. T. Dublin 1984. Behavioural strategies of small mammals under winter conditions: solitary or social? Special Publications of the Carnegie Museum of Natural History, 10:293-299.

Wolff, J. O. 1980. Social organization of the Taiga vole *(Microtus xanthognathus)*. The Biologist, 62:34-45.

212

Ylönen, H. 1989. Weasels *Mustela nivalis* suppress reproduction in cyclic bank voles *Clethrionomys glareolus*. Oikos, 55:138-140.

―――. In press. Zum einfluβ der Musteliden *Mustela nivalis* und *M. erminea* auf zyklische Kleinnager am Beispiel von *Clethrionomys* populationen in Mittelfinnland. Wissenschaftliche Beiträge der Universität Halle.

Ylönen, H., and J. Viitala. 1985. Social organization of an enclosed population of the vole *Clethrionomys glareolus*. Annales Zoologici Fennici, 22:353-358.

―――. 1987. Social organization and habitat use of introduced populations of the grey-sided vole *Clethrionomys rufocanus* (Sund.) in central Finland. Zeitschrift für Säugetierkunde, 52:354-363.

―――. In press. Social overwintering and food distribution in the bank vole *Clethrionomys glareolus*. Holarctic Ecology.

Ylönen, H., T. Kojola, and J. Viitala. 1988. Changing female spacing behaviour and demography in an enclosed breeding population of *Clethrionomys glareolus*. Holarctic Ecology, 11:286-292.

Ylönen, H., T. Mappes, and J. Viitala. 1990. Different demography in friends and strangers: an experiment on the impact of kinship and familiarity in *Clethrionomys glareolus*. Oecologia (Berlin), 83:333-337.

Social Systems and
Population Cycles in Voles
Advances in Life Sciences
© Birkhäuser Verlag Basel

EFFECTS OF DENSITY AND RESOURCES ON THE
SOCIAL SYSTEM OF WATER VOLES

Boel Jeppsson

Department of Animal Ecology, University of Lund, 223 62 Lund, Sweden

Summary.—Water voles *(Arvicola terrestris)* were studied in two different habitats, marsh and grassland, in Sweden. Voles breeding in the marsh moved to burrows in grassland when becoming nonreproductive, whereas voles breeding in grassland remained there all year. Home ranges in the marsh were much larger than in grassland. Males in the marsh had larger home ranges than females, often including several reproductive females within their range. Males with no access to reproductive females had larger ranges than males with access to reproductive females. No difference in home range size could be found between the sexes breeding in grassland. Individuals tended to be territorial in both habitats. However, in the marsh, range overlap occurred between the peripheral areas of females and between males with no access to reproductive females. Increased density in grassland did not result in larger intrasexual overlap, but rather in smaller home ranges and larger intersexual overlap, although intersexual overlap was smaller when a male overlapped two females. The mating system varied from facultative monogamy in the grassland to polygyny in the marsh. During the nonreproductive period almost all animals were solitary and territorial, even during high density. It is suggested that burrows are the key resource for water voles living in habitats where individuals are highly exposed to predation, resulting in different social systems between habitats.

INTRODUCTION

Social organization and thus mating systems are affected by variation in the distribution of resources, which in turn influences the density and dispersion of individuals (Clutton-Brock and Harvey, 1978). Brown and Orians (1970) emphasized that territorial behavior may be adaptive in competition for the resources needed for reproduction and survival. They focused attention on the ecological factors that affect fitness differences among individuals who behave in different ways. In mammals, the disparity in behavior between the sexes is accentuated during the breeding season. Since males compete for matings, their spacing system is determined by the spatial distribution of receptive females (Boonstra, 1977; Clutton-Brock and Harvey, 1978; Ims, 1988; Ostfeld, 1985). Females, on the other hand, compete for resources that increase the survival of their offspring, and thus their spacing system is a result of the habitat characteristics (Boonstra et al., 1987; Ims, 1988; Ostfeld, 1985). The availability of resources affect the degree of competition between females, which in turn influences the dispersion of males and ultimately the mating system.

However, from life history theory we predict that individuals should maximize their lifetime reproductive success rather than their instantaneous reproductive success; therefore, both females and males also should compete for resources that increase their own survival. For females, factors promoting survival and reproduction coincide. Males are, in contrast, subject to a conflict between tactics beneficial for their own survival and tactics to achieve the maximum number of matings.

The aim of this study was to show how the social system of water voles, *Arvicola terrestris,* changed as a result of different resource requirements in different habitats. I emphasize that female territoriality can be a result of reasons other than competition for food and that there is a conflict between instant and lifetime reproductive success for males subjected to predation.

METHODS

The study was conducted mainly in the Revinge area, southern Sweden, about 4,000 ha and rather heterogenous, consisting of permanent pastures with scattered small marshes, forests, and wet meadows. Four different water vole populations were studied. One seasonally migrating population was followed during a 4-year period. During the summer the animals were studied in a marsh of about one ha, and during the winter, in adjacent grasslands. Three populations of water voles that permanently inhabited grasslands were also studied. Two were studied in the Revinge area and a third at Tovetorp field station, central Sweden. The grassland populations were studied for periods lasting from two months to one year. The density for the different populations was calculated using a truncated Poisson distribution based on frequency of captures (Caughley, 1977; Craig, 1953; Jeppsson, 1987). For simplicity, I refer in the following to the relative densities shown in Table 1.

In the marsh, 40 trap stations (modified Sherman traps) were arranged in a permanent grid system with 10-m spacing. Since the water level in the marsh was high, the traps were placed on floating logs. Two traps were placed at each trap station and operated for one 24-h period each week during the breeding season (May-August). All traps had nest material (hay) and food (mainly carrots). During the breeding season in the grassland some traps were placed underground at the burrows and some above ground in the runway systems. Traps were placed about 1 m apart where signs of water voles, like mounds, feces, and gnawings were found. The traps were operated for 5 days initially and thereafter as in the marsh. During the nonbreeding season, all traps were placed underground at the burrows and trapping was carried out irregularly.

Table 1.—Densities and reproductive rates for water voles in northern and central Sweden.

Site	Grid size (ha)	Year	Relative density	Estimated density (n/ha)	Reproductive individuals			
					Both sexes		Females	
					%	n	%	n
Marsh site 1	1.00	1979	High	109	40	60	79	24
Marsh site 1	1.00	1980	Moderate	49	32	34	82	11
Marsh site 1	1.00	1981	Low	28	70	23	56	16
Marsh site 1	1.00	1983	Low	15	78	9	57	7
Grassland								
site 1	0.25	1984	High	92	100	18	61	18
site 2	1.00	1984	Low	10	89	9	50	8
Tovetorp	0.50	1980	Moderate	55	73	26	63	19

Captured voles were anesthetized with ether, individually marked with ear tags, and their reproductive condition and weight noted. I have included only reproductive individuals in the analysis of home range size and index of overlap during the breeding season. Males with scrotal testes and females that were lactating, pregnant, or had a perforated vagina were considered reproductive. Overwintered animals were separated from individuals born during the season by the appearance of the pelage.

Movements of individuals were recorded by radiotelemetry. The transmitters used were similar to those described by Tester et al. (1964), modified to suit voles. The transmitters were attached to voles by collars; their weights varied between 2.5 and 5% of the animals' weight. The range of the signals varied between 100 and 300 m, but was shorter when voles were in the water or deep underground. For voles dwelling in the middle of the marsh, radio fixes could be obtained with an accuracy of ±5 m. For voles at the edges of the marsh or in burrows, radio fixes with an accuracy of ±1 m were obtained. Radiotracking was done either by repeatedly registering radio fixes of individuals every 10 minutes for about 3 days and nights or by obtaining fixes almost daily, but more irregularly for several months to one year. To avoid misinterpretations when comparing the data for vole movements, I have excluded situations in which not all stationary, same-sex individuals were radiotracked simultaneously within the study area. The home range sizes were calculated by the harmonic mean measure of Dixon and Chapman (1980). Isopleths corresponding to 50 and 95% probabilities of use were derived and their areas computed; the 95% probability-of-use area will be referred to as the peripheral area, whereas the 50% probability-of-use area will be referred to as the core area. To avoid errors because of shifts in home range and differences in the duration of radio tracking, only areas used during a 5-day period with a minimum of 15 radio fixes have been used in the comparisons of home range sizes, unless otherwise stated.

I have used a modified version of the method described by Ostfeld (1986) to calculate the degree of overlap between individuals with adjacent boundaries. This modification is a result of the tendency of female water voles to exclude males from their nests after the birth of a litter, resulting in a skewed measure of overlap if the index put too much weight on the overlap between core areas of individuals. Thus, the overlap index for a given pair of neighbors i and j is $(P/i_{0.95})(P/j_{0.95})$ for the peripheral area and $(S/i_{0.50})(S/j_{0.50})$ for the core area, where $i_{0.95}$ = individual i's peripheral area; $j_{0.95}$ = individual j's peripheral area; $i_{0.50}$ = individual i's core area; $j_{0.50}$ = individual j's core area; P = the area of overlap between individual i's and j's peripheral areas; S = the area of overlap between individual i's and j's core areas. To anticipate the problem of defining "neighbor" in the derivation of a mean overlap index value, only the overlap index value between the focal vole and its closest neighbor of the focal sex has been used in the calculations of mean values.

RESULTS

Seasonal Distribution and Population Background

The marsh population.—Individuals in this population moved seasonally between a marsh and burrows in adjacent grassland. During winter (September-April) the voles had underground nests and food stores in the grassland, mainly containing roots of dandelion, *Taraxacum officinale,* and roots and rhizomes of a variety of grasses. The burrows were often complex and could extend to a depth of 1 m, where nests often were placed, surrounded by several food stores.

In May, voles overwintering in grasslands moved to the edge of the marsh, often remaining in shallow burrows until June, when they moved out into the marsh. Owing to the high water level and sparse cover of vegetation during May, the marsh was probably unsuitable for the voles at this time. Later (June-August), most voles had nests and feeding sites on tussocks in the marsh, although some females remained at the edges, using the marsh for feeding and burrows for nesting. Preferred foods during this time were water plantain, *Alisma plantago aquatica,* reedmace, *Typha latifolia,* and horsetail, *Equisetum palustre.* In August the voles began to leave the marsh and in September most voles had left.

High elevation and nearness to the marsh seemed to be features of an optimal place for overwintering. Of 48 individuals captured during two autumns (September-November) in burrows within 50 m of the marsh, 77% were captured within 20 m of the border of the marsh. Of these, 54%

were aggregated in a small mound 10 m north of the marsh.

The total number of individuals in the population increased in 1978-1979 and then decreased in 1979-1982 (Jeppsson, 1987). During July 1982 only three voles were captured, all young reproductive individuals. Possibly the numbers were about to increase again in 1983, but almost all animals were killed by a mink, *Mustela vison,* in July 1983. The proportion of reproductive individuals was highest during low density due to an increased number of young voles coming into reproductive condition (Table 1, Jeppsson, 1987).

The grassland populations.—The grassland voles spent the whole year in proximity to burrows. During the breeding season they used runways above ground and also consumed the green parts mainly of dandelion and grasses. During autumn their movements above ground decreased and their way of life during winter was similar to that of the marsh population.

In contrast to the voles in the marsh, the grassland animals were very site-tenacious. Out of 14 individuals captured in one population during November, five (two females and three males) had been captured the previous August. The following May, four were still present within 10 m of their first place of capture, whereas one male had moved 30 m away. In another population, two females were captured repeatedly within an area of 10 m^2 from May to November.

The density was highly variable, even between populations within a distance of about one km (sites 1 and 2; Table 1). All individuals in the population at site 1 were killed by a stoat, *Mustela erminea,* in July, probably due to the high density attracting the predator. The high proportion of reproductive individuals in this population could have been a result of a deficit of yearlings. However, during moderate density in the grassland, a higher proportion of the individuals were in reproductive condition than in the marsh during high and moderate density (Mann-Whitney U-test, $U = 1010$, $P < 0.05$; Table 1).

Home Range Size

Individuals had considerably larger home ranges in the marsh than in the grassland, independent of sex or population density (Table 2). In the marsh, males had larger peripheral areas than females ($U = 1.0$, $P < 0.05$), but size of the core areas were similar ($U = 31.0$, $P > 0.05$). Both sexes had smaller core areas during low than high and moderate density, but the peripheral areas did not change with density (Table 2).

During low density or in late summer, when several females had moved to burrows in grassland, some males had no access to reproductive females. These males moved over larger areas ($\bar{X} = 3,751$ m^2, $n = 4$) than males with access to reproductive females ($\bar{X} = 1,310$ m^2, $n = 7$; $U = 1.0$, $P < 0.05$).

Table 2.—Mean home range sizes (m^2) of radiocollared water voles during 5-day periods. The 0.95 and 0.50 values stand for the 95% and 50% probability area of the harmonic mean home ranges. Levels of significance have been tested using the Mann-Whitney U-test. Data from two seasons ([a]) and three populations ([b]) have been pooled as no difference was found between them (males: $U = 8.0$, $P > 0.05$; females: $U = 2.0$, $P > 0.05$; Kruskal-Wallis test $= 4.29$, $d.f. = 2$, $P > 0.05$).

				Males					
				0.95			0.50		
Period	Habitat	Density	n	$\bar{X}$	SD	P	$\bar{X}$	SD	P
May–Aug.	Marsh	High	3	1775.3	332.5		330.3	91.3	
		Low[a]	7	1314.3	548.5	>0.05	115.1	53.7	<0.05
	Grassland	High	4	33.5	7.4		2.0	0.0	
		Moderate	4	169.5	28.2	<0.05	4.3	2.5	>0.05
		Low	3	104.3	48.6	>0.05	4.0	1.6	>0.05
Sept.–Apr.	Grassland	Low-high[b]	14	41.0	32.2		1.0	0.0	
				Females					
May–Aug.	Marsh	Moderate	4	919.3	298.0		194.8	30.0	
		Low[a]	5	403.0	198.8	>0.05	39.2	15.4	<0.05
	Grassland	High	6	44.3	24.5		4.2	3.4	
		Moderate	4	100.3	41.1	<0.05	2.5	0.9	>0.05
		Low	4	88.5	94.0	>0.05	6.5	2.6	<0.05
Sept.–Apr.	Grassland	Low-high[b]	10	50.0	52.4		1.0	0.0	

In grasslands, no difference was found between average home range sizes of males and females (peripheral areas: $U = 57.0$, $P > 0.05$; core areas: $U = 86.0$, $P > 0.05$). However, sizes differed between populations with different densities (peripheral areas: Kruskal-Wallis test $= 9.4$, $d.f. = 2$, $P < 0.05$; core areas: Kruskal-Wallis test $= 5.8$, $d.f. = 2$, $P = 0.05$). Individuals had larger home ranges in populations with moderate and low density than in a high density population (Table 2).

During winter, no intersexual difference in home range size was found ($U = 63.0$, $P > 0.05$), and contrary to the breeding period, no differences were found between the different populations (Kruskal-Wallis test $= 4.3$, $d.f. = 2$, $P > 0.05$). The home ranges during winter were equal in size to those during high density in summer ($U = 138.0$, $P > 0.05$; Fig. 1), but smaller than those during moderate and low densities ($U = 60.0$, $P < 0.05$).

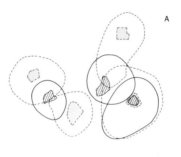

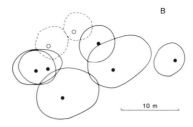

Fig. 1.— Home range areas of water voles based on the 95% and 50% probability area of harmonic mean home ranges in a high density grassland habitat. During the breeding season (A) voles were radiotracked daily for 1 month, and during the non-breeding season (B) voles were radiotracked for 3 months. Peripheral areas are denoted by solid lines (males) and broken lines (females); core areas in (A) by striped areas (males) and dotted areas (females), and in (B) by closed circles (males) and open circles (females).

Space Use and Mating System

The degree of intersexual overlap was considerably larger than that of intrasexual overlap in both habitats (marsh: $U = 4.0$, $P < 0.005$; grassland: $U = 56.0$, $P < 0.05$; Table 3). With two exceptions individuals had almost no intrasexual overlap between their peripheral areas and none between core areas, irrespective of density, indicating a high degree of territoriality (Table 2). Females in the marsh overlapped at moderate density but no overlap was found between the core areas (Table 3), indicating female defense of core areas, but not of peripheral areas.

Radiocollared males in the marsh tended to overlap with more than one female in contrast to males in the grassland ($\chi^2 = 3.27$, $P < 0.1$; Table 4). The variation between males in the marsh with respect to the number of females included within their home ranges was larger than between males in the grassland. Most males in the marsh either overlapped with zero or three to four females, whereas males in the grassland usually overlapped with one female.

Table 3.—Mean overlap index values for radiocollared water voles. Overlap between males where none had access to reproductive females have been given separately ([c]). The 0.95 and 0.50 values stand for the 95% and 50% probability area of harmonic mean home ranges. Data from two seasons ([a]) and three populations ([b]) have been pooled as no difference was found between them (Mann-Whitney U-test, $U = 50.0$, $P > 0.05$; Kruskal-Wallis test $= 3.0$, $d.f. = 2$, $P > 0.05$).

			Males								
			Intrasexual					Intersexual			
			0.95		0.50			0.95		0.50	
Period	Habitat-Density	n	$\bar{X}$	SD	$\bar{X}$	SD	n	$\bar{X}$	SD	$\bar{X}$	SD
May–	Marsh High	3	0.05	0.03	0.02	0.01					
August	Low[a]	7	0.03	0.03	0.00	0.00	5	0.27	0.18	0.08	0.13
		4[c]	0.70	0.15	0.08	0.08					
	Grassland										
	High	4	0.03	0.03	0.00	0.00	4	0.43	0.29	0.50	0.50
	Moderate	4	0.00	0.00	0.00	0.00	4	0.23	0.15	0.38	0.41
	Low	3	0.00	0.00	0.00	0.00	3	0.12	0.10	0.01	0.01
Sep.–	Grassland										
April	Low-high[b]	11	0.01	0.02	0.00	0.00	5	0.00	0.01	0.00	0.00
			Females								
May–	Marsh										
August	Moderate	4	0.22	0.12	0.01	0.01					
	Low[a]	5	0.01	0.01	0.00	0.00	5	0.29	0.15	0.08	0.13
	Grassland										
	High	6	0.01	0.01	0.00	0.00	6	0.29	0.31	0.33	0.47
	Moderate	4	0.00	0.00	0.00	0.00	4	0.23	0.15	0.38	0.42
	Low	3	0.00	0.00	0.00	0.00	4	0.09	0.10	0.01	0.01
Sept.–	Grassland										
April	Low-high[b]	7	0.00	0.01	0.00	0.00	5	0.00	0.01	0.00	0.00

In the marsh, overlap between males without access to reproductive females was considerable and larger than overlap between males in which at least one had access to reproductive females ($U = 0.0$, $P < 0.05$; Table 3). In populations of high and moderate density in grassland, where males overlapped with two reproductive females, the overlap with each of these females was significantly smaller than when overlapping with only one female for both peripheral and core areas (overlap with two females, peripheral areas: mean $= 0.12$, $SD = 0.08$; core areas: mean $= 0.00$, $SD = 0.00$, $n = 3$; overlap with one female, peripheral areas: mean $= 0.53$, $SD = 0.20$; core areas: mean $= 0.88$, $SD = 0.22$, $n = 4$; peripheral areas: $U = 1.0$, $P < 0.05$; core areas: $U = 0.0$, $P < 0.05$; Fig. 1A).

Table 4.—Number of reproductive female water voles captured within the home ranges of radiocollared males.

Habitat	Density	n	Number of females					$\bar{X}$	SD
			0	1	2	3	4		
Marsh	High	3	0	0	1	1	1	3.0	0.8
	Low	7	3	1	0	1	2	1.7	1.8
	Total	10	3	1	1	2	3	2.1	1.6
Grassland	High	4	0	2	2	0	0	1.5	0.5
	Moderate	4	1	2	1	0	0	1.0	0.7
	Low	3	1	2	0	0	0	0.7	0.5
	Total	11	2	6	3	0	0	1.1	0.7

In conclusion, females in the marsh overlapped when density was high in contrast to females in grasslands, which were territorial irrespective of density. Males in the marsh tended to be polygynous, whereas facultative monogamy prevailed in the grassland. During the nonbreeding season, individuals were both intrasexually as well as intersexually territorial (Table 3). The only exceptions among 21 cases of interactions, and which have not been included in the calculations in Table 3, were one case of extensive overlap between two young males (overlap index = 40; Fig. 1B), and another between an old and a young female (overlap index = 100).

DISCUSSION

Water voles are physiologically adapted to a semi-aquatic life (Panteleev, 1971). In this respect they are similar to the muskrat, *Ondatra zibethica*. However, the behavior of water voles living in grasslands was similar to the general pattern for herbivorous, subterranean mammals summarized by Nevo (1979); small home ranges, small intrasexual overlap, and partial intersexual overlap. The potential of these voles to adapt to different environments seems to be considerable.

Water voles are frequent prey for both avian and mammalian predators (Panteleev, 1971) and strongly dependent on cover for survival. In the marsh they were protected from all predators except the mink by the high water level and dense vegetation (Jeppsson, 1987; Woodroffe et al., 1990), whereas burrows were always used in habitats or during seasons with a lack of water and dense vegetation. The only predator that constituted a threat to voles staying in burrows was the stoat, whereas young, dispersing individuals were preyed upon by a variety of species (Jeppsson, 1987; Saucy, 1988).

Several researchers have confirmed the general theory for mechanisms governing the social systems of microtines, predicting that food is the key resource for females and dispersion of receptive females the key resource for males (Boonstra et al., 1987; Ims, 1989; Ostfeld, 1985). Ostfeld (1985) emphasized the importance of food distribution for females (females being most territorial when food is sparse, patchy, and slowly renewed), and of female dispersion for males (males being most territorial when females are clumped or their home ranges overlap). However, studies of *Clethrionomys rufocanus* showed a larger degree of range overlap between females when food was patchy and abundant and between males when females were aggregated (Ims, 1989). Ims suggested that intruder pressure was the most likely explanation for increased overlap between females as well as between males when key resources are abundant but patchily distributed.

Water voles are known to feed on a variety of aquatic, littoral, and meadow plant species (Holisova, 1965; Panteleev, 1971). In the marsh food was abundant and evenly distributed and females overlapped to a certain degree. This behavior was in agreement with the pattern suggested by Ostfeld (1985). However, core areas of females in the present study did not overlap at all, indicating that females were territorial for a reason other than resource defense. Intrasexual infanticide, as found in *Peromyscus* (Wolff, 1985), could be an additional explanation for female territoriality as suggested by Wolff (1985).

Female water voles in grassland were highly territorial against other reproductive females and no indication of extended maternal families as described for the montane vole, *Microtus montanus* (Jannett, 1978), could be found. Space between the home ranges of females was not always exploited even during high density (Fig. 1A), indicating that food was not limited within their home ranges. Voles in this study consumed mainly grasses, which has also been shown to occur in other populations of water voles living in dry habitats (Holisova, 1965; Panteleev, 1971). In contrast to forbs, grasses are evenly distributed and quickly renewed (Ostfeld, 1985, 1986). However, no difference could be found with respect to territoriality between females in this study and the females in a study of a fossorial subspecies *A. t. scherman,* living mainly on forbs (Saucy, 1988). In populations of water voles living in banks of streams with a dense and evenly distributed vegetation, females were territorial and evenly dispersed with large, linear home ranges (about 2,000 m^2; Leuze, 1976). Therefore, female water voles did not fit into the pattern suggested by either Ostfeld (1985) or Ims (1989). Food did not seem to be the key resource inducing territoriality in these females.

Males in the marsh had larger home ranges than females, often including those of several females. The overlap was small between males when at least one of the males overlapped with a reproductive female, indicating a high degree of territoriality between these males. On the other hand, males with no access to reproductive females had large home ranges and a high degree of space sharing, which supports the suggestion that the dispersion of females was the key resource for males in the marsh.

Males in grassland were territorial and their home ranges equal in size to those of females. The strategy used by these males was apparently to maximize overlap with one female or, when home ranges of females were situated close enough, overlap to a smaller extent with two females. Thus, they did not expand their home ranges to include the home ranges of several females, but instead they reduced the degree of overlap with each female, probably at the expense of their ability to control the matings of these females, and thus their certainty of paternity.

Unlike the males in the marsh and grassland, males living in banks along streams overlapped (Leuze, 1976), which is consistent with the predictions made by Ostfeld (1985) that territoriality is least pronounced when females are widely spaced. Thus, for males living in the marsh or along streams, the dispersion of females seemed to be the key resource, but not for males living in grasslands.

In the marsh neither sex used burrows during the breeding season, whereas all individuals living in grassland did. Females living along streams used burrows for reproduction, but males did not use burrows at all except for the nonbreeding season (Leuze, 1976). Evidently, water voles dependent on burrows for reproduction and survival were always intrasexually territorial. It is likely that the key resource for all individuals living in habitats without substantial cover is access to a burrow. The most striking difference between individuals living in grassland, as compared to those in the marsh, was their much smaller home ranges. This 100-fold difference in home range size between the habitats can neither be explained by differential abundance nor patchiness of the food, as shown for several other microtines (Ims, 1987; Ostfeld, 1986; Taitt and Krebs, 1981). The most reasonable explanation for the reduced mobility in grassland, is the dependence on burrows for cover. Possession of a burrow is probably necessary for voles living in a habitat where they are exposed to predation, not only for reproduction, but also for survival during both the breeding and the nonbreeding seasons. Unlike the marsh, where individuals were able to move over large areas due to the shelter of water and vegetation, individuals in the grassland had to remain in the vicinity of their burrows to avoid predation. A possible reason why males in grassland did not increase their home ranges to include several females could be in the difficulty to patrol a large area during high density when there was high pressure from transient individuals without burrows.

Water voles overwintered solitarily, in contrast to the communal winter nesting in burrows reported for the taiga vole, *Microtus xanthognathus* (Wolff and Lidicker, 1981). Digging a burrow is energetically costly, especially in hard mineral soil, and to secure a burrow for the winter could be an additional reason to defend it against intruders during summer. It is noteworthy that voles moving from the marsh during autumn frequently used empty burrows, even those made by moles, rather than digging new ones. Females remaining close to burrows probably increased both their instantaneous and lifetime reproductive success. Habitat constraints on mobility accentuated the conflict between instantaneous and lifetime reproductive success in males in which achieving matings now or surviving for future matings were in conflict.

Mating systems of water voles did not appear to be fixed genetically, but were influenced instead by habitat requirements to which individuals responded. Individuals within a species can be flexible or rigid in their requirements, reflecting flexible or rigid mating systems. Related to this point is the importance of distinguishing facultative from obligate monogamy. Monogamy may be imposed on an otherwise polygamous individual as the result of low density or habitat restrictions. From this point of view, it is important to be cautious in categorizing species as monogamous or polygynous and to determine how individuals respond to population density and variation in habitat characteristics.

In conclusion, intraspecific variation in the social system of water voles was due to individual adaptations influenced by different constraints of the environment. The large degree of flexibility of individual water voles may be an adaptation to different habitats and densities. Since each microtine species might alter its social organization according to density or resource changes, it is difficult to acquire an integrated view of microtine social systems if it is not based on resource requirements.

ACKNOWLEDGMENTS

I wish to thank Rolf Anker Ims, Richard Ostfeld, Jens Rydell and an unknown referee for useful comments on the manuscript, Mats Grahn and Jon Loman for help with computing, Kerstin Persson for drawing the figure and Jonatan Loman for all the interruptions. Grants were obtained from the Swedish Natural Research Council to S. Erlinge and from the National Swedish Environment Protection Board to G. Göransson.

LITERATURE CITED

Anderson, P. K. 1980. Evolutionary implications of microtine behavioral systems on the ecological stage. The Biologist, 62:70-88.

Boonstra, R. 1977. Effect of conspecifics on survival during population declines in *Microtus townsendii.* Journal of Animal Ecology, 46:835-851.

Boonstra, R., C. J. Krebs, M. S. Gaines, M. L. Johnson, and I. T. M. Craine. 1987. Natal philopatry and breeding systems in voles *(Microtus* spp.). Journal of Animal Ecology, 56:655-673.

Brown, J. L., and G. H. Orians. 1970. Spacing patterns in mobile animals. Annual Review of Ecology and Systematics, 1:239-262.

Caughley, G. 1977. Analysis of vertebrate populations. John Wiley and Sons Ltd., London, 234 pp.

Clutton-Brock, T. H., and P. H. Harvey. 1978. Mammals, resources and reproductive strategies. Nature, 273:191-195.

Craig, C. C. 1953. On the utilization of marked specimens in estimating populations of flying insects. Biometrika, 40:170-176.

Dixon, K. R., and J. A. Chapman. 1980. Harmonic mean measure of animal activity areas. Ecology, 61:1040-1044.

Holisova, V. 1965. The food of the water vole, *Arvicola terrestris,* in the agrarian environment of south Moravia. Zoologicke Listy, 14:209-218.

Ims, R. A. 1987. Responses in spatial organization and behaviour to manipulations of the food resource in the vole *Clethrionomys rufocanus.* Journal of Animal Ecology, 56:585-596.

–––. 1988. Spatial clumping of sexually receptive females induces space sharing among male voles. Nature, 335:541-543.

–––. 1989. Causes and consequences of individual variation in space use and timing of reproduction. Unpublished Ph.D. dissertation, University of Oslo, Norway, 26 pp. + published papers.

Jannett, F. J., Jr. 1978. The density-dependent formation of extended maternal families of the montane vole, *Microtus montanus nanus.* Behavioral Ecology and Sociobiology, 3:245-26.

–––. 1980. Social dynamics of the montane vole, *Microtus montanus,* as a paradigm. The Biologist, 62:3-19.

Jeppsson, B. 1987. Behavioural ecology of the water vole, *Arvicola terrestris,* and its implication to theories of microtine ecology. Unpublished Ph.D. dissertation, University of Lund, Sweden, 80 pp.

Leuze, C. K. 1976. Social behaviour and dispersion in the water vole, *Arvicola terrestris,* Lacepede. Unpublished Ph.D. dissertation, University of Aberdeen, Scotland, 243 pp.

Nevo, E. 1979. Adaptive convergence of subterranean mammals. Annual Review of Ecology and Systematics, 10:269-308.

Ostfeld, R. S. 1985. Limiting resources and territoriality in microtine rodents. The American Naturalist, 126:1-15.

–––. 1986. Territoriality and mating systems of California voles. Journal of animal Ecology, 55:691-706.

Panteleev, P. A. 1971. Population ecology of the water vole. Translated edition, D. M. Stoddart, ed. Published by the National Lending Library for Science and Technology, Boston, Massachusetts, 358 pp. [originally published in 1968 in Russian].

Saucy, F. 1988. Dynamique de population, dispersion et organisation sociale de la forme fouisseuse du campagnole terrestre, *(Arvicola terrestris scherman* (Shaw), Mammalia, Rodentia). Unpublished Ph.D. dissertation, University of Neuchatel, Switzerland, 366 pp.

Taitt, M. J., and C. J. Krebs. 1981. The effect of extra food on small rodent populations: II. Voles

(Microtus townsendii). Journal of Animal Ecology, 50:125-137.

Tester, J. R., D. W. Warner, and W. W. Cochran. 1964. A radio-tracking system for studying movements of deer. Journal of Wildlife Management, 28:42-45.

Viitala, J., and I. Hoffmeyer. 1985. Social organization in *Clethrionomys* compared with *Microtus* and *Apodemus:* social odours, chemistry and biological effects. Annales Zoologici Fennici, 22:359-371.

Wolff, J. O. 1985. Maternal aggression as a deterrent to infanticide in *Peromyscus leucopus* and *P. maniculatus.* Animal Behaviour, 33:117-123.

Wolff, J. O., and W. Z. Lidicker, Jr. 1981. Communal winter nesting and food sharing in taiga voles. Behavioral Ecology and Sociobiology, 9:237-240.

Woodroffe, G. L., J. H. Lawton, and W. L. Davidson. 1990. The impact of feral mink *Mustela vison* on water voles *Arvicola terrestris* in the North Yorkshire Moors National Park. Biological Conservation, 51:49-62.

SUBJECT INDEX